GROWING UP
on the SPECTRUM

Also by Lynn Kern Koegel and Claire LaZebnik

*Overcoming Autism: Finding the Answers, Strategies, and Hope
That Can Transform a Child's Life*

GROWING UP
on the SPECTRUM

A Guide to Life, Love, and Learning
for Teens and Young Adults
with Autism and Asperger's

Lynn Kern Koegel, Ph.D.,
and Claire LaZebnik

additional material and illustrations
by Andrew LaZebnik

VIKING

VIKING

Published by the Penguin Group

Penguin Group (USA) Inc., 375 Hudson Street, New York, New York 10014, U.S.A.

Penguin Group (Canada), 90 Eglinton Avenue East, Suite 700, Toronto, Ontario,
Canada M4P 2Y3 (a division of Pearson Penguin Canada Inc.)

Penguin Books Ltd, 80 Strand, London WC2R 0RL, England

Penguin Ireland, 25 St. Stephen's Green, Dublin 2, Ireland (a division of Penguin Books Ltd)

Penguin Books Australia Ltd, 250 Camberwell Road, Camberwell, Victoria 3124, Australia
(a division of Pearson Australia Group Pty Ltd)

Penguin Books India Pvt Ltd, 11 Community Centre, Panchsheel Park,
New Delhi–110 017, India

Penguin Group (NZ), 67 Apollo Drive, Rosedale, North Shore 0632, New Zealand
(a division of Pearson New Zealand Ltd)

Penguin Books (South Africa) (Pty) Ltd, 24 Sturdee Avenue, Rosebank,
Johannesburg 2196, South Africa

Penguin Books Ltd, Registered Offices: 80 Strand, London WC2R 0RL, England

First published in 2009 by Viking Penguin, a member of Penguin Group (USA) Inc.

10 9 8 7 6 5 4 3 2 1

While the author has made every effort to provide accurate telephone numbers and Internet addresses at the time of publication, neither the publisher nor the author assumes any responsibility for errors, or for changes that occur after publication. Further, publisher does not have any control over and does not assume any responsibility for author or third-party websites or their content.

LIBRARY OF CONGRESS CATALOGING-IN-PUBLICATION DATA

Koegel, Lynn Kern.
  Growing up on the spectrum: a guide to life, love, and learning for teens and young adults with autism and Asperger's / by Lynn Kern Koegel and Claire LaZebnik.
      p. cm.
  Includes bibliographical references and index.
  ISBN 978-0-670-02067-6
  1. Autism in adolescence—Popular works.   2. Asperger's syndrome in adolescence—Popular works.   I. LaZebnik, Claire Scovell.   II. Title.
  RJ506.A9K635 2009
  616.85′88200835—dc22   2008041835

Printed in the United States of America

For our Roberts:

We're incredibly lucky to have your skill and enthusiasm supporting us in both our personal and professional lives.

Acknowledgments

First and foremost, we'd like to thank our children (six in total) for bringing so much happiness into our lives and for selflessly agreeing to let us tell some of their personal stories. Extra thanks go to Andrew for his contributions to this book, including all of the illustrations and many wonderful and honest personal essays. We also appreciate the support from our larger family—our parents, sisters, brothers, aunts, uncles, cousins, and friends—who listen, laugh, and cry with us.

We'd also like to express our sincere appreciation to the children with autism whom we've met along the way and to their families. The world is a richer place because of people like them.

Next, we are so grateful to everyone who contributed a personal essay. Our book has been hugely enriched by their expertise and their willingness to share their perspectives and personal stories about the trials and tribulations they've endured in the always unpredictable world of autism.

Thanks to those who proofread this book for us—Bob Koegel, Rob LaZebnik, Brittany Koegel, Lee Kern, Whitney Smith, Rosy Fredeen, and Ashley Koegel—for all their helpful thoughts and comments. We also want to give a shout-out to the wonderful graduate students at UCSB, who are the best and the brightest, who enthusiastically work with people on the spectrum, and who have dedicated their lives to helping these individuals. The future of children on the spectrum is in good hands with people like you. Dr. Rosy Fredeen deserves special thanks for her skill, expertise, constant cheerfulness, wonderful personality, and feedback and suggestions for this book.

We also greatly appreciate Rebecca Hunt for her impressive speed-reading skills, thoughtful comments, and enthusiasm throughout this entire process, and also Alexis Hurley for her continual support and encouragement over the years.

Support for the research described in this book has been provided by the National Institute of Mental Health, the Department of Education, the First 5 California, and the families who have generously supported the UCSB Koegel Autism Center. We'd also like to express special thanks to the Kelly Family Foundation, the Kind World Foundation, and Eli and Edythe L. Broad—their extraordinary support of the Autism and Asperger's Center, housed at UCSB, has greatly enhanced the lives of individuals on the spectrum.

For more information on the Pivotal Response Treatment procedures described in this book go to www.education.ucsb.edu/autism.

Contents

SECTION I

Getting Started

1. Introduction

CLAIRE

In 2004, when Dr. Koegel and I finished writing our first book together (Overcoming Autism: Finding the Answers, Strategies, and Hope That Can Transform a Child's Life, Viking/Penguin), my son Andrew was just entering middle school, and the personal essays I included in the book were a look back at the first ten to twelve years of his life.

He is, at the moment I write this, currently finishing up his sophomore year of high school. By the time this book is published, he will be a junior.

A couple of years ago, I submitted an essay to the New York Times "Modern Love" column that was published the following month. I wrote about my son's growing interest in girls and my fears that his autism might make it hard for him to find romantic happiness. After the article appeared, I received an outpouring of e-mails from parents all over the country who were also worried that their children would never have the social or romantic life that every parent hopes his child will have. Many of them expressed frustration that there was so little guidance or information available for parents of teenagers and young adults on the spectrum.

Kids grow up. The book Dr. Koegel and I wrote four years ago set out to teach parents and therapists how to guide children who couldn't speak to communicate, who couldn't play with others to have a successful playdate, who couldn't dress themselves or control their temper to do both. But those same kids who benefited so much from Overcoming Autism have been spending the last few years getting older, and their issues have grown up with them. Suddenly, the question is not simply "How do I teach my child to do this or that?" but a much more complicated "How do I teach my child not to need me to teach him anymore?"

Kids grow up. A small child with big eyes gets his head patted by the strangers who pass his way, even if he ignores them. But a five-foot-nine fifteen-year-old boy with acne and an inability to make eye contact isn't going to be greeted as warmly. He needs to learn the skills and tact to make his way in a world that no longer coos over the "cute little quiet boy" but suspiciously eyes the "weird" teenager.

The stakes are higher and the risks are greater for kids who can drive, go to parties where alcohol is served, live in college dorm rooms, fall in love—and yet are still far more innocent and susceptible to manipulation than their peers.

Dr. Koegel and I figured it was time to write a new book, one that continues where the original Overcoming Autism left off. In our first book, I wrote about autism from a parent's perspective. In this book, we're going one better: my son is contributing his own first-person perspective. Now an outgoing seventeen-year-old with a driver's license, a summer job, and college looming on the horizon, Andrew can offer something Dr. Koegel and I can't: the ability to tell you what goes on behind the locked door of a teenager who's struggling not only with the emotional and physical changes every teenager goes through, but also with the additional challenge of being on the spectrum.

Andrew's involvement doesn't mean I'm going to shut up: as a parent, I still have something to contribute—although I can't help but notice that as we've been working on this book, much of what I add to these pages is along the lines of "what I've learned from my mistakes." I haven't always followed the advice in these pages; laziness, ignorance, and life's chaos have all gotten in the way of my being the parent I'd like to be. On the plus side, Andrew is a gift of a child, kind and hardworking and supportive and ambitious. He is a success story. I can't take credit for it but I can appreciate it. (And be grateful to my wonderful husband, who has always been far more active than I about getting Andrew out and involved.)

Enough about our family—the reason this book was written is to give the world access to the brilliant advice and interventions of my friend and writing partner Dr. Lynn Koegel. The Koegel Autism Center at the University of California, Santa Barbara (UCSB), which Lynn runs with her husband, Robert Koegel, PhD, has a long waiting list of people from around the world who are eager to be trained in its unique Pivotal Response Training approach to behavioral interventions. Unfortunately, not everyone can make it to the clinic; everyone can, however, buy a book to provide the information that's so eagerly sought.

Throughout this book, I try to speak for all the parents of older kids on the spectrum by repeatedly calling out, "Help! What do we do in this situation?" And Dr. Koegel provides that help, drawing on her years of working with people of all ages on the autism spectrum as she explores the strategies and interventions that parents can immediately begin to use to help steer their children through the difficult preteen, teenage, and young adult years, while also gently and gradually pushing them toward a more independent future.

DR. KOEGEL

Even though we've come a long way, there's still a long way to go when it comes to intervention for children with autism and Asperger's syndrome. While we continue to make breakthroughs in our research, we're also faced with the fact that very few people are adequately trained to work with individuals with autism. This is in addition to the fact that more evidence-based treatments still need to be developed, and it takes at least ten years for the results of successful research to get out to the real world.

On the positive side, more children with autism are being included in regular education and community settings, are able to work and overcome the symptoms of autism. I'm optimistic that in the years to come, intervention will continue to improve so that all adolescents and adults will live socially rich and meaningful lives, and be treated with respect and dignity. Finally, I have hopes that our society will learn to provide families with support, so that they may live their lives without stress, isolation, and anxiety. Individuals on the spectrum are people with talents, humor, and unique personalities that need to be celebrated. Over the course of their lives, they face innumerable daily challenges with communication, academics, bullying, and learning how to read subtle cues, both in their environments and during social conversation. That's got to be difficult! Hope, understanding, and more clinical research should move us ahead in the next decade.

Some Statistics

The Centers for Disease Control (CDC) currently estimates that over half a million Americans under the age of twenty-one have autism. There's been a huge increase in the last few decades. In the sixties, about 1 in every 2,500 children was diagnosed with autism, but now the diagnosis rate is about 1 in every 150. The increase is so great that it cannot be explained by better diagnoses, better tracking, or criteria changes. It is truly an epidemic.

In the early nineties, people became concerned and began regularly tracking the number of children with autism; at that time, the average age of the kids being diagnosed was about five years. These kids, and the decade of children who came after them, are now reaching adolescence and adulthood. Parents and professionals are desperate for more information and support, and have concerns about the future. What can they expect for their children? Jobs? Marriage? Do programs still work with older children even if their parents missed the so-called window of opportunity? Is early intervention the only path to success, or can something be done for older children and adults?

Many children with Asperger's syndrome aren't even diagnosed until late elementary or middle school, because they don't have the early language delays that raise a red flag, and their issues are primarily social. The later diagnosis means their families usually don't have a therapeutic support system in place by the time the kids are in middle school and therefore often don't know where to turn for help.

One interesting change in the past few years is that as children with autism and Asperger's syndrome become adults with autism and Asperger's, in numbers greater than we've ever seen, they've started to demand the world's respect for their differences and recognition of their talents. Our goal is to acknowledge the need to embrace the wonderfully quirky and unique talents of so many of these individuals, while still helping them adapt to society's demands. *All* kids need guidance as they move from childhood to independence. We intend to help you figure out the best way to utilize and develop your older child's strengths, to work on areas that need improvement, and to face the eventual move toward separation and independent living with courage, determination, and hope.

How to Use This Book

We divided the book into five main sections: making friends; romantic and sexual relationships; schooling; life beyond the school years; and finally, improving the issues that come up in daily life. Each section is subdivided into more specific chapters.

We realize that some of these areas may be more problematic or relevant for your family than others. For instance, if your child is in middle school, you're not likely to be worried yet about life after college. And while some parents struggle to instill a respect for personal hygiene in their offspring, others can sleep well at night knowing their child would no more skip his morning shower than any other part of the rigid schedule he adheres to. So we welcome you to pick your way around the book, reading the sections that are most relevant to your child. Of course, you're also welcome to read the whole thing straight through!

Each chapter includes a series of questions and answers at the end. One of the ways in which Claire and I take advantage of our parent/therapist dichotomy is that she can ask the questions that parents still have after reading or hearing my advice, giving me the opportunity to address specifics and go deeper into the subjects parents worry about most.

In this first section, we've included a chapter that explains the terms we use most often and repeatedly throughout the book and gives detailed descriptions of some of our interventions. While we try hard to avoid jargon, we do use terms that describe valuable procedures that you might not yet have been exposed to, so we wanted to take the time and space to describe each of them clearly. We recommend that you read, or at least skim, that chapter and acquaint yourself with all the terms we use before attacking any of the other sections, although you're welcome to use it more as a reference and simply move back and forth when you come across a term you don't recognize.

Scattered throughout the book are thoughts and essays by both Claire and her son Andrew, reminding us that real life frequently alters the best laid plans of mice, men, and clinicians. Other people have contributed their firsthand knowledge to this book as well, in the form of personal essays, and we're more grateful than we can say for their generous contributions, which enrich both our book and our shared knowledge of how best to help our children.

But First . . .

Before you move on to the rest of this book, there are some important things that every parent of a child on the spectrum should be aware of, no matter what stage of life the child is in. So here's some general advice that I'd like to pass on to you:

Find the Right Therapists to Work with Your Child

There are many programs out there and many different people to choose from. To find the right therapy, you need to first make sure that there will be *measurable* goals. If you find that your therapist doesn't have any measurable goals, you may want to consider looking for another one. Measurable goals enable the therapist to measure the pretherapy levels of your child and demonstrate that your child is *progressing* under intervention.

For example, if your child stays in his room on the computer all day long, the therapist will need to make goals to change that behavior and be able to document the steps being taken toward moving him into a more active social life. Or if your child is bringing up inappropriate topics on a regular basis, your therapist should be documenting a step-by-step program for improving the topics during social conversation. In short, make sure the intervention is *practical and working,* and that means monitoring it on a regular basis to be sure that your child is improving.

Similarly, if you find someone whom your child is just not motivated to see, try to switch therapists. Some adolescents and young adults on the spectrum like therapists with a more assertive personality, and others prefer a more "kick back" personality type. Finding the right personality match will help your child stay motivated.

Never Give Up

I saw a nine-year-old last week. He spoke in short sentences and only to request items. The parents told me that the school and other state agencies wanted to cut way back on his services because they felt that he wasn't making gains. He was easy to teach and picked up a few new things just in the few hours I worked with him. I couldn't believe that anyone wanted to give up on him. We also saw a fifty-year-old man recently who was nonverbal. The past interventions he'd had were ineffective. After a few weeks of our working with him, he began using a few words—for the first time in his life. He had simply never had some of the newer and more motivating interventions. As a parent, or a caring professional, you'll need to make sure that no one gives up on your child—especially not you!

Treat Your Child as Normally as Possible

I said this in *Overcoming Autism,* and I want to emphasize it in this book. People on the spectrum need to be treated as normally as possible, even though they have a disability. No matter what age your child is, try to keep her learning things other students are learning, participating in regular school classes, attending social functions, working, and so on. And have the same behavioral expectations of her that you would of any other child.

One thing that's especially tricky during adolescence is balancing enough support for your child with the need to encourage independence. With a younger child, you can control most aspects of his life and still be doing essentially what every parent around you is doing—in other words, it's "normal" to oversee and regulate his diet, his friendships, his schoolwork, his free time, and so on. But as kids grow older, most of them will wrest control away from their parents, and even though for some families it can turn a little dark and ugly, it's a necessary step on the road to independence. Most kids on the spectrum, though, need more support than other kids at all ages, and part of your job now is to recognize when you can fade into the background and trust your kid to find his own way, and when you must intervene with supervision, monitoring, and direction (even if other kids his age are more independent). It's tricky. Your goal is to step back, but sometimes stepping back will only leave your child flailing about helplessly.

We'll try in this book to give you some guidelines for continually aiding and monitoring your child without babying her or squelching her fragile independence, but that delicate balance is something you're going to have to constantly be aware of.

Coordinate

It's now just as important that your older child's or adult's intervention be coordinated across all settings as it was when he was younger. If he still needs intervention, make sure that everyone is consistently doing the interventions and helping your child to use newly learned behaviors.

If you're teaching your child to ask more questions in social conversation, make sure that everyone who works with him or is close to him, including his teachers, knows to encourage him to ask questions when chatting with him. If you think that your child needs to learn a new skill or behavior, make sure that you get everyone on board. Your child will learn faster and maintain the behavior longer if everyone is coordinated.

Think Long Term

Now that your child is older, you'll need to take the long view. If you want her to fit in, for example, make sure that she isn't watching movies that younger children watch. Always insist that the goals for your child are meaningful and will help her in the long term. Finally, you will need to make sure that your expectations are high enough. At home, make sure that you aren't doing too much for her. She'll need to learn skills that will help her live independently and be self-sufficient. So everything you do, every goal you set, and every issue you (and the school) target should be making a difference in your child's life in the long run.

Don't Follow Fads and "Miracle Cures"

This may seem obvious: when you call them fads and put "miracle cures" in quotation marks, everyone can agree that you're talking about something that's probably spurious. The problem is, when you're researching approaches, as all parents do, you'll often hear about treatments, medications, and even medical procedures that sound as if they might be reputable. Maybe someone you know is following some new medical protocol and swears by it. Or a parent you meet tells you how his son improved with some kind of therapy you've never heard of. *Do research before you plunge into anything!* Ask the most established professionals you trust what they've heard about this latest approach and whether they've seen results with their own eyes. Read everything you can—not just the information the proponents of the method are putting out there, but any studies that have been done proving or disproving its efficacy. And if there aren't any studies? That's a problem. No studies mean the method isn't research based, and its success is probably subjective. If no one you trust knows anything about it, it probably isn't the miracle you've been hoping for.

Helping your child isn't about miracles—it's about effort, care, and thought. The ultimate results may *feel* miraculous when you look back over the previous decade or two and realize how far that little boy or girl who once couldn't even speak has come, but you'll have worked for those results every step of the way.

CLAIRE

It's almost funny to look back over the decade and a half since Andrew was diagnosed with autism and remember all the "cures" that have come and gone in that time. I won't bore you by listing them all, but as a general rule, if the latest approach involves pig body parts, don't go there.

I know a lot of people who are doing serious autism research, trying to figure out the genes and the triggers that lead to the neurological damage that leads, in turn, to the symptoms of autism. There probably isn't one single cause, so there might never be one single "cure." I'm not ruling it out, but I'm also not sitting around waiting for it to come along, which is a good thing because, thanks to all the behavioral interventions we did instead of waiting for that cure, Andrew is doing great.

I trust the people I've worked with who are in the field to let me know if there is a real breakthrough. I won't do anything invasive or drastic until I see some hard research and hear from experts whom I respect that it works. And I'm certainly not going to abandon the strategies that have worked for us for so long to go chasing after some unproven dream pill or procedure.

Sure, I've played around with my son's diet from time to time and tried some fun therapies that were recommended to me, because why not? Even the silliest therapy can have a beneficial effect if your child and the therapist really bond and have fun together. That doesn't mean it "works" in any medical sense. It just means that keeping your child engaged and involved is always a plus for his progress. We had a "music therapist" who played the piano and sang with Andrew when he was really little and he smiled his way through the whole thing. Did I think the music had some kind of mystical curative power? Not for a second. But the therapist was warm and loving and Andrew liked to sing. So overall it was a positive and social hour for him.

In the end, though, it's the behavioral interventions that have made the real difference for us over the years, and I think that's true for most of the kids I know who are doing really well. I've known some parents who wanted to "cure" their child so badly that they went chasing after every miraculous claim that popped up. Not only were their hopes cruelly dashed over and over again (usually after a short period of believing they saw the miracle they'd hoped for), but they lost valuable time when they could have been doing the interventions that work, and it slowed their kids' progress.

Hope is a wonderful thing. Expect incredible things for and from your child, but anchor those expectations in the procedures, interventions, and therapies that have proven track records.

DR. KOEGEL

Love Your Child as He Is and Help Him Grow

There are two emotional traps parents of kids on the spectrum can fall into. One is to keep thinking, "This isn't my child; my child is hidden behind this child." The other is to think, "My child is unique and that's a wonderful thing, and I shouldn't attempt to change her in any way."

Don't fall into either trap.

The first is wrong because there is no "real" child hidden behind the child you know. Look at him—that's your kid. Love him—he's your kid. Enjoy his strengths and quirks—they make up the unique person who is your kid. But also help him overcome his areas of weakness—he's your kid and you owe him that.

It's interesting that parents who wouldn't hesitate to teach a typical child better manners or improved skills question the morality of working with their child on the spectrum to make her more outgoing or better able to navigate the world around her. You're not betraying her because you want her to be more comfortable in social situations. You're not forcing her to be "like everyone else." You're doing exactly what a parent *should* do: guiding your child to be the kind of person the world responds to positively, so her life will be easier and filled with friendship.

Don't Be Afraid

That's easy to say, right? But you have to overcome your fear of what might happen to your child out in the world and start encouraging him to be independent and self-reliant. It's easier and much less terrifying to keep your child close to your side and believe that you'll always be there to protect and defend. But—and you know this—as your kid grows up, he needs to find his way in the world without a parent always there to pave the way for him.

Once a Parent, Always a Parent

Once we're parents, we're parents forever. We need to be there for our kids as they grow up. When my kids went away to college, I was surprised how many times they called me and came home to visit. They needed support, advice, and encouragement even as adults. If you read the literature, most people get jobs through connections, and make friends through other friends and family. Kids on the spectrum may need a little more support from their families than typical developers, but all kids need some. It's okay to worry—all parents do. It's okay to keep giving your child advice—all parents do. And it's a great idea to make sure that you have a support system around your child to help her reach her potential in her career, in recreational activities, and with her peer group.

Take Care of Yourself and Your Family

Remember: one important aspect of keeping your goals high for your child is expecting him to be a supportive family member. That means allowing other members of the family as much time pursuing their dreams and goals as he gets. Too often the teenager with special needs ends up dictating what the rest of the family does—a vacation gets picked because "he'll like it and behave," a restaurant is chosen because "he won't fall apart," a parent doesn't show up at a sibling's event because "we're worried about taking the other one." Believe me, we understand how hard it is not to give in to making life easier for your child on the spectrum and simplifying things that way, but you're not doing anyone a service. It's far better to teach your child to control his behaviors and respect other people's needs than to defer to him out of fear or pity. The goal is to make his life and yours as normal as possible.

You also want any siblings to feel just as loved and attended to as the child who's on the spectrum—don't center every family activity around just that one child, but let all the kids have their turn in the spotlight.

In general, the siblings I've met through our clinic work have been wonderful—generous and supportive and proud of their brother's or sister's successes. We've even had several graduate students who went into the field *because* of their experiences growing up with a sibling on the spectrum. Don't take advantage of your kids' good nature, but shower them with praise, attention, and love. If one of them expresses some concern to you that her sibling's behaviors are affecting her life in a negative way, don't ignore her or tell her to "get over it." You need to fix the problem. I've seen kids who've been physically abused by their siblings on the spectrum and others who are afraid to invite friends over because their siblings' behaviors aren't controlled at home. It's your responsibility as a parent to see that interventions are put in place to solve these problems! There's specific information on how to do that in this book, and in our first book, which also includes a long discussion of the stress that an autism spectrum disorder can cause a family, and how best to cope with it. Please, if you're experiencing anything along those lines, read that book as well as this one and take action. Follow whatever steps you need to keep your family close, happy, and functioning.

2. Terms, Interventions, and Techniques

I've started reading some of the other chapters, and you keep talking about "priming" and "prompting." I know how to prime a pump and prompt an actor, but I have no idea what you mean in this context. Please explain.

CLAIRE

I remember one of the first times I met with Dr. Koegel, way back over a decade ago. We had taken Andrew to see her and she was instantly and brilliantly focusing on the areas we needed to help him on. We talked about the need to decrease his "hand puppets" (the way he self-stimulated at the time) and while she said it was fine now and then at home, we could decrease his stimming at school with a "self-management program." I nodded and smiled and agreed that a self-management program was a good idea.

I had no idea what a self-management program was.

Of course, I should have just asked—Dr. Koegel would have happily explained it to me. But I was embarrassed to admit I didn't yet know the term. We took some of the Koegels' books home with us so I was able to look it up later, but I did have to bluff my way through a good part of our first discussion.

Writing Overcoming Autism together was an eye-opening experience for me, because suddenly the terms I had only passing acquaintance with became very real, very useful, very meaningful ways to help your child. "Functional analysis" sounds complicated and technical. It's not. It's really just thinking deeply and rationally about what your child is getting out of a certain behavior, and keeping notes on what you're discovering. It isn't overwhelming—although the resulting epiphany can be nothing short of mind-blowing. ("You mean telling him he has to leave the dinner table is actually encouraging his bad behavior at meals?")

Both Dr. Koegel and I feel very strongly that we want everything in this book to be crystal clear to the layperson as well as the educator. So we're making sure we explain fully any terms we use repeatedly throughout the book.

DR. KOEGEL

A couple of years ago, I appeared on the ABC hit show *Supernanny*, which was seen by millions of viewers around the world. The show focuses on decreasing problem behaviors in typical children. The most common technique used on the show is the time-out.

The producers had invited me to work with a child with autism on the show. They picked a three-year-old boy from Florida who didn't say any consistent words and loved to spin in circles. He could entertain himself for hours on end and didn't seek his parents' attention the way a child without autism would. The producers were taken aback when I told them that their tried-and-true time-out approach to altering behavior wasn't going to work with this kid and that we would have to approach him in a different way—which I subsequently did successfully.

Time-outs work amazingly well with typical kids. You know the drill: the child misbehaves and has to sit alone in his room or in the corner of a room until he's ready to behave. Time-outs are very effective for most children—so effective that when used properly (with praise for good behavior), most kids don't need any other type of program.

Unfortunately, when you're dealing with a kid on the spectrum, a time-out may be the greatest reward you could give her. Remember, one of the criteria for a diagnosis of autism is that the child has to have trouble with socialization—kids with autism don't seek to share enjoyment with others, they don't develop great peer relationships, and they don't often engage in the reciprocal emotional interactions that we see in typical children. So it's no wonder time-outs don't work for our kids—they don't mind being alone! In fact, they usually *like* it. After all, it beats having to engage in some classroom assignment that isn't interesting or in some demanding social interaction that's like speaking a foreign language. (Of course, there are some kids with autism who thrive on social attention and for whom time-outs might work, but they're definitely in the minority.)

Similarly, if they don't have a super big peer group, grounding older kids on the spectrum as a punishment doesn't work either. Most teenagers with autism are more than happy to stay safely at home.

Another thing that doesn't work with kids on the spectrum? The guilt trip. Most moms are great at that. Mine would say, "Is there anything you think you should be telling me?" (in that tone of voice that implies culpability). Um, what could she possibly have found out? But kids with autism don't usually get too bothered by the guilt thing, maybe because they're not as attuned to nuance of tone. Also, we're working with some middle and high school kids on the spectrum right now who have trouble completing assignments, and they don't seem to feel the same kind of anxiety about *not* getting them in that motivates most kids.

So . . . we usually can't use guilt, anxiety, or the desire to be included as a motivating force when working with kids with autism, which leaves us with the need to use a whole other bag of tricks. Some can be applied to a variety of different behaviors, and that's why we've chosen to include them in this chapter of techniques and procedures that every parent should know.

Because we'll be suggesting that you use these methods to tackle different problem areas in many of the subsequent chapters, we're not only defining the terms here but we're also including a detailed description of how to incorporate them into your child's program of interventions. Once you understand the process, you'll be able to individualize these approaches and be comfortable using them for whatever issues may crop up with your child at any time.

Pivotal Response Treatment (PRT)

Years ago, before there were very many kids with autism, my husband was watching a clinic session and pointed out that the kids just didn't seem to be enjoying themselves during intervention. He had noticed that while the kids were learning, neither they nor their therapists(!) looked very happy. Because my husband is one of those people who verbalizes every one of his thought processes, he continued to ramble on about how the only thing they seemed motivated to do was to get out of the session.

You have to remember that this was back when we were having kids sit in chairs for hours at a time while we held up flash cards to teach words, concepts, colors, and so on. When they responded incorrectly, we told them "no," and when they were correct, we rewarded them with verbal praise and a small edible treat.

My husband's brilliant succession of thoughts got us thinking about how long it took to teach each behavior. We started chatting about how typical kids just pick up things without being drilled over and over again. That led us to a long line of research that looked at more effective ways of teaching. Our first publication focused on communication and incorporated motivational procedures that helped children learn to talk faster. That procedure was called the Natural Language Paradigm, or NLP. We soon realized that the motivational components that were helping children learn to talk so much faster also worked well at improving a number of other behaviors, from social interaction to academics.

The other good news was that there were positive by-products of these motivational procedures. In short, the kids seemed to improve all around. This began our long search for "pivotal" areas—areas that, when taught, would result in a broader range of positive changes in the kids. We were, in essence, trying to develop an intervention that was more efficient and more effective. That's how the term Pivotal Response Treatment was coined, and our subsequent research over the years has focused on finding pivotal areas. To date, we have studied motivation, self-management, initiations, responding to multiple cues, and empathy.

Motivation

We talked a lot about motivation in *Overcoming Autism,* and it's just as important with older children and adults. As I mentioned above, after many years of research, we've identified several components that reliably improve motivation—or, specifically, increase responding while simultaneously decreasing disruptive and off-task behavior. Meanwhile, during the intervention, the children smile more, look more engaged and interested, and overall appear happier. These motivational components are as follows:

- **Choice.** No matter how old you are, you appreciate being given a choice. Strive to always give your child some choices in the desired task—they can be about choosing the assignment, the materials he's going to work with, where he wants to sit, the order of work, the writing implement, whom he's going to work with, and so on. The more kid-appropriate choices you can add to any given activity, the more involved and motivated your child will be. Try letting him pick a recipe to cook for dinner (you can also use the recipe to practice his reading and even have him do some fractions by doubling the recipe), or pick out his own outfit, or decide which summer camp he wants to go to. Your child will be a lot happier and more motivated if you give him choices.

- **Interspersing easy and hard tasks.** Let's face it, if you struggled through work every day or picked up a book where every word was one you hadn't heard before, you'd probably avoid that job or that book. That's exactly the situation in which we all too frequently place kids with autism. Too often we find something they can't do, then repeatedly drill them on it until they learn it. Doesn't sound like fun, does it? Now think about giving the kids lots of easy tasks, so they build up their confidence, then every now and then throw in a hard one. Because they have the momentum going, they'll tackle the hard task willingly and surmount it a lot faster.

- **Task variation.** Everyone gets bored doing the same thing over and over again, and teens and young adults on the spectrum are no exception. Learning is much faster if tasks are varied frequently. This goes along nicely with interspersing easy with hard tasks and makes the teaching sessions a lot more fun.

- **Natural reinforcers.** Any time the reward for something is directly connected to the child's behavior, she's likely to respond better. Think about it. Adolescents can spend hours reading directions about how to play the latest video—but give them a required reading book for their English class and it's a struggle to get them to read the assigned thirty pages. Teens can do rapid computation if they're figuring out their allowance—but give them a page full of math problems and it isn't fun. Any time you can develop activities and academic assignments with natural reinforcers, kids will do better. One example I give later in the book is of a boy whose parents wanted him to do chores: setting the table was a great one to start with, because it led instantly to getting to eat dinner—a natural reinforcer. Always look for the things your child enjoys and tie them into the activity directly. If your daughter likes to buy CDs and you want to improve her social conversational skills, have her buy them herself from the clerk and make sure she says a perfect "How are you? May I buy these, please?" The reward of getting the CD she wants directly reinforces the effort she makes to interact.

- **Reward attempts.** If your kid is trying, he needs to be rewarded—even if the attempt isn't perfect. Kids on the spectrum often experience so much repeated failure that they give up trying. If we reward them for every attempt, no matter how imperfect it is, their responding will be greatly improved.

All of the above motivational components have been researched separately, and when they're put together as a package, you'll get far more out of your child. They're critical, because they have so many other positive effects, like reducing avoidance and disruptive behavior. The kids are happier, more interested, work harder and longer, and are just all around better learners if motivational components are woven into teaching.

Prompting

Prompting, put most simply, is a verbal or physical action that increases the likelihood that a child will be successful. Prompts can accompany instructions or can be cues that help him be successful with assignments, social interactions, transitions, or any other area your child may need more help with than his peers. Most children will need some type of prompting when learning a new activity.

Prompting is extremely useful, but it has to be done in a systematic way. For example, if your child spends all of his breaks in the library and doesn't socialize at all, you'll need to determine if he needs someone with him all the time, or if some initial prompting is enough to get him mixing with the other kids. Then you'll need to determine a prompting fading system. This largely depends on the child's behavior and rate of learning—if he's learning the behavior quickly, whoever is accompanying him can fade more quickly.

Prompting works well with promoting social conversation. For example, if you're trying to get your child to ask more questions, you may need to start with a fairly intrusive prompt, such as, "Did you hear that, Johnny? Ricky just said he's hungry. Why don't you ask him 'What do you want to eat?'" Once he's starting to ask questions, you can fade your prompt to "Oh, Johnny, I wonder what Ricky wants to eat." That can be further faded to, "Oh, really?" with a glance at Johnny, and so on. You get the idea. You're moving down the prompting "hierarchy," going from the most intrusive prompting—letting your child know exactly what you want him to do—to the least intrusive—just reminding him it's time to say *something*. Your goal is to fade out completely.

The problem is that most people don't have a prompting hierarchy and they get stuck giving the same prompt over and over again. Teaching any new behavior requires prompting at first, but if you don't work toward fading those prompts, you'll have the child dependent on you for life. Kids with autism have been known to get hooked on prompts, so you'll want to make sure they are as subtle as they can be, and you'll want to fade them as quickly as possible. So remember, prompting is a *temporary* instruction or cue that is designed to help your child learn or engage in a desired behavior.

One trick we've learned is that if you can make the prompt part of the activity, your child is less likely to get hooked on the prompt itself. We learned this years ago when we were teaching letters and were prompting the kids by pointing to the relevant part of the letter, for example, *b* versus *p*. When we pointed, the kids got hooked on the pointing, but when we made the line of the *b* go really far up and the line of the *p* go really far down, the kids understood where we were drawing their attention and learned what to look for right away.

Most important, though, remember that your goal with prompting is for it to fade away entirely. It's a teaching tool, not a crutch for your child to lean on forever. For example, if you're teaching her to greet people, you may need to start out by verbally prompting her: "Sarah, say hi to Beth and shake her hand." Gradually, you'll want to fade out the verbal prompt, perhaps by just saying her name ("Sarah?"), then just looking at her expectantly, with steps in between if she needs to go more slowly. This gradual prompt fading will help her learn the new behavior without getting hooked and dependent on the prompt—a prompt-fading paradigm needs to be in place if she's going to learn to perform the new behavior by herself.

Partial Participation

Partial participation is one of the most important strategies for inclusion, and we want your child to be included as much as possible. Too often I've gone into a classroom and discovered that my student there was given a *completely* different assignment from the other students'. That's not what we want. The idea of partial participation is that the student will learn the same material as his classmates, but it will be modified to his level.

A simple practical example of partial participation can be found in almost any home at dinnertime. After dinner, everyone is expected to help clean up. But you aren't going to have your preschooler load the breakable glasses into the dishwasher. You'll save that job for the older kids and maybe give the toddler the spoons to load. Your toddler is learning how to do dishes, but at his own level.

Now consider your adolescent. You want her to participate in the same activity as everyone around her: if her class is writing a twenty-page history paper, you don't want her off by herself watching video games or doing some simple math worksheets. You want her to write a paper too, at the highest level she's capable of, which may be somewhat lower than the other students'—say, a three-page paper. Your child may also need more specific instructions, such as suggestions at the start of each paragraph, for example, "Write a paragraph here about where the Incas lived"; "Write a paragraph here about what the Incas hunted, ate, and wore for clothing"; "Write here about the pyramids the Incas built"; and so on. This way, your child is learning to write a paper and completing a part of the same assignment as her peers, but again, at her own level. I haven't seen assignments that couldn't be altered in some way to help a child on the spectrum complete it successfully, but it does take a little work, and that's why there is special education staff in the schools.

Partial participation allows your child to be actively involved in the same activity as his peers and to learn the same general concepts, but at his own level.

Priming

I love priming. Almost every kid I work with has priming in her Individualized Education Program (IEP) or as part of her home or community program. In every arena—academics, dating, job training, vacations, even doctor visits—your kid can benefit from priming, which essentially involves previewing materials before you'll need to use them or an activity before it actually happens. We've used priming for all ages and all subjects.

Generally, we try to conduct the priming sessions in a relaxed manner. It should be a fun way of acquainting the person on the spectrum with a future task or activity that might otherwise prove difficult to manage. Usually, priming sessions are scheduled close to the time of the actual activity—like the night before—but they can also be effective if done earlier.

For example, I try to get the next year's textbooks in the summer to review them in anticipation of the upcoming year at school. I have our college students get their books and each syllabus well before the start of the quarter so they can start learning the material. Before one of my clients goes on a date, I'll usually review important skills, such as having him practice asking lots of questions and not talking too much.

Priming sessions are easy to implement, especially if you have an organized teacher who plans lessons in advance, and research has shown that it can be immensely helpful with academics and with socialization.

Modeling

Modeling, or imitation, is a natural part of development. Children imitate what they hear and see. Adolescents and adults tend to imitate people whom they admire or who they believe are similar to them. If you're using modeling as a technique for teaching, you need to make sure that the learner is tuning in to you and imitating the important behaviors.

Often individuals with autism are not spending enough time with peers, so they end up imitating behaviors of the adults they interact with, which can be fairly different from those of kids their own age. So it's critical that they spend time with their peers. Your child may specifically need to be prompted to look at his peers and engage in the same activities. This can be accomplished in classrooms (for example, your child can be prompted to check which page his neighbor has turned to) or in social situations (your child can be prompted to make comments during a sports event just like his peers). Adolescents and young adults on the spectrum are not usually that great at spontaneously modeling their peers, and that's why they often need more intensive programs, but there are usually some specific areas we can teach the kids to model in a peer's or sibling's behavior. These can range from self-help skills to putting on makeup to class activities.

But with adolescents and adults on the spectrum, you need to make sure they have the *right* peer models, and if you're using modeling as a strategy, make sure that they know exactly what's expected so that they're focusing on the desired behaviors you want them to imitate and not on some other potentially less desirable ones.

Video Modeling

Video modeling works well with kids and adults on the spectrum because visual processing is usually a strength for them. It's simple: all you need to do is grab a video camera and shoot footage and then show it to your child. Your approach can range from simply showing her the good behaviors she herself engaged in (so she can increase their incidences) to showing her examples of good behaviors other people are engaging in. Some video-modeling programs also show the client examples of when they weren't so successful and talk about how that behavior could be changed (see the example below), but it isn't always necessary to show unsuccessful examples, unless you feel that it would be helpful in teaching the student how to respond in those particular situations. In video modeling, sometimes the desired behavior is exaggerated and/or done a bit more slowly to make sure the individual with autism is cueing in to the right behaviors.

Video tape modeling is quick and easy, and kids these days are so used to their parents' taping them that you can grab a camera anytime and tape a few minutes without alarming them. The clips don't have to be long—usually in a couple of minutes you'll be able to point out both strengths and weaknesses. When we do this, we always try to show our client more positive segments than negative ones, to keep his spirits up. We usually start and end with a positive one.

For example, if we decide to work on not interrupting constantly, we'll show our client a clip of when she listened attentively and we'll say something like "I just wanted to show you how great this clip looks. You're listening attentively and waiting until the person finishes her sentence before you say anything." Next we might show a short clip of her interrupting and give feedback, such as "In this clip you started talking before the person stopped talking, so he didn't have a chance to finish his thought." Usually about five clips are enough to get the idea across.

As we're reviewing the clips, we try to have the client supply good ideas for any missed opportunities. For example, if we were working on asking more questions, we might first show him a clip where he successfully asked someone an interesting question, and follow that with one with a long painful silence. We'd say, for example, "In this clip, there was a bit of a silence. Since Josh just said he likes Italian food, a good question might have been 'Do you have any favorite Italian restaurants?' or 'What kind of Italian food do you like?'" Then we'd ask our client if *he* can think of any good questions he could have asked the other person, so he gets a chance to develop some questions on his own, which is the skill we're aiming for. We keep practicing and monitoring how well he does during these practice sessions until his behavior improves to the point where the video-modeling sessions are entirely examples of positive behaviors.

Now remember, kids with autism sometimes "generalize" (transfer learned knowledge in one situation to other situations where they weren't specifically taught or practiced), and sometimes they don't. If your child is doing great during the video-modeling sessions but you're not seeing any improvement outside of the sessions, you'll want to use some other approaches to help bring the positive experience into other environments (you can't follow your kid around with a TV monitor and video camera all day long!). Self-management works well to get the behavior out there in everyday settings (see below for more on that). Other reinforcement systems, such as rewarding good behaviors with points or tokens, also can be helpful.

Self-Management

Self-management—learning to monitor one's own behavior in a systematic manner—works beautifully for adolescents and young adults on the spectrum.

Just to give you a little background, some of the first studies on self-management were conducted on college campuses back when students could smoke in class. Researchers were doing studies on how to cut back on smoking, so for a pretreatment baseline they decided to have the students count the cigarettes they smoked during class. It turned out that when they simply counted the cigarettes they were smoking, they started smoking fewer of them. Without any intervention! This was dubbed the reactive effect: simply being aware of your own behavior and monitoring it can make you change it. It's sort of like writing down everything you eat when you want to lose weight or keeping track of those glasses of chardonnay at a party so you don't drink too much.

We've done a lot of research on self-management at UCSB. I did my initial work on self-management when I worked as a speech-language pathologist in public schools. There was one group of children who couldn't say a sound or two, usually *s* or *r*. I only saw the kids two or three times a week for twenty minutes, so they never got enough practice on their sounds. Some of them had been working on the same sound in speech therapy for three or four years. We found that if we provided the little wrist counters that golfers use and had the children keep track of the number of times they used those sounds away from their sessions, they showed incredibly rapid improvement. It really made a difference when they could monitor themselves on an ongoing basis—the kids basically became a crucial part of their own intervention.

Since then, we've set up hundreds of self-management programs for children, adolescents, and adults on the spectrum. It's a great way to get intervention without an interventionist being present. And by making the participants more aware of their own behavior, we increase their ability to control it. Below are the general steps for setting up a self-management program:

1. **Pick a target behavior.** First you'll need to decide on a target behavior. It can be one behavior, such as appropriately greeting people, or a group of behaviors, such as sitting and facing another person, looking her in the eyes, and responding to her questions. Once you've decided what you want to work on, you'll need to decide if it's best to monitor time intervals or instances when the behavior happens. Behavior is

sometimes easier to monitor by time intervals: I once set up a self-management program for my husband for not arguing at faculty meetings and he tallied each fifteen-minute interval of time with no arguing! If the target behavior is a distinct interval, like every time she greets another person, a wrist counter (golf counters work great) can be used to count each occurrence of the desired behavior.

2. **Take a baseline.** The next thing you need to do is determine how often the behavior happens (or doesn't happen). For example, if you're thinking you want to get your child to answer questions people ask him, you'll first need to measure how often he responds *now,* so you can get a baseline that will allow you to monitor improvement. If you're measuring how long he sits and engages in a good conversation, you'll want to have a watch with a second hand so you can note the time intervals. Getting a good idea of how often the behaviors are already happening is important because we always want to start the self-management on a small enough interval or with a small enough number of the desired behaviors so the child or adult will feel successful.

3. **Prepare.** Before you start the intervention, you'll need to create or purchase a recording device: anything from a sheet of paper with boxes for each interval to a stopwatch to a wrist counter (see number 5, "Record successes," on the next page for more information). Figure out what type of reward your child will be willing to work for—this can range from some free time to movie tickets to video games. I know some people don't like the idea of giving rewards, but think of it as a paycheck—there aren't too many people who would be willing to go to work every day if they didn't get a paycheck at the end of the week. And your child will be working *hard*.

4. **Teach discrimination.** Before you can ask your child to start monitoring her own behaviors, you have to make sure

that she understands what she's supposed to monitor and can discriminate between it and what she isn't supposed to do. Remember, we always focus on the positive. So if your child doesn't respond to other people's questions, you'll want her to monitor when she *does* respond to someone. Similarly, if she has trouble starting a conversation, have her monitor each time she successfully does so. If she's monitoring time intervals without engaging in an undesired behavior, like repetitive behaviors (or time intervals of engaging in appropriate behaviors that are incompatible with the repetitive behavior), you can use a watch with a chronographic alarming function or a timer. Don't have her keep track of her failures, just her successes. Focusing on the positive and rewarding success will give your child confidence and a real desire to engage in the appropriate behaviors.

5. **Record successes.** Now that your child understands what the desired behavior is, you can prompt him to evaluate himself. You'll probably need to prompt just in the beginning— over time he'll learn to self-evaluate without the prompts. Each time he engages in the desired behavior, or sustains the determined interval with the desired behaviors, he'll need to record that success. Recording can be accomplished in lots of different ways. You can get a little wrist counter (like a golf counter) from a sports store. Or you can just draw a grid on a piece of paper. If you're recording intervals, such as periods of time without an undesired behavior, you'll need to use a timer or a chronographic alarm watch with a repeat countdown function and a book or sheet of paper to record the successful intervals.

6. **Reward.** As much as we would like our kids to engage in the desired behaviors purely to help themselves, you will probably need to establish rewards for your child. Give her a menu of choices to select from. Of course, you'll want to pair the rewards with lots of heartfelt and enthusiastic praise.

7. **Fade back.** Eventually you're going to want the self-management system to fade. You can encourage this by increasing the number of points or the time increment your child needs to earn the reward. If you do this gradually and systematically, he'll be on the road to independence.

Think about it: self-management is something just about everyone uses. When we were around nine or ten years old, teachers started instructing us to write down assignments and follow up by checking them off. That's self-management. When we were in middle or high school, we started using calendars to help keep our lives organized and prevent us from forgetting important meetings or appointments. When we went out on our own, we kept track of more things, such as shopping and to-do and holiday card lists. We keep lists of birthday gifts, then check them off after we write thank-you notes. Basically, we self-manage all the time. Our self-management systems have become so automatic that we don't need to formally keep track of them anymore—which is what we want for the kids we work with. Most of our kids need the formal programs set up, with some practice to begin with, but once they get going, they can manage themselves, thereby essentially serving as their own "clinicians."

ANDREW

When I was about eleven or twelve, my therapist taught me a technique called self-management. Self-management is a tool that I sometimes use to help me realize when I am doing repetitive behaviors that I want to stop. I have used self-management to help stop talking to myself out loud, biting my fingers, and speech-ticking (using the same word over again in sentences without noticing), which I used to do a lot but I sometimes still do nowadays. What I do for my self-management is that whenever I catch myself doing something that I want to not do too much in the future, I write a check mark down on a piece of paper to remind myself of when I did it. I do that each time I do a repetitive behavior and count all of the check marks I wrote down during that certain time period. If I do a good job with it, I give myself a reward, but if I do not, I just try again until I can stop doing that certain behavior so many times. I mainly use self-management when I feel upset about doing a certain behavior too many times and really feel the urge to stop doing it.

Self-management is useful in many ways. The main reason it helps is because it helps you notice when you are doing a repetitive behavior, especially if you did not know that you were doing it before. The more you notice your behavior, the more it will help you stop doing it. Also, the more you do self-management, the happier you will feel. You will feel much happier not doing those repetitive behaviors.

I also use self-management to keep track of things that I need or want to do, like to finish homework in time, to make sure I exercise, to make sure I call somebody, or to make sure I give something to someone. Self-management is not just putting check marks down on a piece of paper; it can also be as simple as writing down one thing that I need to do or even just writing a few things I need to do on my notepad on my iPod touch.

DR. KOEGEL

It's interesting to note that Andrew counts the behaviors he wants to get rid of—when we set up a program, we generally don't ask people to monitor the undesired behaviors. We try to keep it positive by rewarding periods of time or instances with the desired behavior. However, I have known people like Andrew who keep track of the negative behaviors, and as we said earlier, the first documented self-management programs involved counting cigarettes smoked (a negative behavior), and it did successfully decrease smoking. So again, simply being aware of the undesired behavior, and monitoring when it happens, should also be helpful in making a change.

Functional Analysis

Functional analysis has become popular in the area of positive behavioral support, and we're all glad it has. Previously, people used to punish challenging behavior, not knowing how else to stop it. Often the child learned not to show the problem behavior with the person who punished her, but would revert to it around anyone else. Functional analysis involves figuring out *why* a behavior is occurring, and developing and teaching an appropriate replacement behavior that serves the same function. The main goal of a functional analysis is to replace a problem or inappropriate behavior with one that is socially acceptable.

Functional analysis came out of research showing that almost all behaviors have a reason. One of the most common reasons for problem behaviors is when students are trying to get out of or *avoid* an assignment or task they don't like (I remember my sister used to conveniently have to go to the bathroom whenever it was time to clean off the table and do the dishes). Another common function of inappropriate behaviors for kids on the spectrum is to try to get out of a situation that's unpleasant or uncomfortable. I have seen many kids on the spectrum actually start engaging in behaviors they know are inappropriate just because they want to *escape* the situation. For example, we worked with one adolescent who was moderately social, but when he got tired of interacting, he would start talking about blood and gore, which immediately terminated almost any social situation.

Finally, as we've developed motivational teaching procedures, we've noticed that more kids enjoy socially interacting because we set up the situations so that they're reinforcing and meaningful. Along with that comes a desire to get *attention,* and if a kid on the spectrum doesn't know appropriate ways to get attention, he may engage in behaviors that get attention but aren't socially acceptable. These can vary from repeatedly calling someone to following someone around to behaving aggressively. So if a child is engaging in escape, avoidance, or attention-seeking behaviors, you'll need to make sure she learns and uses replacement behaviors.

Desensitization

You may have heard of desensitization programs for getting rid of pho-
bias, anxiety, or aversions. A phobia can really disrupt someone's life,
especially if it makes him avoid certain situations. We've all heard of
people who absolutely can't get on planes or leave home to do something social.

With many people, the entire desensitization can be completed in
the office by teaching them how to relax, a physical response that is
incompatible with anxiety. We do this through imagery. Once a person can voluntarily relax, we very gradually and systematically work
our way up a hierarchy of least anxiety-producing situations to most
anxiety-producing situations, working on relaxing in each one.

For example, early in a friend's medical career, she was shadowing
a neurologist at a hospital. A young female patient, about my friend's
age, was undergoing a procedure that required a large needle to be
inserted into her brain. During the procedure, my friend began to feel
dizzy and the next thing she knew, she had fainted. The doctor assured her that first-year medical students "drop like flies," but that
didn't help her anxiety. In fact, she briefly wondered if medicine had
been the right career choice for her and she avoided the hospital for
weeks. We were able to overcome this problem using desensitization.
We developed a hierarchy involving steps that started with lying on a
beach in Hawaii or shopping at a mall and ended with watching
someone have surgery or someone else have a needle poked into her
brain. Of course, there were dozens of steps in between those ex-
tremes. Throughout the process, she worked on relaxing—a response
that was incompatible with her anxiety. After just a few sessions, she
had mastered the self-relaxation techniques to replace the anxiety
and was able to go back to the hospital without that dizzy feeling.

Well, that's the general idea, and the procedure works well with
individuals on the spectrum. For kids who have less communication,
we've been able to use a variation of the procedure by having the child
move closer and closer to the item or activity that causes anxiety
while engaging in a fun activity. For example, I've worked with many

kids who screamed bloody murder when they were having a haircut. Sometimes it can get so bad that the mere sight of a pair of scissors throws them into an utter panic. But we can desensitize them to the scissors by having them play a game or eat a favorite snack while we move the scissors closer and closer until they're right in front of the child; then we open and close the scissors, and then we move them closer and closer to the child's head, and so on.

We have also effectively used desensitization with children who had sound sensitivities and other types of fears, so if your child has any type of fear, or is overly sensitive, you may want to consult a psychologist and consider desensitization.

One last note—if you're considering desensitization for someone who's lacking a skill *and* feeling anxiety, it's best to teach the missing skill first. For example, if your child has anxiety about dating, and he has successfully learned the incompatible response of relaxation but then goes on a date that's a disaster, you may well be right back where you started. So it's best to use the technique for behaviors that are specific and not caused by general skill deficits. Those need to be addressed with interventions that teach the skills.

Finally, desensitization works at different rates, and it doesn't seem to be related to how long the person has had the anxiety or how intense it is. Just be patient and keep moving through those steps, gradually and systematically, and if your child starts to demonstrate some mild anxiety as you're moving up the hierarchy, move back and add a few more steps.

Peer Recruiting

Peer recruiting is essentially calling on your child's peers to work with you and the teachers to help support your child's efforts out in the real world. As we mentioned in a previous section on modeling, peers play a crucial role in showing your child (and you) how kids her age are communicating and socializing. Classmates can be an invaluable source for helping your child navigate through the most difficult part of the school day (usually free periods, like recess or lunch) and can be called on to provide company if your child is being isolated. But it's important to approach them in a methodical, thoughtful way, as outlined below.

If your child knows that he's on the spectrum or if he has some behaviors that make it clear to his peers that something isn't right, *and* if you or he feels that the kids aren't being nice to him, a classwide chat about autism might be very helpful. For parents of middle and high schoolers, we recommend first asking the school administration to allow you to address the students in your child's class and then following the steps outlined below. Children can also be approached in smaller groups, but a classwide discussion is something we've orchestrated fairly often with good results. Generally, this session is conducted without the child on the spectrum attending. Below is a suggestion for how to organize this approach:

1. **Introduce yourself.** Tell them what a pleasure it is to be there; say something nice about the school, the art on the walls—anything sincere.

2. **Talk about individual differences.** Some people have blond hair, others black. Some people have fair skin, others have darker skin. Some people are tall and others are short. Everyone is different.

3. **Talk about common disabilities.** Talk about vision problems and how some people wear glasses. Discuss physical disabilities. Ask them if they know anyone who has to use crutches or a wheelchair. Get them talking about different disabilities they may have seen in their families or among their peers.

4. **Now bring in the topic of disabilities you can't see.** Talk about the brain and how many people may be better at one thing than another.

5. **Discuss the symptoms of autism and Asperger's syndrome.** Let them know that many children are born on the spectrum and that it affects them in many different areas.

6. **Share with them personal information about your own child.** Tell them about what causes your child difficulties and why. Discuss the things that have happened in your child's life as a direct result of the disability. Bring up bullying if you're aware that it's been going on.

7. **Ask them to openly and honestly discuss things they have noticed that are different about your child.** Write down what they say or just express concern. Tell them if you have also noticed those things.

8. **Here's the important part: discuss ways that they may be able to *help* your child.** Let them come up with suggestions. You can also give them suggestions, but always ask them if they think those would work for them. When you leave, do it on a positive note, with their thinking of ways to help out your child.

9. **Thank them for their time and commitment to helping your child.** Have some time available afterward for the kids to talk with you individually, and give them your e-mail address or phone number. Many teens and adults find it easier to talk in a one-on-one situation than in a group.

For the story of one family's successful class discussion and peer recruitment, please read Section III, Chapter 2 on making the most of your child's middle and high school experience.

Making and Maintaining
Good Friendships

1. Introduction and Some General Rules About Friendship

My son is entering high school and doesn't seem to have any friends. He spends most of his free time at home on his computer. We (and his teachers) have worked so hard to help him academically, but I think that we may have failed at helping him socially. He has a wonderful personality but the other kids just don't seem to want to be around him. Is there anything we can do to help?

CLAIRE

When you first have a baby, you are that baby's best friend. You (and your spouse, of course) give him all the socializing he needs as you feed, cuddle, sing to and hold him. Once your baby is old enough to go out into the world, you'll probably seek out friends who have babies roughly the same age as yours; odds are good your toddler's friends will be the children of your friends.

Even in preschool, you have a lot of say over whom your kid hangs out with. If you happen to like a mom and enjoy talking to her, you and she might well agree after school to whisk the kiddies off to the ice-cream parlor, where you'll expect your kid to play with her kid while you and the other mom talk. (And talk. And talk. And talk . . .)

In elementary school, kids start to form their own opinion of their classmates, but parents are still in charge of socializing and can quietly manipulate things so that somehow that play-date with Louis (who shoves other kids on the soccer field) never quite materializes, whereas there's always time to get together with Joe, who's cute and sweet and whose mother is incredibly nice.

And then, sometime toward the end of elementary school or the beginning of middle school, there's a real shift as your kid becomes aware of how friendship works and demands control over whom she plays with. Not only will she insist on playdates with specific friends and refuse to play with others no matter how hard you push, but she'll also probably be picking up the phone to make her own plans. (Oh, she'll check with you—but only to make sure you're available to drive.) That's when it hits you: you are no longer in complete control of your child's social life. All you can do now is hope that you've taught her to appreciate kindness and substance over popularity and flash and that she'll stay away from bad influences—and the opposite sex—for as long as possible.

This gradual shift from parental control to teenage indepen-dence needs to happen for kids with autism just as it does for typical kids, but there are, as always, special challenges for them and their parents. First, once parents stop acting as their children's social secretaries, kids on the spectrum may not have the skills to set up their own after-school activities and may therefore be shut out of plans the other kids are making directly with one another. Second, kids on the spectrum tend to be "younger" and more innocent than other kids their age and of-ten can't see through kids who seem nice but are really manipu-lating them. So we parents worry that if we leave it to them to find their own friends, they might fall for the wrong ones. And finally, if you have a kid who prefers being alone to being with others (who finds it easier and less stressful), then there might be a good chance he'll simply opt out of a social life altogether if you stop arranging things for him.

So how does the parent of an older kid on the spectrum help her child find her way to a healthy, happy social life now that she doesn't have total control over her friends and activities? Can't we just go back to making them play with our friends' kids?

DR. KOEGEL

The value of having friends cannot be overstated. Friends offer com-panionship and protect us against loneliness and depression. Friends nurture and support us during difficult times and rejoice in good times. We can open up to friends, revealing the hopes, dreams, and fears we would never tell a stranger. Friends reassure us, advise us, and occasionally even gently rebuke us. Friends offer protection against bullies and mean people. And friends teach us how to get along with others, which ultimately helps prepare us for a happy ro-mantic life and marriage. But as we parents are all too aware, many people on the spectrum have difficulty making and keeping friends. Making and keeping friends isn't just an extra bonus for these kids—it's vital to happiness and something parents must help them work toward.

Over the years, I've frequently heard comments from supposedly competent school staff along the lines of "He seems happy, so why not just let him play by himself?" or "We feel she needs time alone to de-stress," or "We shouldn't try to force him into interacting if he doesn't want to." I must admit that this is a pet peeve of mine. *Students of any age who are having difficulty interacting need support.* And if you're reading this and you're worried about your child with autism or Asperger's syndrome having to interact when he doesn't want to, I want to make it perfectly clear that if intervention is done appropriately and systematically, helping your child learn to socialize should *not* put him in a situation that will make him uncomfortable.

Read on to learn how to help your child in ways that will only lead to greater social happiness, not discomfort.

Understanding Why Friendship Is So Important

Let's look at the research. It's been proved that adolescents who socially isolate themselves have more mental health issues in adulthood, are less likely to get—and keep—a job, and tend to have fewer leisure activities as adults. You wouldn't want any of that for your child, right? Our goal is to help our children develop into productive members of society with jobs and activities they enjoy and friends their own age they can have fun with.

At our clinic, we work with a large number of adults with autism and Asperger's syndrome, and almost everyone reports that he or she would like to have a friend or more friends *and* a significant other. The challenge in achieving this comes from the symptoms they exhibit, which may include the following:

- hating to make small talk
- talking too much about particular topics that may not be of interest to another person
- not listening enough
- not talking enough

- not knowing how to start a conversation
- not using good body posture or eye contact during conversation
- talking about inappropriate topics
- not using the right intonation and voice level

We'll discuss each and every one of these areas in the next few chapters, but before we launch into specifics, let's discuss some general rules that will help your child survive all the complexities of making—and keeping—friends.

Basic Rules for Making and Keeping Friends

Learn to Show Appreciation

Many friends of people with disabilities report that it just doesn't feel like the person with the disability appreciates them. Interestingly, this is also a pretty common complaint some of my married friends make about their husbands! But they didn't complain while they dated. What changed? Well, over time spouses often forget to keep telling each other how wonderful they are or to do all those little special things they did when they were dating.

With this in mind, you can help your child show appreciation for the friends he or she already has. Have him pick out a birthday card and a small gift on a friend's birthday, even if he's not going to a party. Have her take an extra piece of dessert to share with a friend. Have him Facebook a compliment or a comment, such as "Hey, that was funny when you spilled that drink last night at the party—glad we got it cleaned up before anyone noticed—I had fun hanging out with you—we should do it again." Encourage her to mail a friend a postcard while you're on your family vacation. If he read a good book, suggest he lend it to a friend who likes to read, and if he's driving home or you're picking him up, tell him to offer a carless friend a ride. Find ways she can help a friend with a chore, like moving or editing a paper. And anyone can learn to give a friend a compliment. Just make sure that it sounds sincere and not just memorized. (More on that in the next chapter.)

Follow Your Child's Interests

Make sure your child has access to situations and places that will lead to contact with those who share both his age and interest. If your child enjoys chess, find a chess club or let him have chess parties at your home. If your child excels at math, have him join the school's math team. If your child enjoys cooking, throw a little cooking class. This may seem obvious—after all, it's not dissimilar to the advice people would give any of us if we were to move to a new town and want to make new friends as quickly as possible. Finding people with similar interests by pursuing those interests in a class, club, or group is a pretty classic and well-proven way to connect. But your child on the spectrum may need you to make that extra effort even if you haven't just moved or changed schools or anything like that. Most kids will make friends just by being at school with other kids, but your child may well need the extra social boost of connecting with peers who share similar interests—and will probably need you to help him do this.

Similarly, find your child's strengths and put her in situations where her strengths can shine. Think about what your child is good at: computers, math, cooking, gardening, singing, reading, memorizing . . . Then make an effort to find or create a club, class, or event where her strengths will impress people. We once worked with a twenty-two-year-old woman who found social interaction challenging, but she could find any virus in a computer and repair it. She hung out at the university, and the college students were *so* happy to see her each week because she saved them many a problem finding and killing viruses. She found a way to be sought after and admired, and you need to find a similar strength for your child.

Seek Out Same-Age Peers

Throughout our lives, we tend to hang around with people from our own age group. With some rare exceptions, it's generally a problem if your teen or adult child is spending a lot of time with people who are much younger or much older than he is. I have one client who's in his thirties and who's constantly hitting on undergraduate college students. While a fifteen-year age difference may not seem like much to us, it does to a twenty-one-year-old. And so far, this hasn't helped his social life at all, except to get him repeatedly rejected, and I've gently suggested that he work on asking out someone closer to his own age. We also worked with a young woman on the spectrum who met someone online, who ultimately turned out to be a few decades older and was preying on her naïveté, so her parents had to intervene. One high schooler we knew had difficulty getting dates with girls his own age, so he started hanging out with elementary school girls. This was a potential disaster, so we put an immediate stop to it and worked with him to improve his interactions with girls his age.

If your child is hanging out with the wrong age group, you'll need to investigate why this is happening and steer him in a different direction while working with him to improve his appropriate social connections.

Don't Give Up on Your Child's Social Life

You can't give up. Ever. Most schools do very little to help children socialize, especially as they get older. In fact, if your child is socially isolated but not causing any trouble, the likelihood is high that the school will never address this isolation—it's the "troublemakers" who get the attention, not the loners. And after high school, society does even less to help socially isolated kids who have been rejected by their peers. So it's vitally important that you try to facilitate social interactions for your child. And remember—it's never too late. No one is sentenced to a life of isolation. The future can always be better than the past.

Remind Your Child About the Responsibility to Step Up

At some point, the person with the disability is going to have to move forward on his own. As much as we love and want to protect our children, maintaining friendships, falling in love, and getting married are all things they ultimately will want and must take responsibility for. This doesn't mean we should cut the strings and let them sink once they reach a certain age—it just means we need to encourage our kids to help themselves.

I've worked with many individuals who were so motivated to improve socially that they practiced all the time, and others who just wouldn't take that last step, who wanted us to do all the social work for them. Guess which ones ended up getting married? The crucial movement toward independence didn't have anything to do with cognitive level, but everything to do with motivation. A willing and motivated person on the spectrum is likely to have much more success than someone who's fighting you all the way. And you can help with that. Help your child understand the importance of having friends and relationships. Figure out what's rewarding for your child and discuss why socialization is important. For example, I worked with a college student with Asperger's syndrome who wanted to get married *so* much but resisted my feedback all the time. So if I said I didn't think that he should wear the same clothes day after day, he really didn't care, but if I said, "You know, if you want to meet a woman, she's probably not going to go out on a third date with you if you wear the same clothes the second time," that made a difference.

Similarly, we had an eighteen-year-old who wanted to work for us. His most motivating goal was to earn a paycheck. However, he rarely responded to others and never initiated any conversation. When I offered him the opportunity to work a few hours a week *only* if he could greet people appropriately and answer questions others asked, everything changed. He became a highly social, highly responsive young man.

If you can help your child find motivating reasons to get along and interact with others, it can make a huge difference in how much your child is willing to work.

Frequently Asked Questions

I'd really like to give my daughter some extra support in the social skills area. What do you think of friendship or social-skills groups?

Friendship groups are fantastic, especially if the leaders recruit a peer clique of typical classmates to help out. Middle schools and high schools that have friendship groups as a regular part of their curriculum are usually the best schools, and if yours currently doesn't, it would be a great idea to help get some started. Often the typical peers in the group will help the child on the spectrum learn targeted social skills and will provide suggestions on areas that still need intervention. I have seen many of these cliques include the child on the spectrum in activities such as sports events, parties, and other pursuits outside of the arranged friendship group, which is usually held at lunchtime.

I have also had parents report mixed feelings about social-skills groups that include *only* kids on the spectrum. On the one hand, some parents report that the group has provided their children with friends whom they can call and sometimes hang out with. On the other hand, some parents have reported that their child has begun to hang out with children who have more or different social challenges and this has caused a problem when their child imitates other inappropriate social behaviors. Another problem is that typical children may not want to hang out with children in the social-skills group. So those are things to keep in mind. I prefer social and friendship groups with typical peers, and this can be written into your child's middle or high school Individualized Education Program (IEP).

My daughter has one really close friend, a girl who's very similar to her. They get left out of pretty much every social event, but as far as I can tell, they're fine with that, since they have each other. Can I relax and just leave them to each other? Or should I worry that they don't have more friends?

No one fully understands how friendships work, but we do know that different things work for different people. I usually worry—a lot—when one of the kids I work with has *no* friends. In fact, one of the most frequent reasons parents call me is because their children are spending all of their free time alone. So I would say that having any friend at all is great. But what you may want to think about is what happens if that friend is sick, moves, or just decides she doesn't want to hang out anymore. Has your child developed the skills she needs to make new friends? To converse appropriately with new people? To get along with other kids? To engage in activities the other kids are engaging in? If you answer those questions with yes, then it's great that your daughter has a best friend. If you answer no, then I wouldn't relax. I would make arrangements for her to get intervention for helping her develop better socially.

Is it okay that all of my son's friends are outside of school? He's not close to anyone in his classes and sits alone a lot, but no one is mean to him and the school is serving his academic needs very well. He has several good friends who go to other schools. Is that okay or should we be working harder to find friends in his class?

Kids need to have friends both in school and outside of school. Having said that, I think you need to think about how you're defining "friends." If your child is hanging out with other kids during lunch and breaks but just chooses to get together with other friends outside of school, it may not be anything to worry about. However, if your child is spending time off by himself at school, even if the kids aren't being mean to him, it may mean that he isn't learning or doesn't have the prerequisite social skills to have peer relationships. In that case, I would suggest that you talk to your school staff.

Finally, since we're talking about middle and high school, think about possible changes in peer groups. If your child is in a new environment or has moved to a new school, he may take a little more time to meld with the other kids. We decided to place our daughter in a small private middle school while all of her best friends went to the large public junior high. It took her many months to adjust to already existing peer cliques and a whole new set of friends. If this is the case with your son, you may want to be a bit more proactive with trying to arrange fun outings for his new subgroup of peers.

My daughter has always had maturity issues and now that she's in middle school the kids make fun of her because she's still interested in childish things, like cartoon characters. Part of me is glad she's so "young": I don't want to see her grow up too quickly and am just as happy not to have her exposed to the sexually themed interests of her peers. But am I being too protective?

I know it's difficult for parents to see their children lose their innocence, but your daughter needs to be exposed to age-appropriate materials and items. Mind you, I don't mean *inappropriate* materials— I'm often shocked at how many parents think nothing of bringing their twelve- or thirteen-year-olds to R-rated movies full of graphic violence. Similarly, when my children were in third and fourth grades, I was often unpleasantly surprised to see their classmates on "dates" at the movies. We don't need to encourage or even permit our kids to grow up too fast, but on the other hand, if your daughter only watches kiddie cartoons and she's in middle school, she probably won't fit in. So do try to pick replacement activities and suggest she give away or donate all those DVDs with cartoons. Find magazines, CDs, TV shows, and movies that are age appropriate and acceptable for your middle schooler. Other mothers might be a good source of suggestions.

2. The Art of Conversation

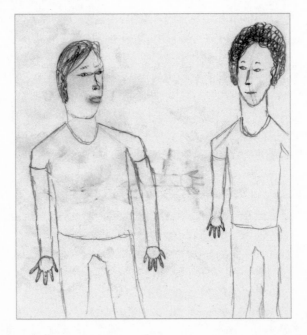

My son desperately wants to have friends, and we've tried hard to put him in situations where he's likely to make them: team sports, chess clubs, church youth groups, and so on. There are definitely some kids out there who share his interests and who seem as if they might be potential "friend material." I know my son wants to reach out to them because he'll talk about them all with great enthusiasm. But when I spy on him in these groups, he's either completely silent (and therefore ignored), or when he tries saying

something, it's so off topic that the other kids give him strange looks and then go back to ignoring him. How do we keep his delayed conversational skills from ruining his social life?

CLAIRE

Take your average kid on the spectrum and put him in a movie theater filled with other kids his age. While they're watching the movie, ask a friendly stranger if he can identify that child. He probably won't be able to, although he might make a wild guess or two. The girl who's nervously biting her nails? Maybe but maybe not. The guy who's rocking a little in his chair? Could be. Not necessarily, though. The kid who's staring intently at the movie, so absorbed he seems oblivious to his surroundings? Possibly. But not definitely.

Okay, now take that same kid and plunk him down at a school lunch table with three other kids from his class who are all chattering away about something—a TV show or a teacher who's irritating them or a party that's coming up or maybe just how awful the food is that day. How long do you think it'll take your imaginary friend to pick out which kid is on the spectrum?

I'm thinking not long. Chances are he's going to figure it out pretty quickly, whether it's because the kid speaks haltingly or because she suddenly starts talking about a completely different topic that no one else seems interested in or because she doesn't make any eye contact when she's speaking or because it sounds as if she's reciting something straight out of a book—and if she's interrupted, she starts right back at the beginning of the recitation.

Making social conversation is hard, and it's even harder if you're someone who has to learn by rules and guidelines the things that other people have an innate sense for. Chatting is more complicated than you realize: people converse one way when they're talking to their grandparents and another way when they're talking to their peers. Conversation is filled with subtle, hard-to-read cues, like the ones that tell you when it's okay to change the subject and when it's rude. Sometimes those cues aren't even oral—they're just a look or a yawn.

We parents of kids on the spectrum have all at some point watched our children struggle to keep up with their peers' conversation. We know what it's like to see our child try to join in—only to have the other kids roll their eyes at the attempt. We've tried to steer our kids into popular interests that will help them make connections, only to hear them instead bring up their one pet obsession over and over again. Those of us who helped teach our kids how to acquire spoken language in the first place (and once swore we'd be happy if we could just hear them say "Mama") are now just as determined to teach them how to make interesting, age-appropriate small talk and conversation, but are stunned by how challenging and complicated it is to do so.

How do we solve all the problems so they can really, truly join in?

DR. KOEGEL

Making conversation is one of the hardest things for kids on the spectrum. Idioms are confusing to them, small talk can be painful, and initiating a dialogue effortful. Even those college students we've worked with who appear totally socially appropriate will usually admit that making conversation is actually excruciatingly difficult for them. But they also say that with practice, it gets easier and can even become enjoyable.

To help make it easier to work on, I'm going to break down the ability to make conversation successfully into several components. Each component, from initiating a dialogue, to active and engaged listening, to maintaining a longer conversation can be addressed if your child could use improvement in that area. Read on.

Initiating a Conversation

Sometimes initiating a conversation—simply getting one started—is the hardest part of making friends, especially for kids on the spectrum. Here are some fairly simple ways to help your child reach out to others throughout the day. Some of these suggestions may seem a bit rudimentary, but kids with social difficulties frequently forget the little basic pleasantries that make a conversation successful, so it's still worth working on them. It won't help your child to be able to discuss quantum physics if it doesn't occur to him first to greet a friend with a pleasant "How's it going?"

Greetings

One easy way to make people feel good is to greet them when they walk into the room—saying "Hi" is just a warm, friendly thing to do. Remind your child to greet his peers—preferably by name—when he sees them for the first time of the day. When you do this, make sure your child is using the same greetings as his peers. We worked with one middle school boy who would walk up to a friend and say, "Hello, Jason Smith, how are you doing today?" While that was polite, and adults appreciated it, the other kids at the school were much more likely to say, "Hey J," with a quick head nod (the one my husband hated when our daughter's boyfriends did it to him). Remember, context is important, and a teenager will and should greet a peer very differently than he would a teacher.

If your child is a little shaky with his classmates' names and identities, you may have to get out last year's yearbook for review or even take some pictures and help him learn to put names with faces.

And if your child just doesn't seem to want to greet people, sometimes it's helpful to connect greeting someone to another activity in his routine, so it becomes automatic. For example, you can teach him that every time he takes his seat, he should say "Hi" to a neighbor, or when he goes to the lunch table, he should say "What's up?" to a classmate. Even video modeling works to teach greetings, especially if your child is one of those kids who really enjoys watching things on TV or DVDs.

Asking Questions

Nothing conveys "I'm interested in starting a conversation with you" like asking a relevant question. You can help your child learn to ask appropriate questions by prompting him. You can start by giving him specific ideas when he's with you, such as "Can you ask me how my day was?" or "Can you ask me if I've seen any good movies lately?" or "Can you ask me what my favorite food is?" You can even pretend to be another kid at school when you do this, if you think the role-playing will help him—and he's willing to go along with it.

Questions can be about anything, but keep in mind that some children do better with concrete questions about things they can actually see ("What did your mom pack you for dessert?") and may be less comfortable with something more abstract. With practice, the more abstract ones will come. And remember, some questions, like "How are you?" are so common that they're almost expected. And if your child actually waits for an answer, he's doing better than most people!

Comments

Comments are also a good way to get a conversation started. There are many things your child can make a comment about, including his or her favorite anything ("Houston's is my favorite restaurant"), family ("My little sister drives me nuts"), food ("I hate peanut butter sandwiches"), weekend plans ("We're going to Disneyland"), weather ("It's so cold today"), teachers ("Mr. Jones is such a hard grader"), and so on. If your child needs a crutch, have him or her carry a picture in his wallet or her purse of someone special or some place he or she went to show others and then comment on it (this is also useful for individuals with more significant communication challenges).

If you're teaching your child to comment, make sure that the comment comes at the right time. Sometimes it's okay to bring up a new subject, but if there are too many out-of-the-blue comments, it may make your kid seem more awkward. You might want to spend time with your child listening to the conversation going on around her and give her some clues when it's appropriate to make comments, such as when the other kids are talking about something relevant or if there is a pause in the conversation. And if she does tend to make out-of-the-blue comments, at least ask her to say, "I know this isn't related to what we've been talking about, but who's the most famous person you've ever met?" or any other selected words that will help the conversation transition to a new topic.

You can also teach your child simply to look around and comment on something he sees around him ("Look at that beautiful Porsche in the parking lot"). This is easy to practice when you're out and about. It can almost be a game: "Hey, look at that bird! I wonder why it's flying south right now." Sort of an adolescent or adult version of I Spy.

Tag Questions

If you want to take it one step further, have your child make a comment, then add a tag question. A tag question is simply a short little question added to the end of a sentence that requests information or clarification from another person, and therefore keeps the conversation going. For example, she can say, "She's a new student, *isn't she?*" "You read that book, *didn't you?*" "It's a hot day, *isn't it?*" or "I like the food here, *how about you?*" Simply adding a tag question can get the other person going during the conversation.

Compliments

Who doesn't like a nice (sincere) compliment? Your child can start a conversation and make someone feel good just by saying "Cool jacket" or "Awesome shirt." You can teach this by picking out something concrete that your child likes about you—maybe something you're wearing—and prompting her to praise it. But make sure that any comment is sincere—don't teach your child to say, "I like your shirt," if she thinks the shirt is ugly. I've worked with a few kids who gave too many compliments (this can sometimes be the case when students are getting some type of reward to help them increase the number of compliments they give), and it's ultimately off-putting.

For example, we worked with one darling girl who just couldn't bring herself to talk to other kids. We practiced having her pick out something nice one of us was wearing—a shiny pair of earrings, a pretty, new sweater, or a nice pair of shoes—then had her give a compliment. Pretty soon, she was doing a fantastic job of saying things like, "I like your earrings" or "Are those new shoes? They're pretty," and so on.

Next we suggested that she could give a friend a compliment, and if she tallied the points on the wrist counter we gave her, she could turn them in for small prizes afterward. We sent the wrist counter with her to camp, and she came home every day with fifteen or twenty points. After about three days, I dropped by the camp and watched—with some shock—as she cheerfully put on her watch, went up to another child, and literally bombarded her with compliments. In the first sixty seconds, she said, "I like your earrings, I like your necklace, I like your shoes, I like your shirt, I like your hat, your hair looks nice, your eyes are a pretty color," and on and on. Then she proudly announced that she had earned all her points.

We had unintentionally created a situation that was worse than when she wasn't saying anything at all to the other kids! Fortunately, once I had observed her, we explained to her that sometimes too much of a good thing isn't better, and that while one compliment may be great, too many is insincere. Make sure you get that message across early on, so you won't make the mistake we did.

Maintaining a Conversation

Once your child knows how to enter into an exchange with a greeting, question, comment, or compliment, he'll start finding himself committed to conversations he then needs to sustain.

I'll often see long awkward pauses and uncomfortable silences when I'm observing adolescents and adults on the spectrum talk to their peers. I've even worked with a few individuals who make facial grimaces or stare blankly when it's their turn to talk—usually because they know that something is now required of them, but they're not sure what to do or say. Empathetic responding is something we often have to practice, but with practice we usually see very rapid improvements.

I've broken successful responding down into learnable components, as follows:

Active and Engaged Listening

Listening seems as if it should be easy for someone on the spectrum—or at least easier than making conversation. All you have to do is stand there, right?

Not really. When people say they like to be listened to, they also mean they want to feel as if they're getting comfort and support from the listener. It's important to be an *active* and supportive listener. In other words, you *can't* just stand there!

Posture

Toward that end, pay close attention to body posture and make sure your child is sending the right signal with hers. Some individuals on the spectrum appear to be outright bored when someone else is speaking: they'll look around, turn and face another direction, and sometimes even walk away when the other person is talking. They have to learn a basic and easy rule: *face the person who's talking and look him or her in the eyes.* That will instantly increase the appearance of interest and rapt attention and will make the speaker feel far more listened to.

Well-timed smiles, frowns, and quizzical expressions also demonstrate a real interest and can be practiced at home. This can be accomplished in several ways, and you'll have to try them to figure out what works best for your child. The easiest way is to simply let your child know when he does or doesn't appear to be interested in what you're saying—make him aware of his affect. You might need to model the desired expressions to help your child really get it and then you can let him know when he's using the right face. If that doesn't work, video modeling or self-management is often helpful. (See Section I, Chapter 2 for precise descriptions of how these methods work.) Remember: always focus on the positive, successful moments and reinforce those with praise rather than criticism.

Learn Appropriate Timing and Cues

Conversation is filled with subtle cues that your child needs to have explained to her. She'll need to learn, for example, that if a person has stopped talking and is looking at her, it's her turn to speak, even if no question has been asked, and that if more than a second or so goes by, the pause will seem painfully long and may reduce the likelihood that the peer will hang in there for more conversation. Similarly, she needs to learn that if she's spoken without pause for too long a period of time, it's time to give the other person a chance to speak.

For kids who are having difficulty maintaining a conversation without long pauses, I often play a game of "How quickly can you answer?" I ask lots of questions and time their responses. If they answer in less than a second, I give them positive feedback. If it takes longer, I have them try again. If your child or adult needs an incentive to keep him motivated, you can work up one together. Video modeling also works well, so he can see which areas need work. By videotaping your child, you can figure out exactly where the problems are.

Finally, learning to read other people's body cues can help. Is the other person looking away, smiling, looking uncomfortable? Individuals on the spectrum often have to be taught what these cues mean. We often start by exaggerating the cues, like yawning or looking in a completely different direction. It's helpful sometimes to teach your child to ask if she's getting the cue right. For example, she can say, "I see you're looking at your watch—do you have to run?" or "Are you interested in *Family Guy* or would you rather talk about something else?" Improving all of these areas can help to get the timing right during conversation.

Ask Relevant Questions

We've noticed that many adolescents and adults on the spectrum really don't ask enough questions. Well-timed and concerned questions are key to making and maintaining friendships, so teaching your child to ask appropriate questions will fill in the gaps, keep the conversation going, and ultimately help him socially.

Earlier in this chapter we talked about initiating conversations with questions. That sometimes takes a lot more work because your child will have to dream up something to talk about. Asking a question within the conversation can be easier because your child can bounce a question off the previous statement.

It's important that your child show interest in what the other person is saying, and an appropriate question will make it clear he's really listening. You can work on that. For example, if you say, "The food here is really bad," you can practice having your child say, "What did you have?" so she can learn how a related question will keep the conversation going. You can also teach her that a great time to ask a question is when there are a few seconds of silence during a conversation.

When we work with our adolescents and adults, we usually have them come up with about three questions they could have asked in a given context. If they can't think of any, we give them suggestions. For example, if the conversation is about the weather and the adult on the spectrum can't think of anything to ask, we may prompt her to ask if the other person likes snow, or what his/her favorite kind of weather is, or if he/she knows what the forecast is. With practice, and brainstorming, asking questions gets easier.

We all want our friends to show that they care about our well-being and aren't just wishing we would move on to another topic when we're expressing some distress. To put it simply, what a worried or sad friend wants to hear is "Are you OK?" and *not* "He wasn't right for you anyway," "You'll be fine," or "It doesn't sound like that big a deal." You need to make sure that your child learns how to ask the kind of questions that show real concern about the other person and uses a tone of voice that sounds sincere.

Reflecting the Response

Not only does your child need to learn to wait for a response (after asking a question or giving the other person a chance to speak) but he also needs to learn to reflect that response in some way, to prove that he's been listening and is interested. This can take the form of either a question or a comment. For example, if your child asks, "Did you see *The Happening*?" and the peer says, "No, I don't like scary movies," your child can reflect on this by asking another question: "Oh, you don't like scary movies, what kind of movies do you like?" Or he might comment: "I don't like them either, although the *Scream* movies were kind of fun." Reflecting a response not only lets the other person know you're a good listener but can also buy some time while you're thinking up a question!

Many of our kids answer questions as briefly as possible. For example, if someone asks, "Do you have any sisters or brothers?" they might simply say yes and nothing else. Or if someone asks what their favorite class is, they might just say, "Math." We've had success overcoming this brevity by teaching our kids the strategy of (1) making a statement, (2) adding some information, and (3) sharing a feeling about it. Then we add that it's time to let the other person respond.

So if someone says, "Do you like math?" we teach them to say something like, "Yeah, I like math—we're working on quadratic equations. Mrs. Berry explains them really well." Or if a peer asks if they have any brothers or sisters, they might say, "Yeah, I have a brother; he's two years younger than me, and he's really into baseball." The three rules are easy to remember and help to keep the conversation moving. We often practice by writing a little diagram of these three steps: **topic→more information→feeling.**

Visual aids, like the above, can help provide a framework for practice and often facilitate the understanding of the process for kids on the spectrum. While these longer utterances may sound a little awkward initially, with enough practice your child will internalize the idea, and become a much better conversationalist.

While many of our kids have trouble getting the conversation started, we also have some kids who go on and on and on and on. The strategy we discussed above—(1) making a statement, (2) adding some information, and (3) sharing a feeling, and then waiting for the other person to respond—works great for this group too. They often don't pick up on the conversational partner's clues that they are giving far too much information, but if we teach them to limit many of their responses to those three pieces of information, they can learn to maintain a much more even give-and-take.

Stick to the Topic at Hand

It's important to teach your child to really listen to what others are saying and not just wait for a chance to talk about what interests her. Make sure your child's responses in a conversation are related to what preceded them. For example, if a peer says, "My grandmother is in the hospital" and your child responds with "Do you like ancient Egyptian art?" that's not likely to make her friend want to continue the conversation or seek her out in the future. In contrast, if your child responds with "That's too bad; I'll bet that's really difficult for you" (or perhaps the more contextually appropriate "That totally sucks"), she will be considered an empathetic conversational partner.

If your child has especially restricted interests and difficulty talking about anything else, you'll need to practice this empathetic listening quite a bit, because it's an important piece of the making-friends puzzle. The other day I was working on conversation with an adult with Asperger's syndrome who really has no friends. The first thing he said to me was, "Would you rather be a pilot on an aircraft or the captain of a submarine?" When I replied, "Probably neither, since I don't like being too far above or below ground level," he said, "What do I do if someone just doesn't want to talk about the things that I want to talk about?" Anyway, we talked about how important it was when asking questions to make sure the other person is interested in the topic. Eventually, he asked enough questions that he hit on a topic of interest to both of us (specifically, the latest fiction books I had read).

You can practice staying on topic and then give your child feedback, or use self-management or video modeling to work on these areas. Feedback and redirection can be helpful, but be sure not to criticize your child—he's trying hard to socialize in the best way he can and needs support, not criticism. And it's always more effective to point out the successful moments than the unsuccessful ones. It's kind of like when someone tells you not to think about elephants and then that's about all you can think about. So if you focus on strengths rather than weaknesses, your child will remember the pluses. Newly learned behaviors are more likely to be used if the person is working for something positive (like a compliment) rather than avoiding a punishment.

Finding a Natural Rhythm of Speech

Maintaining a dialogue isn't just about the words exchanged, but also about tone and nuance. Using the right intonation, pausing at the appropriate times, speaking at varying speeds, and emphasizing certain words all contribute to making a person interesting and easy to listen to while adding to the emotion of any message. Most of us instinctively learn how to monitor our voices from feedback that friends and family have given us. In fact, certain people make a living from the manipulation of their voices—think of our favorite TV characters, such as the soft-spoken psychologist who asks all the questions or the fast-talking deal maker or breaker. Prosody conveys message, meaning, and feeling. Unfortunately, many of our kids have prosody problems. Some talk too quickly, some too slowly, some too loudly, some too softly, and some simply have very unusual intonation patterns.

I have found that many individuals on the spectrum respond well to intervention in this area, but you have to devote a lot of time to practicing if they still persist in the teen and adult years, because—let's face it—they've been talking that way for a long, long time. Basically your child will need to practice until the new speech patterns become a habit. We worked with one university student who had no pitch variation in her voice: she talked in a monotone. We started working on the rising and falling intonation people use when they ask a question, and she said it felt very awkward and exaggerated to her (although it sounded great to us). It took a lot of practice until she felt comfortable using the right voice modulation, but she did get it in time.

Here's an overview of some of the different types of prosody problems that are common with kids on the spectrum, with advice on how to work on improving them, and some real-life examples:

1. **Talks too quickly or slowly.** Many people on the spectrum talk too slowly. It almost feels as if they start to say something and their mind just wanders, leading to really long pauses in the conversation. The intervention we use also works well for people who talk too quickly. Basically, we're teaching them a good pace. Here's how you do it.

   a. **Gather materials.** The first thing you'll need to do is gather together some materials that will help the person you're working with get ideas. They can be any combination of pictures from family albums, books, magazines, postcards, and so on. Put them together in a pile for easy access. If your child needs a little extra incentive, decide on a specific number of points he needs (like twenty) to earn a little prize, which could be a break, a treat, or a fun activity you'll do together when you finish—whatever appeals to him.

b. **Start small and easy.** Now take those items, and pick out one word to say about each item. For example, if it's a family photo album, you can say "Mom" for one picture, then "Dad" on the next picture, then "vacation" on the one that has the last family trip. Have your child repeat each word after you and tell her, "That sounded great" if she says it with the right pace. Do this until she can repeat twenty words in a row with a good-sounding pace. If it doesn't sound right, ask her to try it again and repeat the word you want her to imitate.

c. **Do it alone.** Now it's his turn to say the words at the right pace by himself. Remember, you aren't going to model the word for him this time through. Go through the pictures or cards again and praise him ("Wow! That sounded great!") every time he says a word with a good pace. If he doesn't sound so great, don't criticize him or take points away, just matter-of-factly ask him to try again.

d. **Up the ante.** Now you're going to repeat steps b and c, but with two words. Instead of saying "Mom," you're going to add a word, for instance, "Mom's shirt" or "my dad" or "family vacation." Have her repeat the two words and when she does so at the right pace, praise her. After she says twenty in a row at the right pace, have her redo those twenty all by herself while you give feedback after every utterance.

e. **Move to phrases.** Now it's time to move up to very short phrases—no more than three or four words. You can add something to each two-word combination, for example, "Mom's new shirt," "my dad fishes," or "our family vacation." Again, first have him repeat after you then let him say the phrase by himself once he's repeated twenty in a row at the right pace. Remember, compliment him on how great it sounds.

f. Start sentences. After phrases, you can move to sentences. So this time you're going to have her repeat your sentences, such as, "My mom has a new shirt," "My dad fishes at the lake," or "Our family vacation was fun." Give her verbal rewards for nice-sounding sentences and have her try again if they're too slow (or too fast). After she can repeat twenty sentences in a row with good pacing, have her say twenty sentences by herself.

g. Move it into conversation. Now you'll need to practice with very controlled conversation. Start by letting him know you're going to be working on the pace, or "how he sounds" (use whatever key words you feel comfortable with to describe it), while you just chat. Feel free to use the pictures and ask him to just say a couple of things about the picture or to use a sentence or two to answer your questions. If he has a problem with the pace, have him stop and repeat the sentence he had trouble with after you. So, for example, if he says, "We always have (long pause) fun on our family vacations," you can say, "Honey, can you try it like this? 'We always have fun on our family vacations.'" Then have him repeat the sentence. Practice this until you can have a nice conversation where he's using the right pace.

h. Move it to different locations. One thing that often causes a problem for kids on the spectrum is using the newly learned speech rhythm in everyday contexts—they may be used to speaking at the right pace in the one room where you've been practicing, but take them to the store or a restaurant and their newly acquired ability may disappear. So you'll need to continue practicing in lots of different places.

i. **Practice with different people.** You'll also need to practice with lots of different people. You can do this from the get-go or you can do it after your child is speaking at a good pace. You can get your child's relatives and friends involved if that's comfortable. Anyone other than the person who did the original teaching will work.

j. **Continue to check for good pacing.** If your child is talking at the right rate in all of her settings, you're finished. And remember, the most important time to check is when she's with her peers. Adults can be a lot more forgiving and patient. If the good pacing only happens when the setting is somewhat controlled, she may need to self-monitor her pace. Check Section I, Chapter 2 for the specific procedures, but she'll probably need to use a wrist counter to monitor every sentence or few sentences. Simply being aware of the rate throughout the day will improve her speed until the right pace eventually becomes unconscious. Once she's self-managing, keep monitoring to make sure the rate is right in all kinds of places with all kinds of people.

2. **Disfluencies.** Disfluencies are a close cousin to rate problems, so the interventions that work are very similar. A disfluency is any repetition, whether word ("I want to go go go to the store"), phrase ("I wanna go, I wanna go"), insertion ("I want to um, um, um, go"), break, or other irregularity that interrupts the flow of a sentence. While virtually everyone has some disfluencies, when there are too many, you may need to intervene. It's also important to note that many children, especially boys, tend to go through a period of time (usually in the preschool years) when they have more disfluencies, which they often outgrow. However, most of the children on

the spectrum I have worked with seem to have disfluencies because their mind wanders midsentence. They may have a perfectly logical thought, but while trying to express it, they think about something else, and the sentence just doesn't come out right. The intervention for rate works well with disfluencies for kids on the spectrum. Go through each step listed above, then, if necessary, have them self-manage each sentence with a wrist counter.

3. **Talks too loudly or softly.** A small percentage of kids on the spectrum habitually speak at the wrong volume. I had dinner once with an adult with Asperger's syndrome, and he told me more details than I wanted to know about his previous girlfriend in such a loud voice that I swear everyone in the whole restaurant knew all about his love life by the end of the evening. Since modulating how loudly or quietly you speak isn't related to breaking up the speech into smaller parts, like rate and fluency problems, you can usually start at the sentence level. Here are some suggested steps:

a. **Repeat it:** Have your child repeat sentences at an appropriate volume level. You can start with sentences or a few sentences that your child can remember well enough to repeat back. Do this in a variety of settings, where there are different amounts of background noise: the car, a restaurant, a coffee shop, a classroom, a party, and so on. Give him feedback after every sentence: "That sounded great; you were talking at just the right volume" or "I couldn't hear that one—could you say it a little louder?" Do this until he can repeat at least twenty sentences in a row at a perfect volume.

b. **Say it alone:** Repeat step a, above, but this time have your child say the sentences by herself. They can be comments, questions, or statements. This is just to give her a chance to practice without the direct model. Remember to give feedback after each sentence, telling her whether it was the right volume or if she should try again. Do this in a variety of places, just like the last step.

c. **Self-manage:** Now give your child a wrist counter and have him monitor the volume of each sentence or phrase. Practice by engaging him in conversation. Ask questions and have him monitor each sentence for the right loudness level. Do this in a variety of settings.

d. **Use it everywhere:** Have your child use the wrist counter in other settings when you aren't there. Read Section I, Chapter 2 for details about how to set up a reward system and check for success in these everyday settings. And make sure you check with people in those everyday settings to make sure she's actually continuing to monitor the right volume you've worked on.

e. **Troubleshooting:** If your child still continues to have trouble with volume, you may want to use some prompts. You can verbally or visually prompt him, but don't forget about prompt fading (described in Section I, Chapter 2). For example, a 1 can be an indoor voice when it's nice and calm and quiet, and a 5 can be the outdoor voice when he's trying to get everyone's attention on the baseball field or basketball court. A 3 can be halfway in between. Then you can quietly let him know ahead of time (or during an event, if necessary) which level he should be using. You can also come up with some hand signals so it's discreet and doesn't attract attention. The right signal between you and your child can help him with the ever-changing appropriate volume levels whatever situation he's in.

4. **Talks in a monotone.** When people don't vary their tone or voice inflection during conversation, they sound boring, no matter how interesting their subject matter is. Although we all

dread the moment in scary movies when a loud and sudden noise makes us jump out of our chairs, it does add a bit of a thrill to the flick. Similarly, variation in voice keeps our interest. When an actor gets a sudden high shrill in her voice, we know she's scared. When a parent sternly admonishes his child, we know he's serious. When you chuckle a little while telling a story, we know it's going to be funny. But kids on the spectrum often speak in a perfect monotone, with seemingly no emotion. Like anything else, we can teach people to break that monotone habit. Here's how we do it:

a. **Break it down.** Start with one type of speech area, like exclamations—pick ones that kids use at school a lot, like "Awesome!" or "Cool!"—and model how they should be said, then have your child repeat them with lots of inflection in his voice. Have him keep doing it until it sounds natural, not forced. I usually have kids repeat each expression several times before moving on to the next.

b. **Do it alone.** Now see if your child can use the right voice inflection on her own. You can write down the words, or just prompt her by talking about situations when the expression would come up, then ask her to use it on her own—not repeated. If, for example, you've practiced using the response "Awesome!" you could ask her what she thought of this week's episode of her favorite show. Do this several times for each expression.

c. **Practice during everyday activities.** Once your child is able to use better intonation on expressions, you'll need to work on his using them in everyday contexts. You can play games and have him say "Oh no!" with plenty of expression when he gets a bad spin or loses a game. Practice this until it becomes a habit and you don't need to remind him.

d. **Check his use in other natural settings.** Next, you'll need to check to make sure he's using the right intonation in everyday settings without your prompting. If not, keep practicing. If necessary, recruit friends, teachers, or peers to help in natural settings.

e. **Move on to the next area.** Next you can practice with greetings, questions, and comments. Do it the same way you did the expressions and remember to go through all the steps while paying particular attention to whether your child is using the right intonation in his everyday settings—not just with you when you're practicing.

It's important to remember, with all these interventions, that kids progress at different rates. Sometimes a few practice sessions then reminders are enough. Other times it takes many months to relearn to talk using the right prosody. So be patient and provide lots of positive support for your child. But be consistent and practice as often as possible. If reminders don't work, try self-management. Don't worry if you need to go back a step for your child to be successful. As long as you're making gradual but steady progress, she will sound better.

Read on for a case history example of a young adult whose speech was quickly but dramatically improved by these interventions.

Diane's Program

Diane was an extremely intelligent person whom I met when she started college here at UCSB. She had a diagnosis of autism and had started talking at a very late age and had also had some social difficulties throughout her life. Diane was probably the smartest undergraduate computer science major in the whole university and she had no shortage of guys asking her out (the nice thing about college is that people value intellect and are well past the adolescent gotta-be-cool stage). But Diane talked in a monotone, and I was concerned that it would make people lose interest in what she was saying.

I started working with her on asking questions with the right intonation patterns. Most questions have rising then falling intonation, like "How are you?" and "What are you doing?" To give her a visual, I drew a diagram with the rising then falling pattern. Next, we practiced dozens of flash cards with questions I'd written out by hand—first I had her imitate how I did it but soon I had her try it alone.

It didn't take Diane long to get the idea. Next we had to bring it into the real world. We started out taking short walks and having her ask questions of fellow students and staff around the Center. Interestingly, she told me that she felt awkward using the nonmonotone voice. She said it sounded so exaggerated to her that it almost felt as if she were a cartoon character! But she sounded great to me. Because of her reluctance to use the new intonation patterns, it took about six months of daily practice until it began to feel natural for her, but it was worth it: it made a huge difference in how she sounded and ultimately in how people responded to her.

CLAIRE

For many years, I was so relieved that my son could speak at all that it took me a while to realize that his speech was still strictly literal: he could exchange information very well and deliver pleasantries, but the second the dialogue veered into anything even vaguely witty, it confused him. When his younger brother started getting an edge to his tone, it hit me: I had to teach Andrew how to be sarcastic. Yes, sarcastic—the very thing we parents usually try to get our kids to stop being.

The thing is, teenagers communicate almost entirely with sarcasm. It gives them emotional distance from what they're saying, which feels safer than just being straight and serious. Not just kids, either—I've seen a fair number of teachers use sarcasm in the classroom ("I don't suppose it occurred to anyone to actually do the work I assigned?"), and I definitely didn't want my son to be bewildered or wounded by it, or to take it too literally.

So I set out to "teach" sarcasm. I started by using it gently with Andrew and then immediately commenting on it. I might say something like "Guess that plate is too heavy for you to clear, huh?" and then I'd quickly say, "I'm being sarcastic. I really just want you to clear the plate." As he got the idea, I was able to fade out the explanation. I also pointed out when other people were being sarcastic. Now he laughs when I say something sarcastic, knowing immediately it's a joke. He's still less likely to use sarcasm than, say, his younger brother (who, at fourteen, hardly ever says anything that isn't sarcastic), but he recognizes it when he hears it, he gets it, and he knows not to take everything literally.

DR. KOEGEL

Strategies for Improving General Conversation Skills

Here are some strategies for actively promoting your child's ability to interact with his peers.

Carpooling—Yes, I Said Carpooling

The truth is that playing chauffeur can be a great way to learn what your child's peers are thinking and talking about. The fact that the kids are buckled into one place for a period of time means your child gets a real opportunity to be part of a general conversation with you around to monitor and observe.

I learned so much about my kids' and their friends' lives when I drove in the middle school carpool. They would get so engrossed in their conversations that they would completely forget a mom was in the car. From those daily twenty-minute drives, I gathered an abundance of information about peers (such as who was drinking and smoking), siblings, exes, dates, grades, tests, and just about any other topic a parent would or wouldn't want to know about. The experience really helped me get to know what qualified as "normal" thought and behavior for kids that age.

If you dread the carpool because your child is having trouble making appropriate conversation, try to tough it out by remembering that it is your chance to learn ways to help him. Pay attention to what your child's peers are talking about, how they initiate conversation, what types of questions they ask, and so on, and then work on those areas with your own child. I would suggest starting to work on them at home (priming) first and then making suggestions to him just before you pick up his classmates, for example, "When the others are in the car, maybe you could tell them about the movie we saw last night." If your child still isn't participating, you can try giving some help after everyone's in the car by saying things like "Jeanne brought some doughnut holes today" or "Bradley, did you want to tell the kids about the songs you downloaded on your iPod last night?" But only step in if talking with your child beforehand isn't working—you don't want to do too much of this. Even little things like having your child ask which CD the other kids want to listen to can help start a conversation (make sure the CDs are *their* music, not *yours*).

One sixth grader we worked with seemed to be totally uninvolved in any social group whatsoever. His mother tried and tried to get him with a group of friends, but he repeatedly resisted. By chance, she volunteered to drive on a field trip. Jamie's mother astutely noticed that when he was buckled in with a group of peers, he had totally appropriate conversations with great turn taking. Armed with this information, she volunteered to drive in the carpool. After a few weeks of driving the kids home, she asked them if they would like to go out for ice cream. Of course, she chose a special ice cream parlor on the other side of the city to create an extra twenty minutes of conversational opportunity. Shortly afterward, the carpooling turned into study sessions then expanded into the kids' hanging out. In this way, Jamie's mom capitalized on a successful situation to develop a peer group for him.

Practicing and Priming

Every time you speak with your child, you have another opportunity to help her improve her conversational skills. Prompt her to ask you questions and then help her learn to respond to your questions the way she should with anyone else.

A conversation practice session between you and your child might go something like this:

YOU: "Ask me how my day was."

YOUR CHILD: "How was your day?"

YOU: "It was great! Now ask me what was so great about it."

YOUR CHILD: "What was so great about your day?"

YOU: "I went out to lunch with a friend."

YOUR CHILD: "Cool!" (Prompted by you if he doesn't say anything immediately)

YOU: "Can you ask me another question about my lunch?"

YOUR CHILD: "What did you eat?" or something like that. (If your child can't come up with anything on his own, give him some suggestions, like, "Do you want to know where I went?" or "Do you want to know who I went out with?")

You get the idea. Your child will need practice. And in order to help your child, you'll need to figure out which areas are difficult for her. That way, you can work on one or even a few things at a time in the specific area that your child needs the most help in.

Priming works very well for phone conversations. We often have the child on the spectrum call our staff members and relatives before making an actual phone call to a friend. Even practicing ordering pizza or takeout can be helpful in preparing him for a future social call.

Priming also works great for outings. For example, if your child is going to take a date to a special exhibit at an art museum, it's helpful to go there beforehand so he or she is familiar with the show and has something to talk about—you can suggest some ideas for topics while you're there. We had one adult who went to a car show and accumulated a vast amount of information about the cars, then invited a friend. Unfortunately, he proceeded to correct his friend every time she said something that was inaccurate about the car! So remember to teach your child how to use knowledge in a helpful and kind way. Individuals on the spectrum are often very bright, and like any bright person, each one needs to learn how to share information without sounding superior or like a know-it-all.

Remember, these conversational strategies take time to learn. Keep practicing with your child and also ask friends, family, and instructors to practice with her and give her feedback. Breaking old habits takes a lot of time and practice, so be patient. Keep your tone supportive and encouraging: remember, you want your child to *enjoy* talking with others, not see it as a chore that she always gets scolded about for messing up. Commit some real time to this. You, she, and all her present and future friends will be glad you did.

Self-Management
Self-management can be very effective in reducing speech habits that need to be broken or encouraging new habits that will vastly improve conversational skills. Read on for an example of how it helped one young man improve his ability to make conversation.

Tristan was an amazing kid, very self-sufficient and perfectly able to communicate. Unfortunately, social conversation wasn't his favorite activity, and he had figured out that when he answered someone's question, she would probably just ask him *another* one, which was the last thing he wanted, so he found it easiest not to respond in the first place.

To solve this problem, we bought him a little wrist counter and taught him to click the wrist counter every time he responded when someone asked him a question. We practiced it with familiar adults and staff from the Center until he regularly answered questions from all of us. Shortly after that, we sent him out into the real world to see how he would fare (we had people he didn't know there for support in case he ran into a problem). He did amazingly well. Once we sent him into the grocery store to buy a few items, and the bagger asked if he wanted paper or plastic. When Tristan responded, "Plastic," he immediately gave himself a point! Before the self-management, he had rarely responded at all, but with the self-management he learned to answer without having a therapist or parent nagging him. After several months of improvement, we were able to gradually start fading the counter.

I've kept in touch with Tristan and he continues to be responsive to others, and is quite conversational, even after many years. And this was a kid who, when he was younger, at best only answered half the time.

Video Modeling

Video modeling is another great way you can help your child work on conversation skills. To use it specifically for promoting conversational skills, you would videotape your adolescent or adult having a conversation with someone, then locate the sections where there is good conversation going on as well as the sections where your child needs more help. You and your child can then go over the clips and discuss better ways of responding in the situations that are causing her difficulty. And remember, start with a positive example and end with a positive example. We always want to emphasize the positive, especially in the beginning. You can then practice increasing the successful interactions and decreasing the negative ones, videotape again, and review it all again.

Video modeling is a rapid and effective way to improve conversation skills, and we generally see pretty quick changes with it, as we did with Jake. Jake was a young adult we worked with who, although tall and good-looking, felt very insecure about his ability to talk to others. We videotaped him conversing with peers, and when we were watching the tapes, we found that most of the conversation went fine, except for one problem: he rarely asked any questions. He was able to make comments and engage in long, back-and-forth interactions, but because he didn't ask questions, there were long, awkward pauses in the conversation. For Jake's video-modeling program, we showed him short clips of the few times he did actually ask a question and contrasted that with clips of long silences.

We then suggested different types of relevant questions he could ask during future conversations. For example, we said that if a friend mentioned liking Italian food, Jake could then ask him what his favorite Italian restaurant was or if he also liked to cook Italian food. Or if someone said she liked to read, he could ask her what books she had read lately or what genre of books she preferred.

Because we were able to pinpoint the problem, and because Jake was bright and motivated, it only took about three or four videotape feedback sessions before he was able to get the idea. And without those uncomfortable pauses, Jake was a perfectly fine conversationalist.

CLAIRE

We've found that most of Andrew's minor verbal differences have improved with simple reminders. He's so motivated to be part of the social mainstream that a simple "You're talking a little loudly" will instantly inspire him to modulate his voice. (In fact, he's become so sensitive to volume control that he often—and quite accurately—tells his younger siblings they're being too loud.)

Back when he was in middle school, we needed to remind him fairly frequently that it's okay sometimes just to listen. Because most of Andrew's interests were different from his peers', we noticed that he would sometimes use any break in the general conversation to swing the subject away from what they were talking about—World of Warcraft, say, or some TV show he hadn't seen—and onto something that interested him more, like theme parks or people's relative heights. The problem was, a lot of times the group wasn't ready to move on to a new topic, and even if it had been, his topics probably weren't the ones they would have chosen, which meant they would all ignore him or roll their eyes at one another. Obviously, we didn't want that, so we had several discussions about how, when a group of friends are talking about a subject you can't contribute to, it's really okay to listen and take in what they're saying and maybe ask a relevant question or two—and not worry about contributing.

Here are his thoughts on the subject of making conversation:

ANDREW

Whenever I am trying to communicate with someone, it always feels like I am playing a game of operator. Operator is another name for the game telephone. In that game, you are

supposed to come up with some phrase and pass it down all the way (by whispering) around until the person before you gets the message. People always misunderstand what phrase is getting passed on to them. In my opinion, that is what conversations are like for me a lot of the time. What I mean by this is that sometimes it is hard for me to fully understand what someone else is saying in a conversation. I tend to think that someone is saying something else that he/she is not trying to say. Sometimes during conversations with a big group of people, I misunderstand what topic people are talking about and whenever I try to jump in to talk about the topic I think they are talking about, other people end up getting frustrated with me and ignore me.

Talking one-on-one is much easier for me (which I am sure it is for most people) because then you do not have to worry as much about interrupting others, and it is easier for you to know when it is your turn to say something.

Sometimes it is harder for me to understand what people are saying because they slur their words, they talk too fast or too slowly, or they are from another country and do not know a lot of English. When I encounter a group of people, the only conversations I find boring are the ones that have to do with sports, about other kids who I do not know, TV shows that bore me, or if a conversation is way too much about video games. It is hard for me to be involved because I could not say anything about those kids, and I also do not know much about sports and find them incredibly boring. I also do not like to join conversations that include mean kids who make fun of me a lot.

I do like to join conversations about celebrities, music, cities, computers, theme parks, gossip, *The Simpsons* TV show, sometimes video games, sometimes politics, or about kids I know. I am a huge theme park fan (as I probably said before) and like roller coasters and other thrill rides. I also am a huge entertainment fan and like movies, music, and talking about how great or screwed up some celebrities can be. I am also a big *Simpsons* fan and like to talk about that with others, especially the fact that my dad is a writer for the show. I am also into computers, Web sites, and animation and like to talk about that kind of stuff as well. I also like to talk about video games I like and sometimes about the 2008 election going on (right now as I write).

Whenever I am talking to a group of friends, however, I try not to make them talk about what I like to talk about too much. I want to be flexible and talk with other friends about what they are interested in, but at the same time, some topics can be boring, so then I start to talk about something else by politely changing the subject and not interrupting anyone. For others who struggle making conversation, I would suggest that you find people to talk to who you relate to and who are nice. That way, it will be much easier to make conversation and have fun with it.

Frequently Asked Questions

Now that you've made me aware of it, I'm realizing that my son doesn't ask enough questions. I want to teach him some good, basic questions to start conversations with—or to keep one going—but I keep drawing a blank. Can you help me out here?

Below are some topic areas and examples of the questions your child could ask within that area. This may seem a little basic, but in my experience the biggest hurdle for kids with social difficulties is making simple conversation, so it's worth making sure yours has mastered these social pleasantries. I've listed a few really common topics to get you started.

• **Past and future activities.** People ask lots of questions about past activities: "Did you go on vacation?" "Did you watch TV?" (or any specific shows), "Have you read any good books lately?" "Have you seen X movie?" "What did you do over the weekend?"

"What are you going to do this weekend?" "Do you want to hang out this weekend?" And so on.

- **Sports.** Many people are either into sports or play sports. You can have your child ask about particular games or what kind of sports the other person does. "Do you play any sports?" "Did you see the Lakers game last Sunday?" "Do you want to play basketball at lunch?"

- **School.** If you have a middle schooler, high schooler, or college student, school is always a relevant topic area. Kids talk about teachers, classes, and curricula: "Have you ever had Mrs. X's class?" "Don't you think Coach X is tough?" "Who's your favorite teacher this semester?" "How did you like the lecture in history today?" "What classes are you taking this quarter?" These questions usually lead to long conversations.

- **Food.** This is probably the most popular topic in middle and high school lunch periods, but it also works for adults in restaurants and general conversation: "What are you having for lunch?" "Do you like what your mom packs?" "Do you want a cookie?" "Do you like tuna, because I don't!"

- **Favorites.** You can really find out a lot about someone by asking about their favorites, for example, "What's your favorite TV show/movie/book/holiday?" and so on. Even a question as simple as "What's your favorite color?" can lead to an interesting conversation.

My daughter is quite verbal and very comfortable expressing herself in a conversation—maybe a little too comfortable. She's so assertive about her own opinions—even and especially when they're different from those expressed by the person she's talking with—that she turns people off. She doesn't do it to be disagreeable—she just thinks she's carrying her side of the conversation. But I've seen her peers lose patience with all that contradiction. Any advice?

This is another excellent opportunity to use video modeling to make it clear to your child what the problem is.

We once worked with a young man named Adam, whose mother was concerned because he stayed on the Internet in his room all day long and she really wanted him to make friends. Unfortunately, his peers weren't crazy about him. We videotaped him making conversation and when we analyzed his tapes, we found that in general, he engaged in quite intelligent, interesting, and captivating conversation. The only problem? He was often unintentionally rude.

The rudeness was really argumentativeness. For example, if Adam said that he didn't like Greek food and the person he was talking to said that she liked it, Adam would go into a lengthy diatribe about everything not to like about Greek food. For some reason, he couldn't just accept a different opinion. If his favorite color was blue and someone else's was red, Adam seemed to feel he had to argue about why blue was the better color.

Since the initial intervention goal was to make him aware he's often unnecessarily argumentative, we began by pointing out the moments in the tape when he was being pleasant and a good listener, and then moved on to more problematic examples. Adam wasn't thrilled with this part of the process, but eventually he did come to recognize how uncomfortable it made other people when he "attacked" them for their opinions or simply insisted that his own opinion was superior. As we often see with our kids, just being aware of the problem helped him to overcome it, which is why the video modeling works so well.

When my daughter tries to maintain eye contact, she opens her eyes a little too wide and tries a little too hard. Any advice on keeping it natural?

Again, she'll need feedback, but try to focus on the positive. Emphasize the times when she does use great and natural eye contact. Self-management or video modeling may work well for her if the feedback isn't enough.

When my child is talking to a friend or a group of friends, should I prompt her then? Or fade back? I worry that she's not making conversation "the right way" yet, and I know I could whisper some good questions to ask—but I never know if I should when other people are around.

This is a good question, and it depends on the situation. But first, I would recommend *not* whispering. That is likely to draw more attention to your child. Generally, we try to make a more subtle comment like "Oh, Kiki, did you hear that? Samantha loves cooking; that's just like you. I wonder what she likes to cook." If you feel that even that is too intrusive, you and your child may need to practice at home. Finally, if she just isn't getting it, you may want to recruit a few peers to help out, as long as you're comfortable letting them know your child needs some extra support. Tell them what you're working on and ask them if they could give your child some gentle, helpful feedback. All kids give their peers feedback—whether they want it or not—so you're just asking them to help in specific areas.

I've noticed that most of my son's peers are kind of rude: they use a lot of swear words and can be downright insulting to one another. I want my son to fit in and be "one of the gang" but I really hesitate to teach him to talk like that. What would you suggest?

Let's think about swearing from an intellectual point of view. Most adults swear when they're frustrated or angry and are unable to control their emotions. They know it's taboo and inappropriate and would never do it in a business meeting or with friends, but when a car cuts them off or they drop something precious, those expletives just explode uncontrollably. And physiologically, that's exactly what happens. A different part of the brain seems to process those emotional words that come out in a crisis situation, as opposed to when you're intentionally formulating a word or group of words. That's why they just seem to slip out.

Now take the swearing teens do. It isn't accidental and unintentional—swear words regularly serve as adjectives, nouns, and verbs in teens' communication. That's all a part of trying to fit in, be cool, and deliberately flirt with what's taboo. But it appears that once the kids start using the swear words in their intentional communication, it becomes a habit and it's more difficult not to use those words in other contexts when it isn't appropriate. So I would say *don't encourage it*. Let your son know that the other kids will stop swearing when they grow up. And be a good role model. Don't let those unintended words slip out in your own vocabulary. Teach your child to expand his vocabulary with interesting and unique words that aren't offensive. And finally, remind him that swearing is offensive to some people.

My daughter is basically a sponge: she can memorize anything. The problem is, she treats a lot of conversation like a script she can't deviate from. So, for example, if someone asks where she lives, she'll launch into the exact address, complete with zip code, and then give directions to get there—and if anyone tries to cut her off before she's gotten through the whole recitation, she'll start all over again from the beginning! How do we teach her to approach conversation more fluidly?

Your daughter may be a great candidate to work on the **topic→more information→feeling** that we discussed on page 64. By using this system, she'll be able to figure out exactly the important parts of the conversation that are meant to be shared. Don't forget, though: if there's some way to work her ability to absorb information around to her advantage, find it. A club, recreational, or work setting where memorization would be a useful tool may be the perfect place for her.

Summary

We've spent a lot of time and pages on social conversation because it's so incredibly crucial to forming friendships—and it becomes more important as people get older. Because it tends to be one of the hardest areas for someone on the spectrum to master, social conversation often demands a huge amount of effort and focus, but don't even think about neglecting it. Being able to carry on a pleasant conversation ties into everything your child will need and want in the future, from romantic relationships to jobs to academic success to feeling comfortable out and about in the world.

3. Outings and Get-togethers

My teenage daughter is getting too old to still have playdates at home with dad always hovering nearby—all the kids in her class meet at the mall and the movie theater and places like that. I want her to join them, but she's not used to going out on her own and, frankly, I'm not sure she's ready. On the other hand, it would probably be social suicide for her to be the only kid hanging out with a parent at her side—nor do I particularly want to spend my limited free time with a bunch of thirteen-year-olds. Help!

CLAIRE

Andrew was very eager to go out alone with friends once he was in middle school, but I have to admit that I had some concerns about letting him be alone in public places without an adult supervising. We gave him a cell phone and told him we expected him to check in at regular intervals—usually every hour on the hour because that was easy to remember, or if he was seeing a movie, right before going into the cinema and right after coming out. I explained that his future independence would be based on how responsible he was. If he called us at the expected times and let us know everything was fine, then we'd allow him greater freedom in the future.

For those first few outings, we also made sure a trustworthy adult was somewhere nearby with a cell phone. Nothing ever went wrong, but I felt better knowing that if anything did, some-one I trusted could be there almost immediately.

Andrew turned out to be remarkably responsible about call-ing at the set times (a definite advantage to his being a rule follower!) and I really did feel fine about letting him go for lon-ger and longer periods without checking in. Which isn't to say that there weren't times when he forgot to call and I tried him and somehow he didn't hear the phone ring and I ended up pac-ing the floor, feeling frantic. (I learned to insist he always keep the phone on both vibrate and ring.) Overall, though, he did a good job of staying in touch. I feel strongly that for any kid it's important to make the connection between responsibility and independence—that is, the former "buys" you the latter.

We have had occasional problems arise when Andrew has gone places without us, but nothing that we haven't been able to discuss and resolve later. For example, one friend talked him into cutting in line at a theme park, and they so annoyed some people that Andrew almost ended up in a fistfight. Fortunately, we found out about it and let Andrew know that that behavior was absolutely unacceptable. We made it clear it would be the end of his going without us to theme parks unless he gave us his word he would never cut in line again.

We still try to get Andrew to schedule specific activities with his friends, for example, dinner and a movie rather than just hanging out, but at least now we feel he's had enough experi-ence out alone in the real world to navigate most tricky situa-tions without our constant interference.

Dr. Koegel, of course, has more specific advice on the sub-ject. Read on.

DR. KOEGEL

When you're ready to encourage your child to be a little more inde-pendent and feel she's capable of going out with a friend without direct parental supervision, here are some suggestions for making it work. Your goal is to get your child used to going out with others (to malls, movie theaters, and so on) without you at her side—but also without getting into trouble. Don't forget that store owners and security cops eye teenagers with real suspicion, and if your child has an uncommon affect, she may draw an even greater scrutiny. Adolescents and young adults have to be better behaved and more careful than other age groups because they're watched so closely and with such wariness.

We know one teenager who got his mother's permission to leave the large warehouse store where she was shopping and go for a stroll. When he later tried to rejoin her, the security guard refused to let him in without a membership card and threatened to have him escorted off the premises when he tried to explain he needed to get in because his mother was expecting him. It eventually occurred to the boy that he could call his mother on her cell phone, but only *after* he tried sneaking in behind another customer and got a huge tongue-lashing from the guard. If the boy had been eight and separated from his mother, the guard would probably have been sympathetic, but she was deeply mistrustful of a teenager.

So how do you make sure that your child navigates the real world successfully when he's out on his own or with a friend or two? Once again, structure is your friend. The rules for a successful independent outing are similar to the rules for parties: make sure the outing involves a specific activity your child likes and is competent at and that will provide enough structure to minimize the social stress for him. And keep the outings short and sweet.

We've all heard about teens who get into trouble at the mall, so don't drop your kid off for hours on end without any type of supervision. That's just asking for trouble—even if your child *doesn't* have special needs. If she is going to a mall or similar place, make sure she has enough to do while there to fill up the hours and won't be vulnerable to bad ideas because of boredom or lack of supervision.

Staying in Touch

One advantage we parents have today that previous generations didn't have is the ability to stay in constant touch with our kids through cell phones or text messaging. One of the best ways to navigate the stage where your kid is too old to have a parent guide him around, but too young (at least developmentally) to be completely independent, is to provide him with a cell phone and then make sure that a responsible adult is within a block or two of where he's hanging out. Then you can have regular check-ins (or just save it for emergencies), knowing that help is at hand should he need it.

Discuss *All* the Rules

Before letting your child go alone to stores and movies, talk to him about behaviors that can lead to trouble. I was very surprised when my daughters told me that one or two of their classmates stole things in malls. These were nice kids from nice families who could afford the items they stole, but they were doing it to impress their peers. Other kids will brag about paying for a PG-rated movie and then ducking into an R-rated one, or just seeing two movies for the price of one. Talk with your child about behaviors like these and how important it is to be an honest person and how some inappropriate behaviors are really inconsiderate to other people. Make it clear that someone usually has to pay for other people's dishonesty, that nothing in life is actually free. Reinforce his sense of empathy.

Even if your child doesn't want to "discuss" these things, you can still drop in a sentence or two to let her know about what is expected and appropriate behavior. You can say something like "It's too bad so many store owners at malls don't like teenagers, but I guess all teens aren't as nice as you and your friends. Some of them steal things." Even if this doesn't lead to a discussion, your child will get the message. Again, gradually help her to become independent and praise her for her successes.

Motivating a Socially Unmotivated Child

Sometimes social situations can be scary, especially if your child has anxiety about interacting and wants to avoid his peers. If this is the case with your child, you can gradually desensitize him. To do this,

you will need to make a list of activities that are low-anxiety producers, medium-anxiety producers, and high-anxiety producers. Then
start with those low-level ones. For example, if a movie, concert,
sports event, or school play would suit your child just fine (especially
because you don't have to talk much), then start with that. If the next
level is a one-on-one get-together, move on to that after he feels totally comfortable with the low-level activities. Gradually working up
and having your child feel successful at the low-anxiety level will
usually help reduce the anxiety when you move up to the medium-
anxiety level, and so on. The main point is to move up the levels so
slowly and gradually that your child doesn't experience anxiety. And
if you move too quickly and he expresses some discomfort, step back
and stay at the previous level a bit longer until he really feels comfortable there.

ANDREW

**I have about two or three really close friends and a lot of
friends that aren't as close. I keep adding on new friends all
of the time, so it is hard to count. Most of these other
friends are guys but I know some girls too. I mainly go out
with my friends during the weekends (not every weekend)
and during holidays or breaks. I hang out the most with my
close friends. What I like about my friends is that they are
nice and funny; we share some common interests (which is
not everything of course).**

**When I go out with friends, I hang out at their houses, go
with them to see movies, go to hang out at malls. We have
sleepovers, and every now and then I do other exciting activities with them (such as going to theme parks, paintballing,
vacations). My favorite outings with friends have probably
been going out to malls to look at stores, seeing movies, having sleepovers, and also going out to theme parks every once
in a while. When I go to parties, I usually like going with a**

relatively small group of friends I can relate to and who are nice, but I also like going to big parties with nice kids.

My least favorite outings with friends tend to be when my friends and I are just hanging out at one person's house without really doing anything else, just talking without any activities. The activities that I prefer doing at other people's houses, however, are watching movies or TV shows, playing video games, going online, and going swimming.

My least favorite parties, however, tend to be when I am at a party with other kids I cannot relate to. I have trouble relating to kids who are not very nice, who tend to be bossy, or nice kids who are just talking about people I do not know or only about parties.

There was one party that I went to where I was with kids I used to go to middle school with, where I had trouble socializing with them. Even though I liked these kids and they were nice, all we were doing was talking to one another. These kids were only talking about other kids they knew whom I did not.

The middle school I went to was small, and I did not make any close friends, so it was harder for me to socialize with more kids when I went there. But now it is really not that hard for me to ask someone what they want to do outside of school for the first time. I have met my closest friends at my high school, mainly because I feel I can relate to them more than others. Even though it is not too big, my high school is diverse and everybody is different, so there is always someone you could meet and talk to a lot. I met these kids through talking to them on the school grounds and having classes with them. Then, once we felt like hanging outside of school together, we exchanged phone numbers and screen names. Now we call one another and then do things outside of school together.

Sometimes, it is fun to just go out with one person, which I normally do. However, that is not as much fun as going out with a whole group of people with many people you could choose to talk to. Over going out to a movie or going out to a mall, I would actually prefer going out to see a movie, which I used to do all of the time, but have not done as much nowadays. I would prefer seeing a movie, because instead of just looking around at a mall, you are watching a source of entertainment while you are out, and seeing images that make you laugh, some that use great special effects, and some great actors and actresses, which you do not normally see at a mall.

I really like sleeping over at friends' houses, because then you get to spend more time with your friend. There is one really close friend I have whose house I almost feel at home sleeping over at.

When I am hanging out with friends, we almost never fight. Sometimes, I am flexible and let my friend decide what we do. Most of the time, however, I give ideas and ask my friend to see if he is okay with it or not. People I know definitely have parties I am not invited to, but they don't tend to be my close friends. When I hear about that, I am most of the time jealous, but not that I get really angry. I have thrown a couple of big parties, but not in a while. Most of these parties have been for my birthday. Nowadays, for my birthday, I do not really have parties, but I go on outings where I really just invite my closest friends. For my birthday parties, we would just hang out at my house, go to a theme park (such as Universal or Disneyland), or just have gone out to see movies.

I have also met other friends at a social-skills group I attended. I think these groups are useful for other kids with autism, but I don't feel I really needed to learn anything they taught. It is also a good opportunity to make friends and it is also a good place to express your feelings with other people. However, there can be some kids (who I am not friends with) who have a lot of problems with their social skills, who often have strange behaviors they do in public, and who ask inappropriate questions a lot of the time. In these groups, we did activities, played games, talked as a group, and we would also just hang out. I have gotten together with a few kids I have met in group. There were certain kids with social-skills problems that I have gotten together with in the past, but now I just like to get together with other kids I like and who don't have social-skills problems.

My perfect day with a friend would probably consist of going out to some theme park or movie and having a nice lunch there. Then we would have a pretty expensive dinner at a place with delicious food.

Frequently Asked Questions

I feel as if I want friends for my daughter more than she wants them for herself—I'm always chatting up the girls at school and inviting them to do fun things with us, but she never initiates anything herself (although she does seem to enjoy these outings when they occur). If I ask her to pick up the phone and call someone, she simply won't do it. How do I get her to care about making friends? I'm sick of being in charge of her social life, but if I stop, so will it. Any advice?

Initiating activities is more important than you might imagine and very difficult for kids on the spectrum. We've found with our lunch groups that if we initiate specific activities, the kids on the spectrum are likely to stay with their peers for the rest of the lunch, but as soon as they're left to their own devices, they're back to being alone again. So you've hit on a very important point: we do need to teach our kids how to initiate activities. But calling on the phone and asking a friend over, when socialization is difficult and there's a chance of rejection, is a tough way to start. We want early attempts to have a high likelihood of success and therefore be intrinsically rewarding. So start more simply.

For example, start with having her invite relatives over. You can arrange it all ahead of time so you know her invitation will be accepted.

You can also have her initiate as part of a group. For example, we had one family that planned a party for friends of friends, and the planning group got to send out the invitations. This took the pressure off having just the child on the spectrum doing all the inviting. Even bringing in one other person will make a difference— recruit a friend or peer to organize an event with your child and have them invite people together.

And once your child *is* ready to extend invitations all on her own, still work for her success by making those invitations as irresistible as you possibly can. Have her invite a friend to a specific exciting event rather than just to hang out. That will greatly increase the odds that her peer will say yes.

I'm a single mother with five kids and I just don't have time to organize parties for my son or shadow him on outings or anything like that. But I know he wants more friends. Can you suggest some ways to increase his social life without putting more of a burden on me?

It may be helpful for you to explore the multitude of activities in the community. Some of our most asocial teens are amazing actors in drama classes. Sports teams and chess clubs also provide opportunities for socialization outside of the home setting. Volunteer work can also be helpful in getting your adolescent or young adult into activities that will help him learn to interact with others.

Since most schools have a community service requirement, perhaps your son's school can help you find activities where he'll be able to interact positively with peers. For example, one of our high schoolers goes to the pound after school to walk dogs with a few other students from his class. Another of our middle schoolers reads to preschoolers at the homeless shelter a few afternoons a week.

Jobs can be great for older kids. We have hired a few young adults to help at the university, and this gives them lots of opportunities to interact with peers. So look around, and try to find activities that your child will enjoy and where there will be peers to interact with.

4. Parties

I read your first book and learned how to help my little girl's social life by throwing small, fun parties that made the other girls want to come over. But now that my daughter's in middle school, it doesn't seem as if parents are nearly as involved in their kids' social lives. The girls call one another at the last second to all go to someone's house for sudden, impromptu parties—for all I know, the parents don't even know about them! I want my daughter to be part of this interaction, but I'm not sure she can really handle a party that doesn't have a specific, timed activity and parental help. Can I still control parties even though other parents have stopped?

CLAIRE

Sometimes I feel as if my greatest contribution to this book is in the "what not to do" department. (Remember Goofus and Gallant? I'm Goofus.) Here, for instance, is what not to do when it comes to throwing parties.

Andrew had just started at a new middle school right before his thirteenth birthday, so we figured we'd invite all the kids in his class to watch a movie in our backyard by projecting it on the side of the house. (Cool, right?) We hadn't realized what effect inviting both boys and girls would have on the adolescent boys, who got very rowdy in their efforts to impress the girls. As soon as they got to our house, they started acting up, wrestling and fighting, and disappearing into the dark parts of the back-yard to do Lord knows what. I found myself confiscating various sporting goods, such as baseball bats, which they were using as weapons, and threatening to call parents and send kids home, which did not win me any Coolest Mom of the Year awards.

When we finally managed to corral the kids into seats to watch the movie, the projector wouldn't work. While my husband tried frantically to fix it (with the help of Dr. Koegel's older daughter and a friend of hers who had stopped by to say hi to Andrew on his birthday), I desperately—and I do mean desperately—tried to keep the kids from getting completely out of control by engaging them in guessing games. They were way too old to stay amused with that for long, and pretty soon we once again had twenty kids screaming and running wild in our backyard.

By the time Rob got the projector to work, it was too late: the kids were too revved up to sit and watch and just wouldn't focus on it. Then it started *raining*, so we brought them inside (no more cool outdoor movie—we played it on the TV, which was boring) and *then* some of the boys decided it would be fun to run around outside in the rain with their shirts off even though I begged them to stop. When the parents came to pick them up a little while later, our house looked as if we had staged a reenactment of Lord of the Flies. Not only were the parents annoyed that their kids were wet and half naked, but Andrew told me afterward that a bunch of the kids had told him his mother was too strict and had yelled at everyone too much! It's not often someone gets into trouble for being too lenient and too strict, but apparently I managed it.

Instead of improving Andrew's social life with this party, we actually damaged it—the thing had disaster written all over it—and I went to bed that night (after popping a much-needed Xanax) discouraged and determined never to throw another party again for any of my kids.

Of course we have. But never one like that. Since then, we've *kept our parties small, with a handpicked guest list, and we've always made sure we had plenty of specific activities for the kids to do. In fact, for Leo's recent fourteenth birthday, we had a dinner party with his closest friends and planned a ton of parlor games that kept them busy from the beginning of the party until they sat down at the end to watch a Simpsons episode on our TV (I'm never relying on a digital projector again!)— and it was a total success.*

So the moral is don't invite too many kids (and handpick the ones you do invite), have plenty of activities and a fallback plan if something goes wrong, and remember that adolescents will rage out of control if you give them the slightest opportunity.

And just in case, keep some Xanax in your medicine cabinet.

DR. KOEGEL

Middle schoolers and high schoolers and young adults love to get together in groups, which is ideal for kids on the spectrum, since it takes away the stress of having to maintain a one-on-one dialogue. Parents can definitely still facilitate get-togethers and parties when their children are adolescents, but they need to make sure they fade back and let the kids be in charge of their own events. Their supervision and support should all be behind the scenes.

I remember when my daughter had her first coed pool party. I put pizza, chips, and soda out by the pool, then spent the rest of the afternoon peeking out the window every fifteen or twenty minutes. It started out with the boys on one side of the pool (eating) and the girls on the other side of the pool (not eating). A little while later, one of the girls and one of the boys went for a dip, then the next thing I knew the boys were *throwing* the girls into the pool. Fortunately, that was about the time the parents started arriving, but it made me realize that kids that age should never be left completely unsupervised.

While some kids of this age can just hang out together, chatting and wandering around a mall or someplace like that, kids on the spectrum need a more specific activity so they know what's expected of them and can maintain a related conversation. But once that activity is in place, it's your job to step back and let the kids take over. And by stepping back, we literally mean that—step back, do *not* leave. Kids over a certain age have the potential to get into serious trouble if left completely unattended, and an adult should still be nearby during any get-together, ready to step in the second she or he feels concerned.

Party Time

Here are specific suggestions to make sure a party will improve your child's social life, not harm it:

Provide Some Structure by Way of an Activity

Providing activities will make it more fun for the guests and easier for your child. Ideally, you would find activities that your child is good at (see the specific party examples below for some ideas), but teens and young adults can usually have fun with a fairly minimal amount of preparation. For example, instead of having a pizza delivered, get a crust, a bunch of ingredients, and have the kids put the pizzas together. Or you can put up a dart board or set the lawn up for a game of croquet. Buy ice cream and hot fudge and let them make their own sundaes. Any small activities you can prearrange for the group will take the pressure off your child and make the event more fun for everybody.

Supervise from a Distance

Parties at your home not only allow you to control the activity, but they also give you the opportunity to see how your child interacts and, if all goes well, to gradually fade back. No one wants a parent hovering once he or she is over a certain age, so you need to figure out how you can supervise these events from a distance. If things don't run perfectly, don't waste time fretting about it, but do try to find out where the trouble arose so that you can work on that area before the next get-together.

For example, we knew one parent who planned a swim party for her adolescent son. The first part went well, but after the swim, her son decided to go off and play on his computer. So while all the other kids were socializing and having a great time by the pool, he was absent. After that, the mom made sure that the computer was off-limits to her son unless all the kids—as a group—decided to play on the computer. She also kept the next event shorter and busier so he wouldn't have time to drift away.

Another high schooler we work with found himself in the uncomfortable situation of having a guest bring beer to his party. Fortunately, he was able to nicely decline the alcohol, and made sure none of his friends drove home after drinking. This is a socially tricky situation for any teenager. As parents, we would like to be informed if an underage guest brings drugs or alcohol into our homes. On the other hand, having been a parent of teens myself and having encountered the negative peer consequences from snitching, I realize that this situation has to be handled in a very careful way. This boy made the decision not to tell his parents at the time, not to drink with the others, and to be sure that they got home safely. By telling his parents later, after the party, he was able to have future parties without inviting the kids who were the ringleaders when it came to alcohol. I should also mention that even though responsible parents should make sure that underage kids are not drinking, I have been surprised about the differences in opinions among the parents of my kids' friends regarding underage drinking. Believe it or not, there are parents out there who will actually supply alcohol for their kids. So again, while having the kids hang out at your house has its minuses, it does let you be on top of things regarding what's going on.

Now, if you do find out that kids are drinking at your house, you'll need to confiscate the alcohol. Do this matter-of-factly. Don't yell, don't give them a lecture, and certainly don't make them feel guilty. If you make a big deal about it in front of your child, it will be hard for her to face her friends the next day. Simply tell them that you're sorry, but you would feel terrible if they were involved in a drunk-driving accident or were picked up by their parents while they were under the influence. Let them know you think they're great kids and you want to have them back but suspect that their parents won't let them return if they've been drinking at your house. And if they choose not to come back to your house again because you took their alcohol away, then they were there for the wrong reasons.

The Value of Consistency

Remember, kids don't turn into adolescents in one day. It happens gradually; and if you have always been consistent about curfews, rules—including the facts that kids can't have parties at your house unless an adult is present and that no alcohol is allowed—and so on, it won't come as a big surprise to them during the high school years.

You also need to talk openly with your children about the effects that alcohol and drugs have on people. Talk about the family member who drinks too much and tells personal things that shouldn't be told. Talk about the friend who drinks too much and stumbles around. Talk about people you know who started out drinking socially in high school and now have such serious problems with alcohol that no one wants to be around them. Real stories they can relate to will help your child learn about the consequences of these behaviors.

Keep Parties Short

Let's face it. Your adolescent is having social difficulties, so for him to maintain the interaction is hard work. No one wants hard work to go on for too long! And all kids can get into trouble if they have too much idle time on their hands. Keeping a party short takes the pressure off your child, provides fewer opportunities for troublemaking, and makes the kids want to come back for more great fun. And as the mother in the example above discovered, it can keep your kid from wandering off to do something else when he feels he's had enough.

Enlist Some Cool Help

If you have access to any young and popular adult—a college student or cousin or anyone like that—you might want to see if he or she can help out at the party, so there's an adult keeping a watchful eye on things who doesn't seem parental or controlling. Teenagers tend to admire college students much more than anyone with graying hair!

Party Ideas

Here are some suggestions for successful parties, based on ones we've helped with or observed. Don't limit yourself to these ideas. The point is simply to seize opportunities and focus on activities and areas that will show your child at her best and play to her strengths.

For the Kid Who Loves TV

Most kids have an interest in sports, so centering a party around a game is a great way to bring a group together. Show a game on the TV in your living room and serve pizza, popcorn, and other fun snacks. (This type of event has the added benefit of being fairly simple to prepare for and execute.)

We worked with one college student with Asperger's syndrome who regularly watched a popular reality show, but he always watched alone and didn't have friends. Jason's interventionist—a graduate student—decided to use his interest to create a social event, so she told him to invite some friends over to watch the show at her apartment. Before the show, they made popcorn and bought sodas. She invited some undergraduate students she knew and supported Jason when he invited a few of his Facebook friends to come along. There was just a handful of guests at the first few "reality parties" but the number rapidly grew until close to a dozen kids attended. Watching the show allowed Jason to interact with other students in a comfortably predictable way (talking about the show and guessing what would happen next week) without having to engage in a sustained original conversation, which had always been difficult for him. It also allowed his clinician to observe his peer interactions and provide specific feedback and suggestions for improvement.

Of course, the entertainment doesn't have to be a reality show. You can have weekly get-togethers to watch a sports event or any other popular show. The main idea here is that the kids are getting together in a more structured way so that the social demands aren't as high.

For the Kid Who Loves Food

If your adolescent is involved in a sport, club, or school activity, offer to host a meeting or group get-together at your home. (End-of-the-season

Items Out

Louise Childs Library
05/02/12 10:38AM
973-770-1000

PATRON: DOWD, JACQUELINE
***

Change your brain, change your body : [u
CALL NO: 613 AME
DUE DATE: 05/23/12

_____

Growing up on the spectrum : a guide to
CALL NO: 616.8588 KOE
DUE DATE: 05/23/12

_____

TOTAL ITEMS OUT: 2

Renew online @
www.sussexcountylibrary.org

908 310 9774

team celebrations are a perfect example.) Food is always a crucial part of any party for kids, and it can even be an *excuse* for a party, in and of itself. The mother of one of our adolescents with Asperger's syndrome decided to throw a party for a group of girls, and she got them together with her daughter to draw up the guest list, plan the menu, help cook the food, and then serve at the party. The activities were all specific and fun, so her daughter was able to interact comfortably with the other girls while they planned. She had the girls invite their families to the party, and that led to reciprocal invitations and deeper friendships.

Another student we worked with threw a pizza party. Johnny's mom made the pizza dough, rolled it out into the pans, and each of his friends brought a favorite ingredient for topping the pizza (veggies, pepperoni, olives, and so on). Rolling out and topping the pizza kept everyone engaged and happy—as did eating it. Another middle school girl had a sundae party where each of the girls piled loads of special toppings on her ice cream. Along with that, they made sugar cookies with rolled-out dough and cookie cutters, which kept them busy for hours.

For the Kid Who Loves Movies

Jenna's parents planned a regular Scary Saturday, when they would show mildly scary movies a couple of times a month. The kids (both girls and boys) would huddle in front of the television and scream loudly (and joyfully) whenever an unexpected creature popped out of a closet. The parents happily endured the painfully loud screaming, since it was well worth ringing ears to see their kid with a group of friends every week.

Movie nights are an especially easy way to get a child on the spectrum involved with kids his age, since the need to chat is limited and the kids can sit in companionable silence while they're watching the action. And even after the movie is over, or the next week, the kids can talk about their favorite scenes.

For the Kid Who Loves to Swim

Dana lived in a condominium with a pool and Jacuzzi. Although his parents had invited kids over to swim with him, we noticed that interacting was awkward, and the kids always ended up lingering at opposite ends of the pool. So we decided to add some structure to the activity by teaching Dana some pool games. We taught him how to dive for coins, race across the pool, play Marco Polo and other simple water games. His parents bought a floating basketball hoop and some pool noodles. Having specific activities for the pool made a huge difference in how much he interacted with his guests and kept the awkwardness at bay.

Again, with a little thought and a bit of planning, you can find something your child is good at or enjoys, and structure a group activity around it to greatly increase his or her chances of having a positive group social interaction.

CLAIRE

When Leo finished his kindergarten year, he begged me to throw a party for the kids who rode on his bus. I contacted the bus driver, who was amenable, and he drove all the kids to our house for a couple of hours of junk food and running around the backyard. It allowed us to get to know the other kids on the bus (whom Leo knew incredibly well, since they rode together for over an hour every day, but most of whom I'd never even met), and Leo was proud to be the host and show everyone around his house. It also got his little sister excited about getting to ride the bus one day herself, and ultimately helped her transition to elementary school when the time came.

An end-of-the-year bus party would never have occurred to me if Leo hadn't suggested it—and it probably wouldn't have occurred to Andrew either—so you should really stop to consider whether there are any similar situations you could take advantage of. Adults who run things (such as Girl Scout leaders, team coaches, chess instructors, and so on) are usually incredibly grateful to have another adult participate in celebrating a special event, and it may lend your kid some cachet if the celebration is held at your house. (We've also hosted end-of-the-

year class parties and even a Brownie troop campout in our backyard.) If your place is too small to host the actual party, you can still offer to bring the food or organize the activities or pick up the kids—any of these things will give your child an extra opportunity to interact with the others and give you the chance to spy on how well it's going and figure out ways to improve her social skills.

Frequently Asked Questions

Our middle school hosts a dance once a year or so. I want my son to go, but the one time he went, he was just standing all alone when I came to pick him up and he said he had a miserable time. He doesn't want to go to the big bar mitzvah parties either because he says no one talks to him once we leave him there. I can't host every party, so how can I make other people's parties work for him?

At this point, you're going to need to think about recruiting a peer who is going to the party to keep your child company and help him interact with the other kids. Another idea is to send a local college student or older teen to help at the party—while there, she or he can keep a careful watch on your child and facilitate those social interactions.

My daughter likes to have friends come over for small parties and get-togethers, but without any warning, she'll sometimes just get up and go upstairs to be by herself. I can tell the other kids are really thrown by this. How can I get her to realize that as the host she can't do that?

This is a very common problem with kids on the spectrum. Sometimes they get overwhelmed with social interactions and other times they just don't realize that it isn't polite to leave a guest alone and unattended. Here are a few pointers that might be helpful.

First, make the parties and get-togethers short enough for your child to handle easily. Kids don't need to spend hours together, and setting it up so that they're dying to come back again is better than a painfully long gathering that they can't wait to leave—and they'll all have less time to get into trouble that way too. So start out with an hour-long sundae-making party, or an hour-and-a-half swim party. Or if your child tends to always isolate herself after just a few minutes, start out with get-togethers outside of the home. Take a group of kids to get pizza, to a movie, or a play. Recently, one of our middle school parents whose child has Asperger's syndrome took a group of kids to dinner, then to a show for her birthday. Another family took the kids for a surf lesson at the beach. And another family took their child with a group of friends to a cooking class. Activities outside of the home can be prearranged to increase the likelihood of success.

Second, arrange activities your child likes. That will increase the chance that he will stay engaged in the activity longer. We have one middle schooler who loves to cook desserts. She can do this for hours. Other activities only maintain her attention for ten or fifteen minutes, so we have lots of dessert parties—and those are really popular among both sexes, believe it or not.

Third, practice is important. As we've discussed earlier, priming can make a big difference for any child, and if you verbally or literally walk through the upcoming activities or event, the likelihood that your daughter will have success increases tremendously.

Finally, observe carefully. Which kids are best with your child? Who draws her in? Who makes her feel ostracized? Guide your child toward the right peers, who will be good influences and welcoming to her.

So keeping it short, choosing the right activity for your child, practicing it beforehand, and including the right peers are all helpful in making it work.

5. Dealing with Bullying and Peer Pressure

My son is so sweet and so innocent—and I'm sick over how many kids take advantage of him. In the past, he was shoved around by some mean kids and now he's pretty careful to stay away from anyone who might physically hurt him. But other kids still abuse him in more subtle ways, "borrowing" money they don't pay back or encouraging him to do things in public that will make him

look foolish or get him into trouble. He just can't tell when some-one's friendship is real or phony. Any advice?

CLAIRE

Andrew is a sucker for a good braggart, and back in middle school he believed absolutely everything one especially flamboyant kid claimed to do, like staying up until two or three a.m. every night and roaming freely about the mall with no curfew or restriction on the money he spent. Andrew was just so literal—and so honest himself—that when I suggested this boy was exaggerating, he got angry at me and insisted that every word of it was true, and that he should be allowed the same indulgences. It made me realize how much influence a peer could have on him—and how much influence I was starting to lose.

That's a scary thing for a parent to acknowledge, especially when you think about classic peer pressure scenarios involving drugs and alcohol. Now when we discuss these things, I remind my kids it will probably be a good friend who tries to get them to do these things and not some diabolic stranger. Peer pressure that leads to bad choices will always start with someone your child admires or trusts—otherwise, why would your child do what that person says?

We discovered recently that a kid we had trusted and encouraged Andrew to spend time with had coerced him repeatedly into doing something he wasn't comfortable doing. The betrayal was enormous, not just for our child, but for us too. No one wants to go around suspicious of the whole world, but if your child hesitates to hang out with another kid—even one you like—listen to what's not being said and trust that your child may have a very good reason for keeping his distance.

The most painful part for me of parenting a child who's more innocent than most is having to question the validity of the friendship when a new kid is nice to him. Is the other child really being friendly—or is it all a setup for extortion or a prank?

The funny thing is, I only relax when the new acquaintance is also on the spectrum. Those kids, I trust.

DR. KOEGEL

We all know what bullying is, of course, but peer pressure is a little more ambiguous. We tend to think of it in connection with issues like drugs and alcohol and sexual exploration, but for kids on the spectrum there are also unexpected dangers of being manipulated in less obvious ways. Our kids can be at risk because of their tendency to trust others, their innocence, their lack of experience in social situations, and because they are often used to being told how to act. Sometimes our kids can be coerced into everything from giving up their lunch money to doing things that are destructive and/or embarrassing. You could almost call this kind of peer pressure bullying by friends, and it's a complicated issue for kids on the spectrum, who usually can learn to identify a classic bully, one who's cruel to their face and likely to hit or insult them, but who are likely to find it much harder to recognize the manipulation of someone who seems perfectly friendly. I know one young man on the spectrum who willingly and obligingly handed over a twenty-dollar bill to another student at his school, simply because the other high schooler asked him nicely and said he'd return the money. Of course he never did. An expensive lesson.

Addressing peer issues has to be accomplished as a team, one that ideally includes you, the parents of your child's peers, school administrators and staff, special education staff, and teachers. It has to be done in a way that is sensitive to your child, so it doesn't embarrass him and create a bigger problem. Below we've given you a few suggestions.

Dealing with Overtly Mean Kids

Kids in middle school and beyond *all* have the same goals: to fit in, be independent, be cool, and have friends. Unfortunately, some solidify friendships by joining together to make fun of and bully other children. Bullying is, sadly, an undeniable part of middle school culture—it lightens up somewhat in high school and beyond, but it is rampant in middle school. Research tells us that about 75 to 80 percent of middle schoolers will be bullied—a shocking statistic. Even more upsetting is that almost all kids on the spectrum report that they've been bullied. Fortunately, bullying tends to slow down as kids settle in and find peer groups, but the scary truth is that your child most likely will have to deal with bullying at some point.

I've seen a fair amount of bullying firsthand. Once when I was consulting at a middle school, a boy approached the boy I was watching, said something to him then quickly left. When I asked the boy I knew what had happened, he told me that the other kid had demanded that he give him his lunch money. And he had. This had been going on all year long and the child had never said anything to anyone. Another middle school child we worked with had one of his shoes stolen during physical education class and had to walk all the way home wearing only one shoe. This kind of stuff breaks my heart.

Children with social difficulties are often the victims of bullying. You have to prepare your child to deal with it, so make sure you're on top of things and that your child knows it's his *right* not to be mistreated at school or anywhere else.

Here are some ways to help him:

Talk About It
You, the school staff, and anyone else in your child's life need to let your child know, by openly talking about it, that aggression is unacceptable under any circumstances. Let him know that if he's being victimized, other kids probably are too and he'll be helping other victims by speaking up. Start talking to your child about bullying as early as possible and before he begins to feel self-conscious about talking about it. Use examples of things that happened to you or to other children to get your child talking—you don't have to make it really scary, just get the issue out there. And always keep your eyes open.

Lurk Around

If your child doesn't have the communicative ability or desire to confide in you, and you have a feeling something isn't right, it's time to do some lurking. You can usually find excuses to quietly stand nearby during any after-school activities, and you can enlist someone already at the school to lurk during school hours. Special education staff at the school are trained to observe and can do so discreetly. We have even gotten more staff placed near our students during specific times that tended to be a problem, such as phys ed classes or lunchtime. You may want to request that your child's school counselor, a teacher, or a special education staff member regularly and periodically spend a few minutes with your child to ask her how she's being treated by her peers. And if you put it in the IEP and get regular reports, you won't have to worry about busy and overworked school staff forgetting to check. This doesn't have to be a negative thing—they can start by talking about kids and activities your child enjoys then move on to any "challenges." This regular checking in could make a difference for your child.

Help Your Child Find an Adult at School to Confide In

You want your child to be comfortable confiding in someone if any kind of aggression occurs at any time or place during his day. Teachers can be a great resource when it comes to bullying or harassment. Have a talk with your child about which teachers he feels he can trust and would be willing to confide in if something's worrying him. His first choice may not be his current homeroom teacher or adviser, which is fine. You might want to schedule a parent-teacher conference for yourself if you have concerns. Sometimes confiding in a popular or vigilant teacher can be more productive than trying to handle it all yourself (more on this below).

Many teachers are great about trying to solve social problems, but often the problems need to be brought to their attention. When my oldest daughter was in middle school, she told me she needed a new binder. Then the next week she said the same thing. Finally, on the third binder I started asking questions. Turned out that a boy in one of her classes was ripping up her binders. Unbeknownst to my daughter, I called the teacher and let him know that I was getting tired of buying new binders every week. He was really smart and helpful: he told me that although he was glad that I had brought the matter to his attention, middle schoolers don't like parents talking to their teachers about peer issues. He also said that this particular boy seemed to be smitten with my daughter and the teacher assumed that he was doing it to get her attention (although she wasn't taking it that way at all). So he said that *he* would let the student know that *he* had observed him bothering her and *he* wanted it to stop. Sure enough, the binders always came home in great shape after that, and thanks to that teacher, I didn't have to get involved, which would have been even more embarrassing for my daughter.

Teach Your Child How to Stand Up to Bullies

Research tells us that the kids who stand up to bullies get bullied less in the future. If possible, teach your child to stand up for himself. It may not be a good idea in situations where the kids are physical—we don't want our kids fighting—but they should know how to say, "That's mean. Cut it out!" To get your child comfortable with this response, you may have to prime him. Have him practice ways of responding that are firm and assertive. Remind him that the bully is trying to be secretive and if your child's loud enough, it will draw attention. If your child lets you know that he's being bullied, you can have him practice at home. Prime him as to how to respond, then remind him right before you drop him off at school.

Insist on Accommodations for Your Child

If you discover that your child is being bullied in any way, *insist* that the school make accommodations. If the bullying is occurring between classes, have the school assign a child to accompany her from one class to the next. If it's happening at lunch, the school should assign an extra adult to yard duty, with the sole goal of watching for bullies. If it's happening during class, make sure the teacher provides preferential seating for your child and keeps an eye out for bullying. If you can be specific about when and where it's happening, it will be much easier for the school to make accommodations. If you need to, call an emergency IEP and get it written in. The school staff will usually make this a top priority, since no one wants your child to be hurt in any way.

Find Safety in Numbers

If you can figure out when the bully is getting a chance to harass your child, you can have the school arrange for extra support at that particular time. I worked with one middle school boy who was being bullied in the boys' locker room. The school arranged to have a support person there to make sure he wasn't a victim any longer. Another girl I worked with was being teased while she walked home from school, so her parents hired a local high school student to walk her home. The schools can also take responsibility for getting a peer to walk with your child to the lunchroom, between classes, and to the bus stop, and you can even put it in your child's IEP. (See below for more on recruiting peers to help.) We've also had situations when an aide was assigned to ride the bus with a child because of bullying on the bus. So take advantage of the power of numbers if that will help your child stay safe and happy.

Insist That the School Increase Its Monitoring

Kids don't bully when adults are around. Most kids bully to fit in and be "cool," so they'll do it in front of peers who they think will approve, but not with disapproving adults around. So schools that have a lot of adults cruising the halls and walking around at lunch tend to have fewer problems with bullying. And parents can be a big help here. Since school staff time is limited, you and your friends can volunteer at lunch or between classes to simply walk around. Just your presence will reduce many problems. And you'll get to know a whole lot of really nice kids.

Recruit a Peer Buddy

I have never been to a middle school, high school, or college where I couldn't easily recruit peers to help a child. Sometimes the students are a little reluctant to volunteer in front of a big group, but if you have interested volunteers write their names on a piece of paper, or if you give them an opportunity to meet with you after the group situation, you'll find plenty of eager recruits to help in the halls. In middle and high school, I always suggest that the peer buddy be given a hall pass to get to her own class a little late, if necessary. If you're trying to recruit peers for lunchtime, make sure to get a peer clique. This technique has been more effective than recruiting just one peer.

Ask the School to Set Up Safe Places

You've heard the expression "Idle hands are the devil's playground." Bullying doesn't happen when there is supervision or when the kids are engaged. It happens between classes, at lunch, during breaks, after school, and other times when you've got a group of kids with nothing to do and very little supervision.

Many middle and high schools have clubs at lunchtime, and encouraging your child to participate in these clubs will help keep him busy and safe. A middle school I consulted with in Los Angeles had a game room with dozens of different games and plenty of adult supervision. That room was a great safe haven for kids who preferred some structure at lunch. Another middle school child I worked with helped out as a teacher's aide every lunch period. That kept him safe and gave him some responsibility that also made him feel good about himself. One other high school girl I worked with helped in the library at lunchtime. This gave her an opportunity to be around books—which she loved—and at the same time learn some library work skills. Again, keeping the kids busy limits the amount of time they have to drum up some type of mean or obnoxious behaviors to pull on unsuspecting classmates and can engage them all in fun activities.

Make Sure the Entire School Is Aware of What's Going On, from Top to Bottom

If bullying is occurring, it needs to be brought to the administration's attention, no matter how small or insignificant it may seem. Big problems usually start out as little problems and build up gradually, so you want to end the behavior early on. Usually we start with our child's teacher, but if that isn't helping, it's time to meet with the principal.

There *are* schools that have fewer incidents of bullying, and that isn't an accident. They generally have active programs to decrease bullying and these programs usually are put in place by the principal. If the principal isn't taking effective action, go to the school board. You'll be helping out a lot of innocent kids.

Sometimes the problem is simply that kids don't really understand how hurtful bullying can be and other times the kids bully just to try to fit in, so a school-sanctioned group discussion of the repercussions of bullying can be helpful. Some schools will address the issue in a school assembly. Sometimes a popular teacher will address the issue with her students in class.

Bullying by "Friends"

Recently I got a call from a mom whose high schooler was the victim of a different kind of bullying. It wasn't aggression or theft; instead, the child's classmates were encouraging him to do inappropriate things. One particular child was the instigator, but a whole group of kids would watch the young man on the spectrum engage in these inappropriate things for some sort of immature entertainment. For example, they told him that a girl was wearing a new perfume and wanted him to smell it. Unknowingly, he innocently went up to the girl and sniffed behind her ear. Another time they told him that one of the girls just washed her hair and wanted him to feel how soft it was. Again, he approached her and touched her hair. He didn't fully understand that not only was what he was doing inappropriate, but he was also the butt of a childish joke.

The best way to take care of a situation like this is to first try to make sure that your child has his own sense of what's right or wrong and can therefore resist bad suggestions. You should have daily conversations with your child about personal space, how to distinguish between appropriate and inappropriate behaviors, and the difference between laughing with people and having them laugh *at* you.

It's also important to take a comprehensive approach and talk to the peers about their own behavior. I recently had a child's mom call Anjie, the parent of a young man with autism. This parent of the typical high schooler told Anjie that her own son was deeply disturbed that one of their peers had been getting Anjie's son to engage in inappropriate behaviors, like stealing food from the cafeteria and starting food fights. Since Anjie's son liked the peer attention, and didn't fully understand that what he was doing was inappropriate, he just kept doing it. The young man who had observed all this didn't have the courage to stand up for him at school but was bothered enough to tell his mother, who was willing to step forward. With this information, Anjie was able to approach the school, and the school then took actions to decrease this problem. They had some discussions in class with the kids who were misbehaving, and they provided more staff at the problematic times. They also regularly discussed the rules and how to treat others as a reminder of what was expected. Things quickly improved.

CLAIRE

Make sure when you discuss bullying with your child that she understands that a bully doesn't always wear a scowl and stomp around looking mean. One sweet kid I know was being menaced on a regular basis by a couple of kids in his class—actually being led every recess to a secluded corner of the schoolyard where he was forcibly restrained and repeatedly hit and choked. But they always said to him it was a game and that as their "friend" he should be willing to go along with the "fun." He was so confused—and of course scared—that he never told anyone what was happening. The truth only came out when a little girl in the class saw one of the classmates strangling him and threatened to tell.

A lot of factors contributed to this bullying going on much longer than it should have—the lack of supervision in the yard, the fact that the teacher missed the signs (our friend came in from recess crying one day but made up some excuse, and the teacher didn't pursue it), the fact that he felt outnumbered—but the main thing that struck me in this case was that in the past he had been friends with one of the boys, and that earlier friendship made it difficult for him to recognize that this was a bullying situation he needed to tell adults about.

In movies and books, the bully's a big, tough kid with clenched fists who spouts four-letter words while his equally large cohorts egg him on. In real life, a bully can be the kid sitting next to you quietly all day long in the classroom who came to your birthday party that year and invited you to his, but who mocks you savagely when no adults are around and encourages other kids to make fun of you. Kids on the spectrum who tend to see things very literally may only picture the classic figure when you talk about bullies, so make sure they know that someone who seems friendly can still be abusive and need to be stopped.

DR. KOEGEL

What If Your Child Is the One Behaving Badly?

Peers have more influence as they get older, and many children with social difficulties will do anything to fit in, including taking dares and risks just for attention. You may not feel you have as much control as you once did, but there are still things you can do to help and support your child.

If you're concerned about your child's susceptibility to bad influences, try as hard as you can to permit him to hang out only with peers who will be good influences. If that means you are too "busy" to drive your child to a troublemaker's house on the weekend, so be it. Make every effort to encourage your child to get together with kids you trust and stay away from the ones whose behavior worries you.

If your child has behavior problems, you must do a functional analysis (see Section I, Chapter 2 for a detailed description of functional analysis), even in middle school, high school, college, or beyond. You will need to figure out what's happening *before* the problem behavior to identify any likely triggers, and what's happening *afterward* to identify any inadvertent reinforcers, and then hypothesize as to why it's occurring. As with a younger child, you will probably need to replace the problem behaviors with appropriate ones.

The complicating factor at this age is that the peers may be reinforcing the behaviors. In fact, you may well find that your child is getting attention from his peers by breaking the school rules—it's a classic problem for our kids in middle and high school. If that's the case, it's time to talk with the school staff to have them help you figure out ways your child might be able to get peer attention in a positive way. Can he make morning announcements over the PA system? Can he take roll in a class? Can he tutor? Can he be the president of a club developed around his interests? Your job is to figure out how to replace those problematic attention-seeking behaviors with appropriate ones.

A step further is to recruit peers to actively help reduce the bullying. Constantly reminding kids of positive behaviors and what's expected of them *before* there is a problem reduces future problems. It's best to have teachers work this into their daily routines. Before each nutrition break, the teachers can spend just a minute or so talking about how to treat other people. Just before lunch period, they can talk to their classes about appropriate lunch behavior and how to treat others on the playground. Schools can work good citizenship into their award systems and announce that they will be looking for acts of kindness. Again, it needs to be a schoolwide movement to keep kids safe and content.

One teenager we knew was getting into trouble at school for starting food fights. Myles loved attention—any type of attention—especially if it came from his peers, and he had discovered that throwing food, which usually got other kids to throw food too, would lead to cheers and lots of attention. So he did that a lot. After just about every incident, Myles got sent to the principal. Unfortunately, a functional analysis revealed that the immediate consequence for throwing food was all positive: first he got peer attention and then he got special attention from the principal! (The adults viewed sending him to the office as punishment, but since Myles liked any attention, the visits to the principal were actually reinforcing the bad behavior.) We went to talk to the principal and she agreed not to give him any attention when he came to her office. All he could do was sit there, and that alone greatly decreased his desire to throw food. At the same time, we had to teach him appropriate ways of getting peer attention. Bringing games, like cards, out to the lunch table helped to get him engaged in a positive way. Myles's mom packed extra snacks and put some interesting and cool little things in his lunch bag to share or prompt him to start a conversation. We also worked on having him chat with his friends rather than engaging in disruptive behaviors: we taught him to comment and ask questions. And seating him closer to the lunch monitor was also helpful. In short, we approached the problem from all angles at once, which quickly reduced his desire to get attention in a negative way.

ANDREW

I don't remember really being bullied a lot of the time, however, I have definitely been teased when I was in middle school and in high school. Kids would tease me about how they thought I was "retarded," short, or how I seemed a lot like a younger kid. Most times, whenever kids were mean, I would just try to ignore them. Sometimes, it has been hard for me to ignore them, so instead I would talk back to them. When I talked back to other kids, they just started making fun of me even more and the situation only got worse. Other times, I was smart and went and told a school counselor about it. Not only have I been made fun of by other kids at my school, but other kids in public.

I remember a lot of the incidents really well. There was one time, at the beginning of my ninth grade year, when I was with a friend eating at a Japanese restaurant. There were two older boys next to us who just suddenly started laughing at me. I accidentally said a curse word out loud in that restaurant when talking to my friend, but just did not know any better, so they said they thought that I was "mentally retarded" and started pointing and laughing at me for

it. I did not know them at all. There was an incident, another time in ninth grade, when I was playing a game in my
Spanish class. It was my turn to roll the dice. Other kids in
my class acted like I did not know how to roll dice, so they
started making fun of me. They were lecturing me on how to
do it, but rudely. That incident made me feel really bad
about myself. Also, back when I was in middle school, when
I was really thirteen or fourteen, the other kids thought that
I looked like I was ten. So every day in eighth grade, they
called me "little kid," and whenever I told them I actually
developed a mustache (when I really did), they did not believe me.

Last year, when I was frequently teased in some of my
classes, it got bad enough that I asked my therapist for advice. This one kid would stare at me and would pretend that
I was staring at him all the time, which made me furious.
He would also point and laugh at me whenever I made faces
and also teased me, saying he thought I acted like I was
"retarded." My therapist told me that the best way to deal
with teasing is by ignoring others who make fun of me and
by just not getting involved. At first I thought that it would
not be too effective, but oddly enough, it actually really
worked out well.

I do not remember anyone actually acting like they were
my friends when they really were making fun of me. I have
definitely been peer pressured before though. An old best
friend was a good friend to me in elementary school and
middle school, but then once we went off to high school, he
started making me do some stuff I really did not want to
do. This all happened when my friend came over to my
house. At first, I thought that there was no way to get out of
it. Then I realized that I was actually feeling uncomfortable and did not want to do anything with that friend anymore. So then I told my mom about it. I was worried that
she would get mad at me for all of the stuff I did with my
friend. I was very honest and told her that my friend was

really forcing me to do things that made me uncomfortable. This probably would have easily been avoided if there was more supervision, but whenever I am with friends, I do not like to be watched by my parents the whole time. I actually think that would have made it worse, because in the past, my parents did not know that whatever my friend and I were doing in my room was happening. I did not feel comfortable alerting them about this earlier. The bigger problem was that this kid did not listen to me and bossed me around a lot.

My mom understood my problems and got mad at my friend, feeling my emotions. The one thing I really learned from that was to stand up for myself when I felt uncomfortable doing something. Even nowadays, I still have trouble standing up for myself when I do not want to do what my friends are doing.

I do not remember actually bullying anyone. I have only teased people back who have made fun of me, especially when I have been in a bad mood. I knew it was a bad idea, but there were times when I felt like that would be the most effective in getting someone to stop teasing me. It actually turned out not to be and only caused them to make fun of me more.

Fortunately, I have never gotten in trouble for teasing anybody. I am a nice person most of the time and know that making fun of other people (for no reason) would only make me look like a worse person to be around. One of the reasons for that was that my parents have always treated me kindly and have given me important lessons on how to deal with rude kids, from first grade to now. My parents used to tell me that whenever I was being teased, use my words, and instead of fighting, walk away.

For kids who are being bullied or teased in school right now, if I were you, I would not listen to that person's comments. The best idea is to ignore whatever that person says. If that person has teased you too much, I would also strongly suggest talking about it with a school counselor. I also suggest that you do not talk back to that person; it only makes the situation worse and that will actually tell the bully/teaser to make fun of you more often. Another thing you could do is talk to a good friend about it and ask him/her to see what they would do.

Most of the time, I have stayed quiet when I have seen people being teased because I felt like it was best not to get involved. However, I remember when I was in ninth grade, approaching two kids I did not like who were saying rude things about one of my best friends. At least my friend was not there to hear those kids' conversation. Then I came into the conversation and told them that my friend was a nice kid and that they were just being rude to him a lot of the time. That ended their conversation about my friend and they finally started talking about something else.

Frequently Asked Questions

My son wants to spend time with a boy whom I don't trust. He seems very fast and I'm concerned that he manipulates my son into doing things he shouldn't do. On the other hand, beggars can't be choosers, and my son really doesn't have any other good friends. How can I make sure this is a healthy friendship?

In this type of situation, you'll need to weigh the pros and cons. If the peer is going to lead your child into destructive behavior, you'll need to stop the friendship immediately and work hard to find other peers. On the other hand, if the peer is basically a good kid with just some poor judgment due to lack of maturity or lack of knowledge about your child's disability, it may be time for a little chat. And if you don't want it to seem as if Mom and Dad are too involved at this age, ask a school counselor, popular teacher, babysitter (or are they called drivers in middle school?), or even an older sibling to initiate the discussion.

My son is the gift who keeps on giving. It seems as if every kid at school has either borrowed money from him or asked him if he could buy lunch or a snack for them "just this once." Of course they never remember to pay him back. I've tried telling him he needs to insist on getting his money back, but even when he tries, he comes back with "She said she didn't have the money on her today and she'll pay me back another time." He's just an easy mark. He's so eager to be liked that he keeps falling for the friendly smiles—and the requests that always go with them. How can I get him to be savvier and to distinguish between a real friend and someone who just wants something from him?

First of all, you may want to make a rule that he can't bring money to school. If he doesn't have money to lend, the kids can't harass him. If this means buying lunch tickets, you'll need to do that. Next, if you think some of the kids might really need snacks, throw in an extra bag of chips now and again and let him share them. That way, they won't be bugging him for money, but he'll get to be known as a nice guy. Finally, if he's easily swindled, that's something you'll have to work on. As much as we'd like to teach our children that everyone is good, this may be a great opportunity to teach him the meaning of a true friend. True friends wouldn't take advantage and that's just what the kids you've described are doing. Make sure that your child understands that friendships are reciprocal, and if friends are willing to share with him or lend him money, that's one thing, but if it only goes one way, it just isn't right.

My son has been treated badly by a kid in our neighborhood, and my husband wants to teach him to hit back. Our son is a big kid and with some training, he might even be able to win a fistfight. But his sense of boundaries is shaky and I'm terrified that if we don't have a hard-and-fast rule (no hitting ever!), he may hit the wrong person. My husband says we're basically teaching him to be a victim for the rest of his life. What do you think?

Even though the kids who hit back at a bully are the ones who are less likely to be bullied in the future, it isn't a good strategy to teach. A better approach would be to work on the other fronts and make sure that there's supervision when he's around this kid and that adults are keeping an eye out. And if you can, talk with the bully and/or his parents. It may be high time someone taught him how to treat others.

Making and Maintaining Successful Romantic Relationships

1. Introduction

My daughter, who's on the spectrum, is in eighth grade. I saw on the school calendar that a semiformal dance is coming up. I asked her about it and she said that kids are going as couples and no one has asked her to go yet. Even though I'm slightly relieved—I'm not sure she's ready for this and I know I'm not*—I'm also concerned she's feeling left out. How do I help her start getting asked out on dates?*

CLAIRE

Just when I thought I'd figured out how to parent a kid with autism, nature and time upset everything again and turned my adorable little innocent into a teenager with a changing body and a growing interest in the opposite sex. Puberty waits for no mom.

Up until now, I thought I was doing everything right for Andrew. I'd spent countless hours teaching him the skills that other kids acquire naturally, like how to talk or have a conversation or share an opinion or join in a fun activity or comment on how awful the cafeteria food is, and so on—all the goals Lynn and I wrote about in *Overcoming Autism*. Whatever the situation was, I knew I could sit down with him—or find a well-trained interventionist to do it—and quite literally teach him what he'd need to do at preschool or elementary school the next day.

And then one day I realized that my child wasn't a child. He was a teenager with an ever-growing interest in girls. And I thought about all the things he would need to learn over the next few years. Things like

How to catch someone's eye without looking as if he's trying to catch her eye.

How to flirt, maybe by saying something that's almost insulting—but with a certain impishness that implies he really means the opposite.

How to touch someone's hand just lightly enough so she thinks maybe he meant to do it but isn't sure (but he meant to do it).

How to get his friends to ask her friends if she'd like to go to the dance with him.

How to hold hands with a girl.

How to kiss a girl, but only if she wants him to.

How to know whether or not a girl wants him to kiss her.

The more I think about these things (and the list could go on and on, of course), the more I want to scream, "Wait! I could barely figure those things out for myself when I was a teenager. There's no way I can teach my child with autism any of that."

Well, yes, that is the problem, isn't it? How do you teach what can't be taught? We used to find ways to expose Andrew to new activities before he'd have to do them for real—like playing baseball in the backyard before he'd have to play at school—but we can't take him into a darkened make-out room at a party and show him what he's supposed to do (and not do) there.

Andrew is coming up on an age filled with locked doors and private places, and that scares me. I want to help my son find a great girlfriend and start down the road toward one day being in a happy relationship, but isn't that something he can only do by himself? How can I even begin to help?

The only thing that's clear to me is that when it comes to romance, a parent has to change her approach, work on the things she can work on, encourage her child to take some chances and trust his own instincts (and hope she's already *successfully instilled the right values), and ultimately, know that her child, like you, me, and everyone we know, will at some point suffer in the name of love.*

Fortunately for us all, Dr. Koegel has some more specific and immediately usable advice in this area.

DR. KOEGEL

How and when kids get together romantically varies tremendously. I remember taking my daughter to the movies when she was in elementary school. To my shock and horror, there were kids from her class on *dates*. Real dates, with holding hands . . . kissing . . . arms around each other. And all that with *no* adult supervision. These weren't teens—they were ten- and eleven-year-olds. I think I was in such a state of shock that I spent more time watching them than I did watching the movie!

This was, admittedly, young to start dating. While there is some variation, most preteens still hang out with kids of the same sex. But when they reach about fourteen or fifteen, they start spending more time with members of the opposite gender. At this point, it isn't usually romantically meaningful, and these relationships only last a few months.

From the age of about sixteen on up, teenagers begin to develop more serious relationships that can last several years. As Claire mentioned, most of these relationships happen gradually and spontaneously, so we worry about teens on the spectrum who have had social difficulties and who may not have been full participants in the wildly complex social jungle of peer friendships in elementary and middle school. And while there is some research on the dating and sexual habits of typically developing teens, it's based mostly on self-reporting, which means there's always the risk of over- and underexaggeration, or just plain inaccuracies.

So all we really know is that serious dating *does* start in the teen years, and no one wants her or his child to be left behind. Unfortunately, there just hasn't been any research about how to facilitate dating with kids on the spectrum and therefore little to no guidance for parents who would do anything to help their children find some romance at a very vulnerable age. Here at the clinic, we've watched a number of individuals with autism and Asperger's grow up and develop successful romantic relationships. So we know it can happen. When we study them carefully, we can analyze that success and pluck out some crucial tips for helping your child follow in their footsteps.

One quick note: in both this chapter and the following one on sexuality, we often talk about the "opposite sex." We're simply using that as shorthand for any romantic object—it's important to remember that as far as we know, the prevalence of homosexuality is the same for people on the spectrum as it is for typical people. Any advice we have about romantic or sexual relationships is as true for a homosexual relationship as it would be for a heterosexual one, so even though we may simplify things by referring to the opposite sex, our goal is to include same-sex relationships in any discussion. Please see the Frequently Asked Questions in Chapter 3 of this section for more specific advice for the parent who thinks his child on the spectrum might be gay.

2. Dating

My daughter who's on the spectrum came home happy one day because a guy at school asked her to go out with him. Then he didn't call, and someone told her later he was just joking. She was devastated and I was boiling mad. I promised her that someday a good guy would ask her out for real. I just wish I could do something to make that actually happen. Any ideas?

CLAIRE

A close friend of mine recently got divorced and found herself back in the dating game. The ensuing emotional roller coaster got me thinking about my own ancient dating past, and I vividly remember how violently I careened from the highs (having a great time with someone interesting) to the lows (not having that interest returned). I felt an immediate rush of relief that I didn't have to go through all that again.

Most of the people I know really haven't done that much dating—it's something you do for only a limited part of your life, usually after college (because it's so easy to hang out with a member of the opposite sex in college that you don't really have to arrange "dates" while you're there) and before marriage. And, of course, sometimes between marriages. I'm sure there are people who spend longer periods of their lives dating, but in general, we don't have to do all that much of it.

But during those times, nothing feels more important. It's impossible to put yourself out there romantically and not start feeling judged. You question everything, especially yourself. Am I what he wants? Is he what I want? Am I settling? Am I reaching too high? Is it just physical attraction? Why isn't there more physical attraction? Could this be someone I might one day want to marry? If not, should I bother spending more time with him?

I remember feeling rejected. And I remember rejecting people. That's what dating is all about, right? Sorting through, figuring out what works and what doesn't? You can't do that without discarding people along the way.

It's so hard. Five minutes into most first dates, people have already formed an impression of the person they're meeting alone for the first time. ("Always arrange to have drinks first," a friend once counseled me. "That way, you can get out of it without committing to an entire evening, but if it's good, you can go on to dinner.") By the second date, you're starting to think about getting physical. By the third, you're probably talking about going back to your apartment or his.

At least that was how it worked in my day. The unwritten rule book has probably changed in the last couple of decades, but the one thing that doesn't change is that there is an unwritten rule book.

Imagine going through all this murky, undefinable, judgmental, potentially humiliating mess we call dating with the extra social difficulties that come with being on the spectrum.

My sister loves to quote Cole Porter's "There's a boy mouse for ev'ry girl mouse," and I believe there is (although I feel compelled to add that sometimes boy mice go with boy mice and girl mice with girl mice. I'm sure Cole would have agreed). Our kids can and should find someone to spend their lives with. It's just unfortunate that the process of finding that person requires using all our social skills—the weakest area for most kids on the spectrum.

DR. KOEGEL

As I said earlier, we do know quite a few adults on the spectrum who have very happy romantic lives. Although there hasn't been much research in this particular area, I've extrapolated from each happy relationship to come up with advice that might help your child achieve the same wonderful, universal goal.

Read on for some successful strategies that you can use to help your child start dating.

Priming

As we discussed in the general information chapter (Section I, Chapter 2), priming involves going over an activity *prior* to when it happens—essentially rehearsing it. There has been a lot of effective research done on priming, usually focusing on academic and social activities.

The basic principle behind social priming is that if you run through what is likely to happen in a social situation, like being greeted and needing to respond in kind, you'll increase the likelihood that your child will successfully repeat the practiced behavior when the real situation occurs. While some professionals like to use pictures as prompts, the literature shows that simply rehearsing the situation verbally helps just as much. And for older kids, it is more age appropriate to just discuss the upcoming social situation and appropriate ways to interact in that situation.

This approach can be very effective when your adolescent on the spectrum starts dating.

Sammy's Prom Night

Sammy was a high schooler diagnosed with Asperger's syndrome. He was extraordinarily good-looking but definitely had his social difficulties. He had a smattering of friends here and there, but had had few deep relationships throughout his life. Unbeknownst to his peers, on a regular basis the truancy officers found him cutting school to go to the local Barnes & Noble in search of pictures of naked girls. In addition, his parents occasionally found him surfing the net for stark naked hotties when he thought he was home alone.

There was no question that Sammy was interested in the opposite sex, but his interest was all theoretical: he had never actually had a date, a girlfriend, or even a friend who was a girl.

So it was a big surprise when he came home one day and boldly announced to his mother that he wanted to invite a particular girl to his junior prom. His mother's first reaction was terror: this was uncharted territory for both of them, with real potential for disaster. She tried to persuade him to wait until he was a senior to go to the prom, arguing that it would be more successful if he had his driver's license. But Sammy was determined, so she gave in.

The more his mother probed, the more she became aware that her son didn't have the slightest clue how to ask a girl out. Worried that his awkwardness and inexperience would lead to certain refusal, she decided that before he plunged right in, he should practice (be primed) by doing a little role-playing. She played the part of the girl and he pretended to call her and ask her out.

Mother and son tried out all kinds of scenarios, ranging from the acceptance (which led to working out details of when the girl could expect to be picked up) all the way to the dreaded no and how to respond appropriately and graciously to that by saying something like "I hope we can hang out together some other time." As they rehearsed, Sammy's mother suggested phrases, responses, and questions that Sammy could try out right then and fall back on when he made the real call.

When the time came to actually ask the girl out, Sammy was remarkable. He did a great job of asking and was—to his mother's astonishment and delight—immediately accepted.

Making It Work for Your Kid

Even if we didn't have years of research proving its efficacy, it would still be pretty obvious that priming works. It simply makes sense that prior exposure to a potentially complicated situation gives your child a template to work from when the time comes. That doesn't mean it's always simple to arrange in real life: your child may well play the teenager and roll his eyes and refuse to have anything to do with you when you suggest practicing asking a girl out or any other type of dating situation. It's a common reaction and part of the classic teenage "if my mother or father suggests it, I don't want to do it" pattern they all seem to fall into.

So if you feel strongly that practice will increase your child's chance of success, but you're not the right person to do it, you'll need to recruit someone to help. Think about other people he likes and respects. Does he have an older brother or uncle whom he admires? Is there a teacher at school who would be helpful? How about a college student friend? It doesn't really matter *who* does the priming—the important thing is to give your child the exposure and practice.

Make an Offer No One Can Refuse

Even with priming, sometimes simply nailing that first date is the hardest part of finding a girlfriend or boyfriend for someone on the spectrum. Because they have been isolated from peers—or have isolated themselves from peers—young people with autism and Asperger's often don't learn the subtle cues related to socialization, so they may seem a little awkward and uneasy in social situations. Most of these kids are wonderful, kind, caring people, but their unconventional mannerisms can put off people who don't yet know them. It's especially hard to get over that hump with members of the opposite sex, who just aren't as likely to spend the hanging-out time necessary to appreciate their inner qualities. This leads to a dating catch-22: in order for a girl to get to know a guy (or vice versa), she has to spend time alone with him, but in order for her to say yes to spending time alone with him, she has to get to know him!

Once people get to know these kids, they see their good qualities: how most are never catty and gossipy or overly concerned with superficial things like what someone is wearing or what someone said at a party. They're also incredibly honest and straightforward, which is what makes them great friends and partners. But it takes time to appreciate and value these deeper qualities, and unfortunately, the first impressions may be awkward. That's why it's *so* important to give them any help possible in getting that first date.

Most parents of teenage kids on the spectrum know all too well the heartache of finding out your child has put himself out there, asked someone on a date, and been rejected. One way to increase the odds of an acceptance is to make the actual date event something so extraordinary that no one would turn it down. Read on for Griffin's experience.

Griffin—A First Date to Die For

Griffin was a high school student who was having trouble getting dates. It wasn't for lack of trying. He tried and tried—and was constantly turned down. His mother admitted to me that the rejections had become so painful to her that she was tempted just to tell him not to ask out any more girls. As I was consoling her, I said, "Too bad he doesn't have tickets to something that all the girls would die to go to."

My offhand remark sparked an idea in Griffin's mother. Griffin's dad worked as a stagehand at a large concert hall. At his wife's suggestion, he called in a few favors and was able to score some free backstage passes to a hugely popular band concert. Griffin asked a girl he liked to go with him and she was delighted to say yes. And once she got to know him, she liked him, and they went out many more times.

Making It Work for Your Kid

A concert is just one idea. Most people have friends who do cool things that kids are interested in, and you shouldn't hesitate to ask around—see if anyone you know can arrange something special for your kid. Even if you don't have anyone close to you who can help, there are many people who understand the difficulties of kids with disabilities and will go out of their way to make things happen. I've worked with many families who were able to procure great tickets to events for free just by asking if they could be donated to a child on the autism spectrum. And if you're not strapped for cash, you can also figure out—maybe with the help of a friend's teenage kid—which events in your city are the current hot ticket and purchase admission.

Having that extra special to-die-for date may be just what it takes to get things started.

Teaching Listening

The restricted interests and lack of social awareness that tend to be symptoms of an autism spectrum disorder often lead to what others might see as self-absorption. Everyone likes to be listened to, and no one likes to be with someone who engages in monologues about a subject *only she* is interested in. Because conversational skills and sympathetic listening don't always come naturally to those on the spectrum, you might need to teach them even if your child appears to be past the age where teaching her to talk should be necessary. A good first impression is crucial for getting a first date, and expressing an interest in another person will really improve that first impression.

Nick and His Cars

When I first met Nick, he was a straight-A college student who had been diagnosed with Asperger's syndrome. I'm not sure if he had ever dated, but he definitely wasn't dating when I met him. He wasn't particularly well groomed: he wore dirty clothes, rarely bothered to shave, and had dirty fingernails. But his biggest social problem was that he talked nonstop about fancy cars. He simply had no interest in any other topic—if I brought up a subject other than cars, he immediately reverted to cars.

His mother had brought him to see me because she was worried that he was, in her words, "obsessed" with a female student. He had asked her out several times and she had declined every time, so he began following her. He knew her patterns, whom she hung out with, and what she did just about every minute of the day. His mother was afraid the girl would think he was stalking her. And truthfully, he was.

I felt that if we could help Nick become more socially successful overall, he would stop pursuing the young woman who had no interest in him. It was clear to me that his biggest social problem was his inability to engage in a real back-and-forth dialogue—it wasn't that the other students didn't want to be with him, it was that after a few minutes he drove them crazy talking exclusively and excessively about cars. We started intervention, working on the skills Nick needed to become a good conversationalist (see Section II, Chapter 2 for more specific details on how to implement this intervention): we taught him how to ask questions, listen attentively, and respond to topics other than cars. With some work, Nick gained the ability to maintain a conversation that wasn't only about cars, and that made him much more attractive to college girls.

As his social skills improved and he started to see people responding more positively to him, he became more and more motivated to continue that success. On his own, he worked on improving his hygiene, which led to even more positive responses—and eventually a girlfriend!

Making It Work for Your Kid

Asking questions and listening to the answers may seem like a logical and easy thing, but for kids on the spectrum it takes work and practice. Many of these young kids have trouble asking information-seeking questions, as we discussed in *Overcoming Autism,* and when they're older, they also struggle to get a back-and-forth rhythm going during social conversation. But with practice, they can learn, it gets easier, and it does improve their social lives. As we describe in detail in Section II, Chapter 2, social conversation will require some practice, which often means modeling specific appropriate questions to initiate a conversation or to keep one going.

If your child is at the age when he doesn't want to practice with you, recruit a therapist, friend, or relative to help you out. Sometimes it works even better if you find someone who is closer to your child's age. That way the topics of conversation will be relevant to his age group. And if your child struggles a little at the beginning, don't worry—changing the way you talk takes time and practice, but eventually as your child becomes comfortable with it, you'll see a big difference.

Building on Similar Interests

It's hard to break through the restricted interest of an individual on the spectrum, but if you can find peers who are interested in that same restricted topic, you might have just the catalyst you need to spark a romantic relationship!

For instance, we worked with a graduate student with autism who had just switched her major to computer science. She felt that everything in her life was going well except with the opposite sex. She was interested in guys, but throughout her college years she hadn't met anyone who returned her interest. This happened many years ago before very much research had been done, so we really didn't have any immediate ideas of how to help her. Normally we would have suggested that she seek out clubs, church groups, or intramural sports to meet more guys, but the only thing she liked to do was work on computers.

We asked her to give us a week to search the literature to see if we could come up with any ideas to improve her social life. We were pleasantly surprised when she came back the next week and cheerfully announced that she was the smartest student in all her new classes (which by the way, were filled mostly with males) and that just about every guy in the class had asked her out! Since the guys in her graduate classes were all as interested in computers as she was, they admired her strength in that area and were tailor-made to find her appealing.

JJ's Book Club

JJ was a beautiful teen who had been diagnosed with autism as a preschooler but had improved so much that some of the school staff argued that it looked more like Asperger's syndrome. Whatever it was, she spent all of her free time alone.

JJ loved to read. In fact, it was difficult to get her out of the school library to socialize. To encourage her to interact with other children, we started a book club with some other kids who also loved books. JJ really came to life while discussing books with her peers, and not long after we set up the book club, she began spending time outside of school with one of the boys who had joined it. In addition, after discussing the books, she almost always spent the rest of the lunch period hanging out with the kids in the club. She loved the club and it also provided a catalyst for her to get together with other students her age.

Making It Work for Your Kid

Most individuals on the spectrum tend to have isolated areas of interest, but this doesn't have to isolate them socially. If they are able to focus these interests in a socially appropriate way, they can use them to connect to others with the same interests. You might have to work with your child to find an appropriate activity and venue and possibly even seek out some professional help in finding and setting up clubs and organizations that will give her the opportunities she needs to meet romantic possibilities who share her interests, but when you see your child flourish socially, you'll be glad you did.

Exploiting Strengths

Henry Kissinger once said, "Power is the ultimate aphrodisiac," and there's no question that appearing to be in a position of knowledge and strength increases the likelihood that you're going to impress other people—which, of course, increases your odds of romantic success.

Most teens on the spectrum have areas of strength. If these strengths are used in the right way, the teen with autism can become a valued member of his or her peer group, someone the others look up to and admire—maybe even romantically.

Many people have jokingly said that most university professors are on the spectrum, and the truth is that to get a doctorate, one *does* have to accumulate a vast amount of information, and to get tenure at a university, one has to continue to collect even more information on the specific topic. During the pursuit, one's interests may become a bit, um, *restricted*. Restricted interests? Does that ring a bell?

The important thing to remember is that while professors may become a bit overfocused on their area of knowledge, people respect and admire them for it. Similarly, a teenager or young adult on the spectrum can use *his* area of interest to increase his value in his community, as this next young man did.

Making It Work for Your Kid

Find your child's strengths, whatever they may be, and help him get into situations where he will be valued by his peers for those strengths. If your child is the valued member of his peer group, that will most certainly make the first date easier. There are some easy ways to showcase his strengths. After-school or lunchtime clubs are the easiest (as in JJ's Book Club, previous page). If your child is a great musician, try to get him involved in the jazz band at school. Or if he likes the computer, see if you can get him assigned as an assistant to the computer teacher at school.

Even if your child just has a strong interest in an area but isn't too great at it yet, he may connect with a mentor or a tutor in that subject. And if you can't make it happen at school, there are plenty of opportunities outside of school. Some of our students take lessons, such as drama or surfing. We even have one young adult who is very involved in the local Catholic church's youth group. Just make an effort to look around and find places where your child will fit in and be valued.

Setups

Again, this is all about nailing that first date, so members of the opposite sex have a chance to see past the challenging social behaviors to the wonderful person underneath.

While I have mixed feelings about sororities and fraternities—particularly because I think they spend *far* too much time on social events and not enough time on academics—these types of clubs are sometimes helpful for those who need a little social boost. Both my daughters have been in sororities and they've told me that the kids in the Greek system always make sure that everyone has a date for the parties.

Jordan—Using the Brotherhood

Jordan was a college student who was diagnosed with autism at a very young age. We worked with him when he was young, and he and my daughter went to preschool together. Over the years, he improved significantly to the point where he no longer needed intensive intervention, but our families remained in touch and our children continued to go to each other's birthday parties.

Jordan had developed into a brilliant and athletic young man, but he remained a bit awkward around the opposite sex. He ended up going to the same university as my daughter, so she helped him get into a fraternity by introducing him to some of the fraternity brothers. Once he got into the fraternity, he regularly went to "date parties," where everyone was set up with a date. At these events, the fraternities party with the sororities and each member asks a girl out. Sometimes it's a bit of a blind date because they've never met, but the end result is that everyone goes with a date—no one is excluded. Sometimes getting a little help from friends is what it takes to get that first bond created.

Making It Work for Your Kid

Your child doesn't have to belong to a fraternity or sorority to reap the benefits of being set up. Family and friends are good sources. We know one young man whose older brother was always willing to help set him up. Ask the people you trust if they know any member of the opposite sex who's around your son's age who might be a good fit, because of similar interests, similar temperaments, or maybe even such *different* personalities that they complement each other (see below).

Peer Cliques

When I was a kid, guys asked girls to school dances and we always went as couples, so when my daughters were in high school, I was shocked to discover that they were more likely to go to their dances in one big group, and sometimes that group consisted of only girls. But I realized quickly that it's quite a common practice these days. Kids often socialize in groups, especially when they're first dating.

This is good news for kids on the spectrum: recruiting a peer clique for social interventions is more effective than recruiting an individual. Read on for how it worked for one of our clients.

Brad—Dating in a Group

Brad was in high school when he started to express an interest in dating. Unfortunately, there was no getting around the fact that Brad had some challenges socially. He had poor eye contact, ended conversations too abruptly (sometimes mildly insulting others), talked too loudly, and frequently brought up inappropriate topics, such as a twisted and politically incorrect episode of *Family Guy*. But even though he had social difficulties, his peers loved and supported him. He had a group of friends of both genders who regularly hung out together after school watching TV, studying for tests, raiding the refrigerator, and so on.

So when it was time for a school dance, Brad simply invited one of the girls within his close group of friends. The girl happily went as his "date" for the evening, knowing that the friends would all go as one big group, which made the whole thing less stressful and loaded for both of them. Brad felt good about himself and both he and the girl were comfortable "going together" within the greater structure of their clique.

Making It Work for Your Kid

The dynamics are simply different in a big group. Although Brad might have been able to get a girl to go with him to the dance all on his own, I suspect that he would have had a few more rejections if he hadn't had a peer clique to fall back on. I've met many of his friends and I know they do truly enjoy being with him despite his social challenges.

So if your son or daughter has a group of friends of both sexes, take advantage of that when the time comes for dances and parties. Choosing within her peer clique may be an effective way for your child to start getting experience with members of the opposite sex, without taking her out of her comfort zone or putting too much pressure on pairing off before she's ready for that.

And even if your child doesn't have a fixed group of friends, peers can be amazingly supportive. Teens get such a bad rap, but they can be wonderful to kids who need extra help—I've seen it with my own eyes. Studies have shown that with a teacher's or specialist's direction, middle schoolers will band together as a group to work on specific social areas with kids on the spectrum. And these friendship groups often carry over outside of the school day. We have witnessed many middle and high schoolers who start off volunteering to have lunch and work on social conversation with kids on the spectrum and end up happily extending the friendship by going with them to school sporting events and other outside-of-school activities. While not every child needs formal arrangements, they can be really fun and helpful if your child needs that extra boost in making and keeping friends. (See Section II, Chapter 1 for more on friendship groups.)

Opposites Who Attract

Most young adults on the spectrum find socializing laborious and making conversation effortful. As a result, they're likely to withdraw into solitary activities that don't require them to interact with others. You might assume that the perfect relationship for someone like that would be with someone similarly introverted and retiring (and that certainly can be the case), but I've seen several truly happy romantic relationships that prove the exact opposite. For someone who finds engaging in conversation difficult, being with someone who's so outgoing she can keep the conversation going without any help from him may well be the perfect solution to his social problems.

Juan and the Woman Who Completes Him

Juan had difficulties socializing, but that didn't mean he didn't have the desire. He found social situations awkward and uncomfortable, simply because he was never certain what was expected of him and was always worried he'd let the ball drop. His anxiety over his ability to be social only made his difficulties worse, and he found himself in a vicious cycle of being too nervous about whether he *could* successfully engage to do so.

Then he met Jennie, and his problems were solved. Jennie was outgoing and friendly and carried most of the conversation at parties—she talked enough for both of them! His burden was lifted, and you could literally *see* his happiness and relief when she was re-telling some funny event or keeping a conversation bouncing along with other people. Because her strengths filled out his areas of weakness, the relationship worked and Juan no longer had to dread social situations. The more the pressure on him was lifted, the more he could relax and enjoy himself.

They married shortly after college and both are still immensely happy together.

Making It Work for Your Kid

I was chatting with a mom recently whose adult son with Asperger's is dying to meet someone to date. She is a very social woman and has lots of friends with daughters her son's age. Her son tends to be quite headstrong, and she asked me if I thought that someone who could "stand up to him" would be a good match. Knowing her son, I thought that situation would be disastrous, so I surprised her by suggesting they look for someone who was mellow and easygoing.

If you are helping someone get a date, observation and a little conversation about what's important to him or her is the best strategy. What type of personality does he seem to have the best time with? The more outgoing or the more quiet type? Does she tell you she prefers to be around someone who takes the lead on conversations or someone who is more passive? Does he like someone who laughs a lot or the more serious type? Any help your adolescent can give you (or her friends) on the type of person who's attractive to her makes it easier to find the right first date.

And don't forget to watch your child in social situations to see what personalities work best with his, both with friends and romantic interests. The truth of the matter is that we don't necessarily "know" why some personalities mesh so well—it's kind of a surprise. But by watching your child actually interact with others, you can get a sense. You can see if he gravitates toward the quieter types, or if he seems to find the more outgoing appealing, and which personality type is likely to bring out the best in him. Once you get an idea, you can home in on helping him find that perfect person.

Read on for Andrew's first-person take on what it was like to have a middle school relationship.

ANDREW

There was one girl introduced to me by a friend of mine—a kid I knew from elementary school who lived in the neighborhood. He gave me her phone number and when I talked to her on the phone, she was nice. After I had talked to her on the phone a lot and we had IM'ed some, I met her with that same friend of mine and his girlfriend at a mall. This girl I was hooked up with was really nice and would always say positive things about me, like she would tell me my haircut looked good and that I had a good personality. When we

were going on dates, we would eat lunch or dinner at restaurants, and we would see movies and go to theme parks. I had a good time with her.

The only problem with her was that she was not that pretty; she was very clingy and we were totally different people—she liked to listen to music from musicals and I didn't like that stuff at all. She would also talk nonstop about Harry Potter. Other kids at my school made fun of me for going out with her when they saw a picture of her on my cell phone (this was back in eighth grade). They made me feel like a loser for going out with her. We broke up, because I eventually felt embarrassed that my friends teased me about her. Also, I realized that our interests were really different.

When we broke up, I told this girl nicely that I just wanted to be friends with her after all, but she just broke into tears. I did feel bad for her, but at the same time, I felt like she was overreacting. Then, my friend's then ex-girlfriend was mad at me, but then later apologized to me for getting mad.

When I am looking for a girl, I look for both her personality and her looks. After that, I would always try to ask cute girls from my middle school and high school out, but a lot of them have turned me down. They nicely said that they did not want to go out with me, but even though they were nice, I was not too happy about it.

The next girl I am really trying to look for to date would be a girl who has some similar interests (that do not have to be exactly similar, obviously). I would also like this girl to not only be pretty, but to also have a good personality. I would probably try to get a date with her by talking to her and getting to know her, and then by asking her out and getting her screen name and her cell phone or home phone number, and maybe calling her on her cell phone to make plans. I will hopefully go out with her for about six months to a year.

DR. KOEGEL

Andrew's personal account illustrates a number of points we mentioned above. To start, Andrew's first date happened in the same way that many young people get together—as a setup. Second, no one who meets Andrew would deny that he has a great personality (and he's cute too), so talking on the phone before getting together was a perfect opportunity for Andrew and the girl to get to know each other. Meeting through a friend and arranging to hang out with that friend and his girlfriend had the advantage of a peer clique—a group of friends. That took a lot of pressure off of having to be one-on-one on a first date. And as with most middle schoolers, Andrew's relationship only lasted a short time. We would like it if relationships were independent of what the peer group thinks, but unfortunately they aren't at that age. It isn't surprising that Andrew's friends' comments focused on looks—boys that age tend to do that. And sometimes a blurry cell phone photo is all they need to sharpen their claws and attack.

CLAIRE

There are two things that really struck me as I read Andrew's account. The first was how susceptible he is to peer pressure. I don't think his father or I realized to what extent the other kids' teasing altered his feelings about a relationship he had been really enthusiastic about up until then. He does tend to be very impressionable, and because he takes things more literally than other kids, he'll believe boasts and opinions that most kids would know to take with a grain of salt. I'm glad we're aware of this now—it's something to talk to him about and work on in the future. You don't want other kids to have the power to poison something that makes your child happy, and yet so often they do. One discovery we've made is that while he won't listen to his parents' attempts to contradict what his peers tell him, Andrew will listen to his favorite uncle, and so we frequently ask my brother-in-law to take him out to lunch and casually bring up a topic that we feel Andrew's peers have misled him about.

The other thing is something I had forgotten about but which came back to me as I was reading what he had written: Andrew was truly wonderful on the phone with this girl. I would hear him talking to her and he was a great listener, sympathetic and supportive. ("They teased you today? That's horrible!") I'm not sure he enjoyed those conversations, but he did a great job of holding up his end and I honestly think it's because we worked so hard on his conversation skills when he was little. One of the first directions Dr. Koegel ever gave us was to work on "increasing Andrew's questions." We did, and in Overcoming Autism I talk about how effective that was in improving his ability to engage with others. What's interesting is that its effectiveness continues to this day: he really is a good listener and will ask the right questions at the right time—there are a lot of men out there who could learn from him. We women like to be listened to. (Of course, Andrew gets the credit for being fundamentally a kind and supportive guy.)

A romantic life doesn't appear full-blown and perfect just when you're ready for it. We all had to struggle with some very awkward moments and relationships before we found those that really worked (and of course even our happy endings often turn out to be neither happy nor endings). Our kids will need more support, interference, and guidance than most, but don't rule anything out for them.

Frequently Asked Questions

I really don't think my son is all that interested in a romantic relationship yet, although most of the kids around him seem to be forming pairs (he's a senior in high school). Is it something I should push? Is it possible to wait too long? Or should I wait for him to show interest?

Some individuals on the spectrum prefer to stay single throughout their lives. And that's fine, if that's their choice. Unfortunately, many tell us that they would like to have a relationship, but have either been unsuccessful or just plain don't know how to approach another person. While it isn't necessary to "push" a relationship on your child, it is important to teach him the things he will need to learn to be a part of the dating world, especially if he's showing signs he wants that. And even if he is a late bloomer, if he has learned the skills, he'll have a much easier time. There's no doubt that every person—male and female, on the spectrum or not—goes through an awkward period with the opposite sex—and some are more awkward than others. There are some interesting studies that lay out exactly what young adult and college women want on dates. What women like on a date are

- **Flowers.** Women appreciate the little extra special thoughtfulness. In fact, one of my daughters recently talked about a friend's to-die-for boyfriend: every time the girl is sick, he brings her soup and medicine and whatever else she needs.

- **To be treated.** Forget women's lib—girls these days like the guy to pick up the tab. If the guy has limited funds, it doesn't have to be a five-star restaurant, as long as he pays.

- **To have doors opened for them.** No matter the venue, remind your son always to hold the door open for his date. Women just like that.

- **Fun things to do.** Young women report that dates are more fun if the guy plans two or more things to do. So instead of just dinner, do dinner and a movie. Instead of just coffee, do a museum and coffee. A quick Internet search of things to do in the city usually brings up tons of possible options, and if your son is short on cash, no worries—there are always fun things around town that are either free or don't cost too much.

- **To be picked up and dropped off.** Teach your son to pick up his dates (or meet them and walk if they're at school). And remind him to clean his car out first!

- **A nice end to the evening.** At the end of a date, teach your son to tell his date he had a nice time and that she was fun to be with, and then to give her a warm hug. Young women do have a higher image of dates who say something complimentary and are affectionate at the end of the date.

Although both men and women report that, in general, they want to date for fun and to find a long-term companion, most men report that sex is a main goal of dating. If you have a daughter on the spectrum, that's yet another reason to teach her when and with whom she should have sex. (See the next chapter for more on helping your child on the spectrum deal with sexual issues.)

My son has always been most comfortable around kids who are significantly younger than he is, so a lot of his closest friends are a few grades behind him. But now that he's fifteen and talking a little about girls, I'm wondering if he's going to be more interested in the ones who are a lot younger. It is true that girls his own age seem much, much more sophisticated than he is. But I can hardly encourage him to pursue younger girls—that's just icky. Any suggestions?

This happens sometimes, but it would be a good idea to keep an eye open. While it isn't such a big deal for a twenty-eight-year-old to date a twenty-six-year-old, it does become sticky when an eighteen-year-old is dating a sixteen-year-old (or younger), who technically is not an adult yet. It may be a good idea for you to do a functional analysis on his behavior (see Section I, Chapter 2 for how to do this) to understand *why* he prefers to be around younger kids. If it's because he doesn't have the social skills to maintain relationships with his same-aged peers, then he'll probably need some intervention in that area. But if his friends are truly good matches and not *too* much younger, it might not be a problem. Just make sure he has the proper supervision if either one isn't an adult yet.

My daughter isn't the slightest bit interested in making herself look attractive, but she is interested in boys. She doesn't understand why her friends are asked out and she isn't. How do I get her to see the connection between looking her best and being attractive to the opposite sex without hurting her feelings or creating more anxiety for her?

Looking attractive, whether superficial or not, is a basic part of our culture. You can't go into a department store without seeing a whole section totally devoted to women's makeup. Looking nice on a date is important because it shows the other person that you fixed yourself up for him or her. The best thing you can do is make the goal of looking nice fun for your daughter. Look at magazines (you may want to pick a magazine that will have affordable and reasonable styles) or advertisements and discuss the fashions in them. Talk about her favorite people and what they wear, discuss dressing for work versus dressing for a picnic, have a mother-daughter beauty day, fix her hair while you're waiting for brownies to finish baking, and so on. (For more on helping your child to look good, see Section VI, Chapter 2.) And remember, while some fashion magazines can have a negative influence, they're still a useful intervention tool and can lead to helpful discussions if your child is having trouble in this area. First impressions make a big difference, and I've had adult clients who refuse to trim their nails, don't wash their hair, and sometimes don't even seem to look in the mirror before they leave the house. They have trouble making a really good first impression and subsequently getting that crucial first date.

3. Sex

My son is very delayed socially and academically, but physically he's right where he should be (which is much further along than I'd like him to be). I've noticed him staring at girls on TV, which isn't a problem, and also at girls on the street, which is sometimes a problem. His hormones have definitely kicked in, but I don't think he has the cognitive or social skills to deal with them appropriately. How do I keep him from getting into trouble?

CLAIRE

Ah, sex. The source of so much agony and uncertainty when you're a teenager.

I'm not going to tell any cute little family stories here. There are limits. But I will say this: for whatever reason, I'm fairly comfortable talking to all my kids about sex and I think that's a good thing. No matter who your child is or what issues he's struggling with, it's got to help him to have a parent who can speak comfortably and calmly about the realities of sexuality and who can listen to any questions or concerns without overreacting. Studies have shown that the more sex is discussed openly in the household, the later kids are likely to have sex. The same is true for sex education—the simple fact is that the more knowledge your child has about sex, the longer he's probably *going to wait to have it. And I think we parents can all agree that's a good thing.*

All of my kids—even the littlest ones who find the idea of sexual intercourse absolutely repulsive (as one does before puberty)—have been told repeatedly that sex is a wonderful but serious act that should take place only between two people who love each other, that masturbation is normal but must be done privately, and that you should always use a condom when you have sex. I'm willing to answer any other questions they might have, but I absolutely insist on their knowing those three things, even if it means I have to bring the topic up now and then. (After I took my older kids to see the movie Juno, I immediately launched into my "This is why you should never have sex without a condom" speech, and one of my teenage boys moaned, "Why does everything have to have a moral with you? Can't we just enjoy it as a movie?")

Kids on the spectrum, who are rule followers and absorb things best when they're boiled down to their simplest elements, need you to be honest and direct with them about sex. Kids who aren't on the spectrum need you to be honest and direct with them about sex.

Now on to Dr. Koegel, who's going to be honest and direct with you about sex.

DR. KOEGEL

The bodies of individuals on the spectrum work the same way that everyone else's does. I had a dad tell me one time that his adolescent son with autism came home from middle school one day extremely upset because he'd had an erection at school. The dad replied, "Haven't you noticed how middle school boys always carry their books in front of themselves? That's because that happens to all of them!"

One of the challenges with individuals on the spectrum is that because they have social difficulties, they may not learn about sex the way their peers do. Most of the males haven't talked with the guys in the "locker room," and the girls haven't been included in the group gossip about boys. The kids may not have asked their parents about sex, and their parents may have not brought it up, assuming their kid wasn't ready to talk about it. And to make matters worse, the kids may not have dated as often as their peers—or at all—so they haven't had a chance to learn anything firsthand. Odds are good they're just way behind in every sexual arena.

But as Claire mentioned, it's best to address the subject *before* it comes up as an issue or problem. And if you don't feel comfortable talking about it, get someone else to help. We don't want the only thing our kids know about sex to have come from the small amount of sex education they've had in school. It just isn't enough.

Unfortunately, there's been almost no research done on sex and autism spectrum disorders. As far as we can tell from reports, only a subgroup is likely to marry. On an even more worrisome level, a higher percentage of individuals with disabilities (higher than those in the typical population) are arrested and incarcerated for sex crimes. Sadly, it seems that many of the arrests stem from our kids' lack of social awareness about what is and isn't appropriate and not from any malicious intent. For example, some of our adults have been accused of "stalking" girls they were interested in. One parent reported that her son was beaten up at the beach because he kept staring openly at another guy's bikini-clad girlfriend, completely oblivious to how offensive that was. Another parent called me because his son had been arrested for downloading kiddie porn even though he didn't realize that it was inappropriate (see Section VI, Chapter 4 on managing technology in your household). Claire and I were on a talk show once and a parent called up complaining that her son with autism had unintentionally touched a girl inappropriately, and the girl's family had filed charges against him. Kids on the spectrum rarely mean harm, but they often just don't understand where to draw the line.

As our interventions improve and kids on the spectrum become more and more included and more and more successful academically, the challenge will be to fill in the social gaps, so that they can pursue and enjoy relationships and sex as much as their typical peers—and without risk of offending someone or violating any laws.

Puberty

As we said before, every parent dreads the teenage years, and having been through them twice (and survived both times!), I'm happy to tell you that they're not all that bad. Yes, kids do become a bit more difficult to handle—when they're little, they'll usually change their behavior if you correct them, but during adolescence, whatever their peers think is far more important than what their parents think. They're trying to fit in and they're trying to spread their wings. And they should be. If they listened to everything we said, they would be playing our music, wearing our styles, and talking as we do—which just isn't normal for an adolescent. Whether we like it or not, our kids *do* need to shift from spending the bulk of their free time with their parents to spending it with their peers. Again, this will lead to healthy friendships and healthy romantic relationships.

Around (or shortly after) children celebrate their ninth (for girls) or tenth (for boys) birthday, they'll experience an increase in their hormone levels, which will eventually increase their libidos. Something important to remember is that puberty doesn't happen overnight. It is gradual—over a period of many years—which is great news for parents, because it isn't as if one day they're raising little kids and the next day they're parenting wild, raging, out-of-control creatures who don't want to have a thing to do with them. But it is an awkward time for kids, physically and emotionally.

This whole puberty process starts with girls' developing breasts and boys' experiencing testicular enlargement, and with both sexes' growing pubic hair. While this doesn't seem like such a big deal, every adult remembers the conversations about size back at that stage—the girls talk about who has the large breasts and the guys talk about who's "endowed." And since middle and high schools have made a point of encouraging group showers after phys ed classes, none of this is a secret.

Shortly after puberty begins, boys will start growing facial hair and their voices will change. And girls will start their periods, which makes a few days every month completely uncomfortable and unpleasant. Then to make matters worse, nature throws perspiration and body odor upon them, along with acne for some, and boys experience all of those also, in addition to wet dreams and (very embarrassing) spontaneous erections.

And whom do they have to talk with about all this? You might think you could send them to your family doctor, whom they have known for many years and should feel comfortable talking with about anything having to do with the body. But guess what. Research shows that *almost all* medical doctors *do not* feel comfortable discussing sexuality issues. Further, most medical schools give *no* training in the area of sexuality. So here we are, a society that's obsessed with sex (books, the media, movies, TV, gossip magazines, advertising, and so on), but we're almost incapable of having a frank, open talk about it.

Fortunately, you can help your child by being open and honest when it comes to discussing puberty, relationships, and sex. While kids on the spectrum will have the same physiological changes as typical kids, their difficulties with communication and socialization may result in their not completely understanding normal body changes. If your child doesn't hang out often with friends, he may not have talked with them about the birds and the bees, and if he finds communication challenging, he may not have fully understood the elementary school lectures. So if you think your child may need some extra support in this area, here are some suggestions:

Talk About It Before It Happens

If your child hasn't been as socially active as his peers, he may not have been included in the general changes-of-life discussions they're all having, so he may not have much information and will need you to start from the basics.

If she has challenges with communication, she'll probably need you to simplify things. I had a dad tell me recently that his daughter had attended some sex education classes at her school, and after a big meal she announced to her father that she had a baby in her tummy.

The dad tried to explain that she was just full from the large meal, but she insisted that her stomach was growing so she must have a baby in it! If the sex education class is going to be over your child's head, you need to take the time to discuss it with her in a way that she can understand.

You need to start early so you can prepare your child before he or she gets unnecessarily alarmed over perfectly natural body changes. Tell her that she will find blood in her underpants and what she should do about it, whether it is going to the nurse, calling home, or opening up her personal hygiene kit. Give her this information *before* her first period starts. Similarly, tell your son not to worry if he has a wet dream. Assure him he can just pull off the sheets and throw them in the laundry or let them dry and no one will notice (well, tell him that). Let your kid know that these changes are natural—that periods happened to you when you were her age (and probably still do)—and explain what to expect long before anything happens.

Continue to have ongoing conversations about the subject. Your child will have many questions, and if you only have one formal "sex talk" with him—the kind where you sit down, say a few things, ask if he has any questions, and then it's over—he won't feel comfortable about discussing things regularly as they come up. Always keep the lines of communication open and answer any questions honestly and openly, so your child feels comfortable about asking you questions anytime something comes up.

I remember one of my daughter's friends asking me intimate details about sex. Apparently, her mother hadn't talked with her about sex in the detail she desired, and this poor kid had no idea about what was happening with her body. I was really worried that her mother would be upset that I answered openly and honestly, but I never got the dreaded phone call.

Breast Development

The days of bra burning are over. And that's sad. Not only because of the statement it made, but also because bras can be really uncomfortable. But these days, to fit in, girls have to start wearing a bra as soon as they have something noticeable.

If your daughter is starting to develop, take her shopping and let her try on a variety of different bras. Then make sure putting it on gets into her routine, just like putting on any other piece of clothing. If she needs a self-management chart or a checklist, make sure to add the bra, until putting it on becomes a habit.

Body Odor

A friend told me a funny story recently. She said that after her daughter had participated in a school health education class, she came home and announced that she needed to use deodorant, despite the fact that she hadn't hit puberty yet and had no more body odor than a toddler! But the school nurse had said girls her age needed to start using it, so my friend went ahead and got her some. I recently caught my own daughter lifting up her arm and smelling the pit after a trip to the gym. Once they hit puberty, most kids become aware of needing to put on deodorant on a regular basis, but for kids on the spectrum, it might not click in as naturally as it does for others. If your child doesn't seem to notice that she needs to check those things, you'll need to teach her. Remind her to smell her clothes before she puts them away to see if they need laundering—even if they look clean. Make sure she puts on deodorant every morning. And if she forgets, get it into her routine or start a self-management program. Also make sure she knows that after a physical activity, a stressful class or meeting, or when the weather is warmer, she'll need to check more often.

Nutrition and Vitamins

Kids on the spectrum often have poor diets, and this can delay the onset of puberty. Furthermore, some types of nutritional and vitamin deficiencies can cause increased discomfort during puberty, like menstrual cramping. You can lessen the negative physical effects of puberty by making sure your child eats a healthy diet and gets the right vitamins.

Exercise

We have long been proponents of physical exercise. The benefits can't be understated. We have published several articles showing that vigorous physical exercise can be immensely helpful in improving schoolwork and lowering repetitive behaviors in kids on the spectrum. Physical exercise can also be helpful in reducing menstrual cramps, and for both sexes it can have positive psychological effects during puberty, not to mention provide the opportunities to meet and interact with peers. A lot of gyms are opening up specifically for teenagers these days.

Finally, regular exercise will help with weight, and kids' weight does fluctuate during puberty. Some picky eaters gain weight during adolescence if they gravitate toward carbs, and others gain when they aren't participating in physical activities as often as they should. So do your child a favor and get him on a sports team, in exercise classes, or enrolled in a gym during adolescence and beyond.

Shaving

If your child isn't as socially aware as his peers, he may not think about hygiene and looking good as often as you would like. And the changes that puberty brings do necessitate new grooming skills. Hair starts growing where it hasn't grown before. For boys, it's on their faces (nothing looks worse than those little unshaven straggly mustaches some boys have during puberty), and for girls, hair starts growing in lots of socially unacceptable places (well, unacceptable in our society—in Europe, she can probably get away with hairy armpits).

Your daughter needs to learn to shave her underarms (the hair there can harbor bacteria and lead to body odor) and her legs. If you find she just isn't remembering to shave, start a self-management program. Shaving needs to be a regular part of her routine, and for boys, the same is true for shaving their faces.

Resting

Many kids on the spectrum have sleep problems. Parents report that their kids wake up in the middle of the night, and even if they aren't demanding attention, can be heard moving around for hours. This sleep disturbance may not correct itself in adolescence. One parent woke up in the middle of the night to find her nonverbal adolescent son's bed empty. After an unsuccessful search throughout the house, she called the police. A few hours later, they found her son several miles from his home. He had crossed half a dozen very busy intersections and found his way to a music store. While his mother admitted that going to the music store was an age-appropriate activity and he couldn't express his desire to go there to her, his leaving home in the middle of the night was a completely and utterly terrifying experience for her.

Your child needs an adequate amount of rest for proper functioning—with sleep she'll not only function better, but feel better—and that will affect you too. If your child isn't getting enough sleep due to pubertal changes like wet dreams, menstrual periods, or any other reason, here are some suggestions:

- **Make sure he stays awake during the day.** Many kids catnap during the day. In fact, I visited one high schooler who slept through all his boring classes (we've all been tempted to do that), and woke up bright and cheery for his interesting classes. You may have to enlist the school's help if this is happening.

- **Make sure she gets enough exercise during the day.** Exercise sometimes helps with nighttime sleep. When we were doing our research on physical exercise, we found that many school programs do not require kids in special education to participate in regular physical education programs. To make matters worse, many kids on the spectrum are either excluded from or, for some other reason, don't participate in team sports. Finally, many may not be included in spontaneous pickup games. So you may have to work a little bit to get physical activities set up for your child—at school, after school, and over the weekend.

- **Have a routine.** Every parenting book has a section about getting your toddler to sleep at night and most suggest a routine: for example, bath, then bedtime story, then kisses, then tuck in and lights off. Many adolescents and adults benefit from a routine too. You've heard people say not to read in bed every night or you'll get sleepy when you read at other times. This is because you *can* become conditioned to feel sleepy. Try to find a routine that helps your child get to sleep at bedtime or when he's experiencing middle-of-the-night insomnia, but make sure it's the same routine night after night. For an adolescent, this may involve getting into pajamas, brushing his teeth, washing his face, reading a chapter in his favorite book, then listening to some quiet music. Whatever routine you want to develop for your child is fine—the main point is making sure it's relaxing and that it happens at the same time each night, so he gets drowsy and falls off to sleep shortly afterward.

- **Watch the diet.** Make sure your child isn't having caffeinated beverages or lots of chocolate right before bed. And if she's getting up in the night to go to the bathroom, have her cut back on her liquid intake before bed.

Triggers

One area of research has focused on adolescents and young adults who seem to be doing just fine for many days in a row, then (seemingly) all of sudden one day exhibit disruptive behavior. It doesn't seem to be related to anything that's happening then and there, such as problems at school, work, or family routines. We've discovered that some things that happen rarely and infrequently may trigger a problem behavior.

For example, PMS has been associated with behavior problems. Mom may ask for help with household chores or a teacher may give an assignment that would be fine any other day, but couple that with PMS and we may see behaviors we didn't even know existed in our kids. A child who has communication challenges might not be able to clearly explain that she's not feeling well that particular day. So if your child is having unusual outbursts, try to find out what "growing pains" might be triggers. If you have a daughter, you might want to lighten up a bit during that time of the month. Let her take more hot baths, use a heating pad, exercise a little more, and so on—anything that helps reduce PMS. If your son got turned down when he asked a girl out, give him a little more support. Let him know that you understand what he's going through.

Rules and Limits

For some reason during adolescence, your rules are tighter and stricter than any of your kid's friends' parents. At least your kids think so. There probably are a few parents who have no rules for their kids and a few who are so strict it isn't healthy. But in general, I found that most of the rules the parents of my kids' friends had were pretty close to mine. So don't give in to your kid's complaints that you're being unfair!

Make sure your kid thoroughly understands your rules and their consequences. The very worst thing for a child is if you're wishy-washy, don't stick to consequences, and change your mind about your family rules and limits. I'm not saying that kids can't earn more freedom. If your child always follows the rules, keeps up his grades, and is hanging out with an acceptable peer group, you can give him a little more freedom—and make sure to tell him that's why. But continue to have a curfew and other rules, and make sure that you stick to them, even if your child tells you that he has to be home much earlier than any of his friends. Check with the other parents and agree on acceptable rules, whether it's the dress code, curfew, or behavior at parties—it's a lot easier if all of you have the same rules.

The same goes for you and your spouse: stick together about rules. Kids will ask Mom if they think she'll be softer, and Dad if they think he'll give in. It will save you and your significant other a lot of heated arguments if you just say, "Let me check with Dad first," then discuss it together when something doesn't sound right. A united front is much easier than having your child divide and conquer.

You Still Hold a Lot of the Cards

Even though your child may be putting more emphasis on what her peers think at this age, remember that you are still her parent and you still hold the cards. If your child is behaving inappropriately, you need to think about consequences. If she's being rude to you, you may need to think about not lending her the car that week. If she went on an inappropriate Web site, you may have to restrict her access to the Internet for a few days. Parents forget that older kids still need boundaries and rules, and if they follow them, great—you can lighten up a bit. But if they don't, they still need consequences.

On the other hand, if your child says something rude to you, don't get into an argument with him and don't try to one-up him—it will only make matters worse. Kids still need feedback on their behavior, and if you calmly say, "It hurts my feelings when you talk to me like that," it's going to go a lot further than turning it into a battle of wills.

Every time you start to get frustrated with your child, stop and think. Remember how hard it was when that classmate teased you and how embarrassing it was when your tampon leaked through your clothing (or if you're a dad, maybe it was getting an erection at the worst possible time) or how miserable you felt when you weren't asked to the prom by that special boy? Multiply all those hardships and painful moments big-time for a kid on the spectrum. *Everything* is more challenging when it's more difficult to read others' emotions, and you're being teased more often than the typical peers, and getting your ideas across is challenging. So remember to be the supportive parent he needs at this time.

Find Special Times

The last important thing to remember, which is especially crucial during adolescence when your child is gradually moving away from you toward her peers, is to plan special time together. If you and your child both enjoy going to the local coffee shop for a hot chocolate, keep doing that. If you have the same favorite TV program, keep watching it together. If you like going to the movies, plan to do that on a regular basis. Those special times, when you're both relaxed and having fun, will be remembered forever.

Summary

Again, every parent has to deal with puberty, but if your child is on the spectrum, you may need to help him learn how to deal with the added hygiene responsibilities, society's increasing expectations, and the stronger sexual feelings brought about by the gradually increasing hormones. Remember, even if your child seems socially immature, he's having the same physiological changes as any child. A parent recently told me that she found her stepson looking through her lingerie—she felt that it was all part of his Asperger's syndrome. Well, you know what? All young boys get curious about those kinds of things at that age. It's a normal process of growing up and learning about sexuality. So keep the communication lines particularly open during this time.

Keeping Sex Safe and Appropriate

Again, there hasn't been as much research or information on this subject as I'd like, but as we work with more adolescents and adults, we have learned about potential problem areas we need to address and some ways to improve sexual knowledge and skills.

Inappropriate Touching

I worked with one girl who loved to give hugs. The problem came during puberty. She still kept giving whole body hugs that, sweet as they were when she was tiny, rapidly became inappropriate for her age because she pressed her whole body against the other person. We had her practice giving more socially acceptable hugs—the kind where you stand back a little and put just one arm around the other person. By putting in the time to teach and practice the correct way of hugging, we were able to get her out of the bad habit and into a good one.

We also have kids who have the opposite problem with giving hugs: they stay too stiff and aloof and seem uncomfortable. Appropriate hugging changes with age and familiarity, and getting it right takes practice. If your child resists your attempts to practice, enlist a teacher or therapist to help and give feedback.

Other kinds of touching are even more complicated. When is it OK to touch another person? When is it offensive? If your child is delayed socially or hasn't dated as much as his peers, you'll need to talk with him very clearly about all that. If your child already has some difficulty understanding what is personal space, and when it is and isn't appropriate to touch another person, you may want to deal with it before it becomes a real problem by working with him on it directly. Because he really doesn't understand the rules, you don't want to punish him, but you do want to make the rules clear for him. Just break things down so they're easily understood, such as "Hugging is good for relatives and adult friends, but shake hands with new acquaintances and nod at friends." If your child is visual, you may even want to draw some social circles or write a list and discuss appropriate touching for each social grouping.

We've spoken with a few adults on the spectrum who say they always wait for other people to initiate intimacy, thus protecting themselves from doing anything inappropriate. Unfortunately, it also means they're not learning much about reading their partners' wishes. Adults need to get a sense of whether their physical attentions are welcome or not. One thing we've taught our adolescents is to drop in a question if they're uncertain (and even if they aren't). For example, if they're giving a shoulder massage to their date, we tell them always to ask her, "How does that feel?" Even the kids who have trouble reading facial expressions and subtle cues can learn to ask the questions that will allow them to figure out what their partner does and doesn't enjoy. (More on that later.)

Stalking

A subgroup of our kids become fixated on things—they accumulate tons of information and become very focused on one topic. Unfortunately, we've had a handful of adolescents and young adults on the spectrum who became fixated on a particular romantic interest and began what many people would consider to be stalking that person: following her around the school grounds, sitting outside her dorm, repeatedly calling her even after being told not to do so, and so on. Although there's never any harm intended, the objects of interest understandably freak out at the unwanted attention. We've found that it really helps to involve the person in other activities and meet new people to get his mind off that one particular individual. It's important to recognize that the "stalker" wants a friend (or romantic interest) and so simply trying to make him stop following the object of interest won't be nearly as effective as making other social opportunities available to him so he'll feel less dependent on that one possibility.

I was at a high school recently and one of the students with autism had been friends with another girl in her special education class. Unfortunately, the student decided that she didn't want to be friends with our client anymore. Instead of redirecting the child on the spectrum to interact with other kids, the school staff let the situation escalate until she was following her former friend around constantly. Then their solution was to let the girl leave early from class so she couldn't be followed! There was no attempt to address the main issue, which was our client's desire to have a friend. The school provided no alternative or replacement behaviors whatsoever, so the girl on the spectrum felt she had no choice but to persist in trying to get this one former friend to hang out with her. It turned into a much bigger problem than it needed to because it wasn't addressed correctly. In cases like this, it's vital to work on social skills and increasing the child's peer relationships, using the interventions we discuss in Section II.

Modesty—or Lack Thereof

The other day I visited the home of a middle school girl who was diagnosed with autism as a child but now does incredibly well in all areas. Unfortunately, while she interacts amazingly well with adults, she has very few friends her own age, so we continue to work with her in peer social areas. She was wearing a dress that day and while we were sitting around the table visiting, she tucked her knees up to her chest, apparently unaware that in that position everyone in the room could see her blood-stained underwear. Her mother noticed and quickly ushered her upstairs to change her clothes—but if her mother hadn't been there, I doubt the girl would have realized what she was doing. Her carelessness about how she presents herself to the world may well be off-putting to her peers, especially when it comes to something as potentially embarrassing as this was.

Kids on the spectrum can be oblivious to personal matters of modesty, and so you really have to be explicit and detailed in discussing this area with them. You can help out by purchasing clothes that naturally preserve modesty, like pants instead of dresses for a girl or longer shorts instead of shorter ones for a boy. If your child tends not to notice personal things like a leaky tampon (or an unzipped fly in the case of a boy), teach her to check for them on a regular schedule—but in private, not in front of other people! You can also teach your child certain routines, such as "Always check your fly before opening the bathroom door to leave" or "Every recess break, go to a restroom stall and check your tampon." Getting personal hygiene into the daily routine often makes it easier to remember. (See Section VI, Chapter 2 for more tips on helping your child with personal hygiene.)

Distinguishing Between Public and Private Acts

I touched on this in the previous paragraphs. People on the spectrum sometimes don't have the social awareness to realize that an activity that is appropriate in the privacy of their own room is simply unacceptable in public, including, of course, sexual activities, such as masturbation—and I *have* seen kids with autism masturbate in public. If your child is masturbating in public, make sure he understands that it is something that should only be done in private. Use a self-management program if the behavior is too entrenched to be changed easily. Self-management has been effective in reducing self-stimulatory behavior in public, and teaching your child to monitor periods of time without masturbation may solve this problem.

For more on teaching your child to distinguish between appropriate public and private behaviors, please see Section VI, Chapter 3.

Abuse Prevention

There was a horrible situation in a nearby institution where a young, nonverbal woman with autism was raped by a male staff worker. This sexual abuse might never have been found out if the woman hadn't become pregnant. For many years there had been rumors about abuse of the patients at this facility, which housed several hundred individuals with disabilities, and some of the patients had even run away, but it took the undeniable evidence of the pregnancy to finally close down the place. The staff worker is now incarcerated.

Individuals with disabilities are often victims of abuse because they don't always have the verbal abilities to report it, they might not understand when they are being taken advantage of, and people frequently don't believe them when they do try to report it. When I worked in the public schools, one of the principals molested boys *on the school grounds* for many years before he was finally caught and arrested. Almost all of his victims were disabled children, many of whom had behavior problems, communication delays, and very bad family lives. Because of their personal histories, when they tried to relate what was going on, they weren't believed, and it took years before the man was caught and sent to prison.

In order to prevent abuse, individuals with disabilities need to be taught about personal boundaries in very clear, specific terms. You will need to be very precise about what's OK and what isn't and which people are acceptable to have relationships with. You should teach your child how to say no clearly and forcefully, and tell her to report anyone who's doing anything that makes her uncomfortable. If your child isn't able to verbally communicate, you need to frequently check on the people she lives, works, or goes to school with. If your child is in a residential setting, make sure that background checks are regularly occurring or at least are done thoroughly when people are first hired. And look for signs that something might be wrong—drop in unexpectedly as often as you can.

Making Sexual Decisions

If your child is engaged in an appropriate relationship, he's going to need to make the right sexual decisions. If he's sexually active, make sure he understands about sexually transmitted diseases and their prevention, about birth control options and the necessity of using one every time, and how to have a satisfying sexual relationship. Open and honest communication between two partners and education are the best ways to ensure a satisfying sexual relationship. There are courses and books on relationships, and encouraging your child to feel comfortable talking to you, a relative, a therapist, or another close friend may be the best way to help him in this area.

One thing I've noticed from working with young adults on the spectrum is that they often have had significantly less sexual experience than other people their age. To help compensate for this inexperience, you may want to suggest that your child ask his partner if she's being satisfied (if you're comfortable doing so). You can practice this by suggesting your child give his partner a shoulder, foot, or hand massage and ask her how it feels as he's doing so. Does she like it harder or softer? Is that a good pressure? Is she tense anywhere? Once he's comfortable asking these questions, it's easier for him to ask them when he's being more intimate, and his partner will be more likely to volunteer this information if she's used to expressing her feelings.

Relationships, Marriage, and Kids

To be perfectly honest, we don't know much about intimate relationships, or marriage, or the family life of people on the spectrum. What we do know tends to be anecdotal: individual stories about people on the spectrum who are married and have kids. Without large data sets, we don't have any actual statistics on how many people on the spectrum have successful relationships, children, and so on.

A few decades ago, Asperger's wasn't often diagnosed, so many of us have close friends who we know are on the spectrum but were never diagnosed. Some are dating, some have significant others, and many have kids. We also know that the large number of kids from the current autism uptick are close to hitting puberty, so we'll have to deal with this issue a lot more in the future. And finally, we know that the interventions we have today—for social challenges, conversation improvement, and the inclusion of individuals on the spectrum—are better every year, so the futures of these kids become more optimistic with every passing day. We should have a lot more research and information at our fingertips in another decade or so. But for the moment, here are a few things I do know from my experience as a therapist:

Fewer People on the Spectrum Than in the Typical Population Get Married

Unfortunately, kids with social challenges who are not adequately treated (and this happens a lot) often have problems with socializing as adults. So it's critical that they get support at all ages. As we discussed in the school sections, many, many kids don't have adequate social programs during middle and high school. Some kids don't have any type of social intervention in their natural settings. Having said that, I know many individuals on the spectrum who are happily married. Sometimes they marry a little later, but many do get married.

Many High Schoolers and College Students Need Support in Initial Relationships

While most kids start holding hands, kissing, and flirting as early as middle school, many of our high schoolers and college students have *never* had a date. So that means that they may not be able to read the romantic cues. They also might be a bit awkward, as anyone is on first dates. It's important in these cases to find therapists who are trained to help them learn how to read social romantic cues, when to touch (or not touch) another person, how to strike up a conversation with someone they are interested in and how to take it to the next level. Learning how to satisfy a partner is important for any couple, but if your child has difficulty reading the social cues, he may have to be taught to ask more questions and be more open about his relationship with his significant other. We tell our adults that it's okay to say, "Sometimes I have trouble picking up on other people's feelings, and I just wanted to know if you enjoyed yourself last night?" It's important to make that effort, because if the date simply assumes he's being insensitive to her feelings, *that* is a certain relationship stopper.

Early in my career, when autism was rare, I almost never saw families with more than one child with autism. In fact, when people asked me if they should have another child, I almost always said it was very unlikely that they would have another child with autism. I don't say that anymore. Now that there are more kids being born with autism, we are seeing more within the same families. And we do know that genetics plays a role in autism, because if one identical twin has autism, the other one is almost always on the spectrum as well. In fact, in the last decade I have seen triplets, two girls and a boy—all with autism; four siblings—all with autism; and a number of other families who have more than one child with a disability (although not all had autism). The studies vary somewhat, so it's hard to put an exact number on the likelihood of having more than one child with autism in the family, but the odds are higher of having another child on the spectrum if you already have one child with autism.

That brings us to the likelihood of having a child with autism if one or both parents have autism. We do know a few things. There seems to be a possibility that some environmental components may be linked to autism. For example, there have been a few publications suggesting that older parents may be more likely to have a child with autism. And if your child is a late starter at dating, she may also be a late starter on the baby front. So that's one possibility that may lead to an increase in incidence—not just because she's on the spectrum but because of her age.

But we need to keep in mind that one of the problems of interpreting these studies is that they don't usually specify the degree of autism—it's either a "yes, he has it" or "no, he doesn't." The participants are often grouped, so we don't know if it's more or less likely to happen in kids who require more support. Further, if a parent isn't very social, his child may not be exposed to opportunities for socialization, and therefore may appear as though he has symptoms, but may just not have learned how to socialize.

So the bottom line is that an adult with autism or Asperger's seems to have a higher likelihood of having a child of his own on the spectrum. But these are just numbers and statistics. There really isn't enough information yet to clearly determine just how likely it is.

Kids of Kids on the Spectrum

As we mentioned above, another thing to think about is that there really haven't been many studies that look at different subtypes of autism when it comes to the genetic link. We know from experience that there are many "autisms," and kids with this diagnosis can be as different as night and day. A child who shows no symptoms of autism by age five is different from a child who is still severely disabled as an adult, and they're both different from the child who's fine in every way except socially. The studies that have looked at family links usually lump everyone together and get a statistical probability out of the lump.

So if your adult child decides to have children, it's a good idea to get genetic counseling before the pregnancy and then, once the baby is born, to stay alert for any early signs of a disability and get intervention as soon as possible if there are any symptoms present.

And if the parent isn't that social but wants his child to be, he'll need to make an extra effort to get her involved in afterschool activities, clubs, and other social networks outside of the home setting. By staying informed and active, the parents and grandparents can overcome any potential environmental factors.

Frequently Asked Questions

My daughter is dating a boy who seems like a nice young man. We're thrilled—she's had so many social difficulties over the years that it's wonderful to see her successfully dating. My husband is worried, however, that the boy is going to pressure her sexually and it does seem unlikely that they won't get into at least some heavy petting, given their age. I honestly don't know what to tell her to do. When I was that age, I had a feel for how far I was willing to go and how to make sure things didn't go any further. But she's such an innocent—and so eager to please him—that she might let him do things she shouldn't. I'd like to give her some clear-cut rules for how far she can go, but I'm not sure what those should be or how explicit I should get. Any advice?

Open discussion is the best thing. She needs to understand that she shouldn't rush into anything. If she's an adult and doesn't live at home, discussion is the best you can do, but if she's a middle or high schooler, make sure she's adequately supervised when she's with this guy. It doesn't make sense to leave adolescents alone for hours on end with no supervision—they'll most likely dig up things to do, and at that age, some of the things will be sexual. You also need to stay on top of the supervision situation at the other child's home—you may think you have things perfectly covered as far as supervision is concerned, only to find that the parents of your daughter's boyfriend don't supervise at all.

Talk to her about what you feel are appropriate behaviors for her age and the values you would like her to have. If you feel that it's OK for her to hold hands and kiss her boyfriend, let her know that's all she should do. At this age the boyfriend may not last long if she isn't willing to have sex, but she may also have a lot less heartbreak if she isn't sexually active.

My son is on the spectrum and even though he's a young adult, he shows no interest in women. It occurred to me for the first time recently that he might be gay. It's not something we've really talked about with him and in our efforts to simplify rules as much as possible, we've only talked about sex and appropriate touching between a man and a woman. Now I'm wondering if we've completely confused him. Any advice on where to go from here?

Like typical kids, a percentage of kids on the spectrum will be more interested in same-sex relationships. This doesn't change the fact that they need to understand that they shouldn't be taken advantage of, that they need to protect themselves against STDs, that they shouldn't rush into things, and so on—all of the important information you'd impart to any kid reaching this age. In other words, you're already telling him the right things, but it wouldn't hurt to say specifically that sometimes these things take place between two men or two women.

Neither my husband nor I am comfortable talking about sex with our child. Is there another way we can help our child learn about sex without specifically having to discuss it?

First, you're not alone. Many people find it difficult to discuss sex with their children. Fortunately, there are many books you can purchase for your child that explain sex in a simple way and are tailored to his or her particular age. Also, if you have someone you trust, a relative or therapist, that person may also help with discussing sex and answering your child's questions. Finally, since your school's sex educators are trained in this area, they may be able to provide your child with a little extra help.

Making School Successful

1. Introduction

School has always been the hardest area for our child—and for us. At home, I can watch over every aspect of his life, but when I send him off to school, I have to depend on other people to make sure he's being taken care of and stimulated. I want him to like school and I want him to grow and learn. How do I get the most out of his schooling experience?

CLAIRE

I can (and later will) discuss at great length all the ways that school is hard for Andrew and other kids like him, but for a moment I'd like you all to consider how hard school is for the parents of kids on the spectrum. The kids have to learn to read; we have to learn to advocate. They figure out how to solve math problems; we have to figure out how to structure an IEP. They try to memorize history facts; we try to memorize the rights we're entitled to under state law so we can demand a better education for them. They have to deal with the occasional unsympathetic teacher; we have to deal with frequently unsympathetic public school administrators who view the children we love as an extra burden they'd just as soon not have. They have to navigate the social jungles that are the lunchroom and play yard; we have to . . .

Actually, there's nothing as hard as that. They win that one.

The point is, if you're a parent who's fighting for your kid's education, you're working your ass off on a daily basis. You may feel frustrated, impotent, angry, and overwhelmed. But know that you're not alone. And know that there are ways to approach the schools to make everything a lot better.

DR. KOEGEL

Being the first . . . being a pioneer . . . bringing new strategies to an outdated system . . . it's fun, right? Not when it comes to educating a child with autism. It's stressful, fatiguing, and humiliating for parents who want their children to get the best education possible but know that if they don't, it could mean losing their child forever. It *should* be easy—the research clearly shows that kids who are included in regular education programs do better socially and academically. Researchers have shown that the typical students in classrooms that include kids with disabilities do better too. Research also shows that if kids on the spectrum get an intensive intervention program, they're likely to have much better outcomes down the road. So getting your child what he needs from his school should be simple, shouldn't it? But it isn't. I still can't believe how hard parents have to fight for the basics. I remember writing letters for Claire and Rob just so the school district wouldn't reassign Andrew's aide when he was doing so well. (Their actual school was very supportive—the change order had come from the central office, which knew nothing about the individuals involved.) And I've testified in many fair hearings—and not lost one yet—all pertaining to getting basic inclusive and social programs for kids on the spectrum.

But it's worth it. Children on the spectrum need to be fully included at any age; they need modifications to help them get through assignments; they need parents and staff to work together to provide a comprehensive and unified program across all of their waking hours; and they need to be in a school system that embraces them as part of the community—one that doesn't just stick them in a different building, a different classroom, at a different lunch table, but welcomes and includes them as an integral part of the student body. It should be just that plain and simple.

We said in our introduction that one of the tricky things about parenting kids in this age group is figuring out when to step in and when to step back. So we want to be clear about this: making sure your child's school is working for him in all the right ways cannot and should not be left to chance. Don't hesitate to meet with teachers, administrators, and staff to advocate for your child when it comes to his or her academic environment.

2. Middle and High School: Supported Independence

My son just graduated from elementary school and next fall he'll be going to our much bigger local middle school. I'm worried that the transition will be too much for him: he's going from a place where the kids have known him since kindergarten (and are therefore used to his quirks) to a place filled with strangers, most of whom will be older than he is. And back at elementary school, I was able to establish a real relationship with each year's teacher and monitor his progress with her. But at middle school he's going to have a different teacher for every subject and parents are simply not as involved. How do we navigate this strange new world?

CLAIRE

Things really changed when Andrew graduated from elementary school. For one thing, he had had a one-on-one aide up until then, the same one every year. We used to joke about how Dawn was his second mom because she took such good care of him in an unobtrusive way, always facilitating his social interactions with the other kids and making sure he understood what the teachers wanted from him. But now he was doing so well that we were sending him off to middle school without any special support. We had chosen a private middle school over our enormous, zoolike local public school, because it meant smaller classes and a more nurturing atmosphere—but it also meant no IEP, no special education staff, nothing but regular teachers and administrators who were going to expect him to keep up on his own.

The biggest change for us was the transition from one class-room teacher to many teachers of different subjects. Each September in elementary school we would meet with his new teacher and go over Andrew's academic strengths and weaknesses and let her know that we welcomed any communication throughout the year. Now that Andrew was going to have a half dozen or more teachers who would only see him about an hour a day, we knew we wouldn't be able to make and maintain that same kind of connection.

It's been an interesting journey since then. Not every teacher in middle and high school has been the perfect match for Andrew, but I will say that all but one have offered unqualified and enthusiastic support. When he's had a problem in class— and believe me, we've had quite a few of those over the year, ranging from awkward partnering situations to failed grades on tests—they've been willing to work with us to improve it, whether that meant dealing with it themselves at school or giving us the information we needed to help out at home.

Socially, middle school was hard. Because it was a small school, the pool of boys was tiny and Andrew just didn't find any soul mates in it. For the first year or so, he managed to stay socially afloat simply by being cheerful and a good listener, but by the end of his last year of middle school, things were deteriorating and he was starting to get picked on and teased. We were relieved when he graduated from eighth grade and could move on to a new school.

We were fortunate to find a high school that doesn't just talk about diversity—it truly embraces it. Andrew was welcomed for who he was right from the start and his friends are as quirky and offbeat as he is.

Nothing's perfect. There are still kids at school who tease him and make him uncomfortable. One ungracious teacher *made his ninth grade year stressful, ignoring our requests for help in figuring out why Andrew was struggling in her class and never giving us the information (graded tests, future subjects, and so forth) we needed to help him at home. Several group projects have turned disastrous, with Andrew either doing too much of the work or not enough. Some girls told him and his best friend to call them and then deliberately and maliciously ignored their calls. And so on.*

It's probably impossible to get through middle and high school without some discomfort, but Dr. Koegel's advice can reduce it to a manageable amount.

DR. KOEGEL

You can ask pretty much anyone you know, and he or she will tell you that the years in middle school were not altogether a wonderful experience. Some may say it was a total nightmare and others might say it was a mixed bag, but rarely will anyone tell you that middle school was paradise. My own experience wasn't something I'd like to repeat, even if I knew then what I know now. I was under five feet tall and looked as if I belonged in third grade, and the other kids at school had no reservations about regularly letting me know that I looked too young. Of course, now that I've been celebrating my twenty-ninth birthday for the last two decades, I would fully appreciate someone telling me how incredibly *young* I look. But context is everything, and back then looking young was embarrassing and humiliating.

Actually, come to think of it, context is everything when dealing with kids during their middle and high school years. My friends would complain to me about how impossible their adolescent kids were with them at home, but they always seemed perfectly delightful to me. And I remember overhearing my adorable, sweet niece talking to friends on the phone and sounding like a refugee from an X-rated movie: every other word was bleepable. Most kids *do* have many different behaviors in their repertoires. They're not rude and argumentative to everyone—their parents are usually the lucky recipients of those behaviors. That's important: kids need to understand contextual appropriateness, and you'll need to keep that in mind when helping your child socially. Kids pretty much learn, without any special intervention, how to act in specific situations, but kids on the spectrum may have difficulty with that, especially when it relates to peer socialization. While they may do just fine with adults, their adult-pleasing behaviors may not win them any same-age friends. We'll talk about how to deal with some of these issues in this chapter.

As parents, we often think about ourselves when our kids are in middle and high school. We're nostalgic about the days when our kids wanted to be with us over anyone else, willingly complied when we asked them to do something, and eagerly shared triumphs and tribulations with us at the end of each day. We were there to fix their pains, both psychological and physical. Now they're less willing to share information with us and often totally disagree with our point of view. But we need to remember that as difficult as it is for us, it's infinitely more difficult for them. Kids in middle school are trying to fit in, and this may mean doing things we wouldn't have dreamed of, like dressing in outrageous outfits, drinking and taking drugs, and shutting out adults. What we have to remember is that our children are changing physically, mentally, socially, and emotionally.

Mother Nature brings on a lot of those changes. Girls begin to develop and start their periods. That's a big deal. They may be experiencing discomfort about their bodies and PMS. Boys are also hurtling into puberty, each of them on his own private time line, so the difference in size and development can vary hugely from one boy to the next.

The change in school is huge too: middle schools and high schools are usually much bigger than elementary schools, and there are many new kids to deal with as well as a different teacher for each class. In some ways that last part is good, especially if your child ever got a not-so-great teacher in elementary school whom she was stuck with every day, all day, for a whole year. But changing classrooms and teachers every period has its own set of challenges, which are primarily social—kids hang out together in the halls between classes and walk from one class to the next with their friends, so it's potentially another challenging time for children with social difficulties.

Despite some of these radical changes, it's important that you understand that your child doesn't change and become a teenager overnight. Children gradually grow and gradually want more independence. That's healthy and appropriate. And it's healthy and appropriate for us as parents to accept and even encourage the changes. When they're in those middle and high school years, they shouldn't still be clinging or begging us to walk them into their classrooms or to call their friends' parents to set up playdates. If they're not coming to the joys of independence on their own, we need to help them get there.

You've Got to Have Friends

During these years it's more vital than ever for the socially awkward child to make friends. Fortunately, there are lots of things parents can do to help their teens in the middle years—read Section II on making and maintaining friendships for specific ideas.

One thing to keep in mind is that for many kids in this country, middle school is the toughest time socially. None of us want our kids to have a bad two or three years, but it's rare to get through this time without a few painful moments, even if you're not on the spectrum. It's important to remind your child—and yourself—that social life almost always improves in high school, where the kids are more mature and more comfortable with differences. Kids stop needing to be like everyone else and start celebrating their varied interests. High school classes also tend to be bigger than those at middle school, and I've heard many kids say that while they never felt that they fit into a social group in middle school, they found a great group of lifelong friends in high school. So tell your kid to hang in there if middle school feels lonely—things *will* get better—and let him know he's not alone.

The Good News About Middle and High School

In many ways, it's actually *easier* to have a child who's on the spectrum in middle and high school than in elementary school: you don't have to worry about your child having one potentially unhelpful teacher all day, every day. At most middle and high schools there are a number of different teachers for each course, and some of them really welcome children on the spectrum.

Most middle and high schools have more electives and more class choices. This gives your child an opportunity to enroll in classes she may find more interesting. Being able to choose both the teacher and the course can make middle and high school a much more enjoyable and successful experience.

But here are also some important things that parents need to think about with their middle and high schoolers on the spectrum:

Inclusion Is Still Important

I've noticed that many middle and high schools do less inclusion than preschool and elementary school. They often place the kids in "special," less demanding classes or in career development courses. There is no reason why a child should not be fully included in middle and high school—both academically and socially.

We had one mother who got so frustrated with the school system that she started homeschooling her son. While I'm not opposed to homeschooling for some children, children with social difficulties need to learn how to interact with their peers. This particular mother didn't have that component in her homeschooling program, and consequently, although he was very bright, he didn't have any peers to model his behavior on—only his mother. So as a teenager, he acted just like her. Because women in their forties don't have the same topics of conversations, the same activities, or the same interests as fourteen-year-old boys, he was quite the misfit. Even the jokes he told weren't jokes that fourteen-year-olds tell. While this is an extreme case where the child had no social opportunities at all with other children, it illustrates the importance of maximizing opportunities for your child to interact socially with his typical peers.

It Needs to Be the Right School

These days, more and more schools are providing the opportunity for interdistrict transfers, and if your child is on the spectrum, you may have an even more legitimate reason for selecting a specific middle or high school. Remember, principals and teachers make the difference. If the school isn't receptive to (and, ideally, enthusiastic about) working with your child in both academic and social areas, and if the staff there doesn't have ideas—lots of ideas—for how to support your child as well as previous successful experiences working with kids on the spectrum, keep looking. We've seen firsthand that the principal's values and the teachers' dedication are crucial to making our kids' programs work.

I recently visited a high school where, in the course of chatting with me, the principal referred to the kids on the spectrum as "*those kids*" and talked about "*their* programs" in "*their* special education classroom." It was as if these kids were aliens in "*his*" school—there was no sense that they were part of the community. Not surprisingly, that school didn't offer any good programs for kids on the spectrum.

Schools that celebrate diversity and are committed to the best education for each child, regardless of learning styles and needs, best suit our kids.

They Still Need Support—But Also Their Space

No matter where she falls on the spectrum, your child still needs support. This may be particularly important for socialization. At elementary school, there are lots of games, sports, and other activities going on around the playground, but in middle and high school, the kids are mostly just hanging out. They also spend a *lot* of time hanging out during nonschool hours—typical teens spend close to twenty hours a week hanging out with friends outside of school. While just sitting around shooting the breeze and complaining about teachers may not play to your child's strengths, do try to find as many opportunities as possible to get her together with friends, even if you need to structure that time to make it successful.

If your child isn't making friends, try to find clubs and fun classes he can take outside of school that will get him involved in a peer network. (Read Section II on making and maintaining friendships for more about that.)

Kids on the spectrum are often more willing than their typical peers to go to the movies or out to dinner with their parents. I've even had high school parents talk in detail about their child's social difficulties *in front* of them while they sit and listen with no sign that it's embarrassing for them (and it really may not be). As nice as it may be to feel that your child isn't yet pushing you away—as most teenagers are doing to their parents—you also don't want her to seem babyish at a time when teasing and one-upping one another are such a huge part of the daily interaction. Save parent/child time for when you're at home together and encourage your child to be as independent as possible around her peers.

Be a Team

Teens, whether they're on the spectrum or not, figure out really quickly whom to ask for what. If he wants a later curfew, he knows Dad is likely to say yes. If he wants a bigger allowance, he learns that Mom's a soft touch. My husband and I figured out early on that our kids were dividing and conquering—trying to get a yes out of one of us even when the other said no—so we made a policy of discussing any big questions together before either of us would commit to an answer. Teamwork makes anything stronger. Consistent programs coordinated across both home and school environments will ensure that your child is getting his work completed and his homework finished, that everything that is supposed to get home from school gets there and everything that is supposed to get back to school also gets there.

To make sure this happens, you'll need to have regular communication with those most intimately involved in your child's education by e-mailing regularly, checking in on the phone, and holding monthly team meetings. Open communication and regular meetings will help you address any potential problem before it becomes too big to handle.

You want to make sure from the very beginning that the principal and school staff are willing to provide a friendly environment that will support your child. I have been at schools (most recently a high school) where the principal clearly viewed the kids on the spectrum as irritants and wanted them sequestered in the special education classroom. This isn't teamwork. Support from your principal is critical to your child's success, and if the principal isn't supportive or willing to give you any time, you'll need to either find another school or have a third (more educated) party attend meetings as an advocate. I have attended many IEP meetings in schools where principals or other staff members were not willing to provide needed social support and/ or inclusive settings.

Continue to Reward Your Child for Good Behavior

One thing parents often forget, especially during the teen years, is that kids need just as much praise and positive reinforcement now as they ever did—and maybe even more. Even if they roll their eyes when you praise them, keep doing it. Figure out what's rewarding to your child during the middle and high school years and provide this abundantly when your child is behaving. Remember, kids on the spectrum often have to make more of an effort than their typical peers to socialize or stay tuned in or write that essay. Don't ignore the effort. Praise and rewards at this age are still incredibly important.

Studying, Academics, and Homework

Kids on the spectrum can vary wildly in regard to academics. Some are at the top of their class across the board, some are good in certain areas but not in others, and some need help in just about every area. I've learned that there are a few things that are really important when it comes to supporting your child's schoolwork.

First, in regard to curriculum, many special education staff members are happy to have middle and high school students engage in work without any regard to whether they're actually learning anything or not. In fact, I have seen special educators dumb down the curriculum so much for some fully included kids that they weren't learning anything at all, making the classwork so easy that it was no more intellectually stimulating than sitting in front of the television all day. Make sure your child is *learning* in school. Make sure that she's acquiring new and useful information during her hours at school. And make sure that the school is expecting the most of your child. To do this, you'll need to check over her work and periodically observe.

If your child is essentially being babysat and not taught during school hours, you'll need to call an emergency IEP and make sure that the goals are changed. Then keep on top of the school—make sure they document the acquisition and maintenance tasks and that everyone who interacts with your child is aware of the new goals.

Homework

We know that making homework meaningful and practical increases the likelihood that a kid will complete it. If the teacher is open to suggestions and can easily make changes to the assignments, suggest that he use the kids' names and fun examples on the problems—those little connections can really capture the kids' interest while they're doing their work.

But making sure homework gets done is *your* job. You don't have control over what the teacher assigns, but if your child doesn't like the assignment, you can improve his motivation by giving him choices, like where to sit while he does it, the order in which he completes his different assignments, the type of writing tool he uses, and so on. If it's just too much for your child, you can always request that he be required to complete a only portion of the homework. And remember: always let him do a fun activity after he's finished his homework, something that's worth working for.

And last, organization is critical. Time management will help her the rest of her life. You don't want to be a constant nag, but you do want to help her learn to organize herself so that you only need to check over things. Many kids on the spectrum are dependent on adults to move them through every step of doing homework. If your child expects you to walk her through her work, there are several ways to deal with the problem. First, many schools have afterschool homework clubs on campus. If your child needs to learn to do homework independently and to gain organizational skills, those can be IEP goals. If your child's school doesn't have any homework clubs, see if she can get a study hall where the teacher will work with her on independent completion of assignments.

If you want to work on this at home, first you'll need to coordinate with the school to make sure your child is actually writing down the assignments and bringing the work home. Teachers can be a great help with this. Have them let you know *immediately* if your child isn't completing assignments. We had one middle school girl who told her parents she had finished her assignments every night. It wasn't until the open house that her parents learned she was the only student who didn't have her work up on the board. While her parents fixed the problem by hiring a college student to help with organization and homework completion every day after school, many weeks had passed before they even knew there was a problem.

One quick note: many middle and high school teachers now post assignments online, which is a great fallback if you or your child wants to double-check what's due. Unfortunately, online assignments cannot be relied upon completely because not all teachers post online and some forget to post assignments on a daily basis. Your child needs to get in the habit of writing down her homework assignments for each and every class—it's an important skill and the most reliable way to stay on top of things.

After you make sure your child is getting the assignments and the work home, you may want to do a functional assessment to figure out *why* he's having trouble with his homework. If it's because the work is just too difficult or he's missing key academic areas that make it impossible to complete, you'll need to talk with the school staff about filling in those gaps and helping him with strategies to complete the homework independently. If it's because he likes the attention when someone is helping him, then you'll need to systematically and deliberately give him loads of attention every time he *completes* his homework independently.

Start with very short periods of time of independent study and work up to longer period gradually. You can even use self-management to monitor gradually increasing periods of time that she works independently and then reward her for those periods.

It's also possible your child is interacting with you to *avoid* doing the homework, engaging you in conversation and using comments or even disruptive behavior as a means of putting off getting down to work. If that's the case, you'll need to set up a reward or incentive system for getting started. This can be done by simply giving him a special treat or allowing a favorite activity after some predetermined amount of homework is finished (remember—start small). And finally, remember to include those motivational components we discussed in Section I, Chapter 2.

So the bottom line is stay connected. Make sure your child is learning and make sure she's getting work completed. Stay on top of things—don't wait until it's too late.

CLAIRE

Schoolwork can be so hard for Andrew. He's incredibly bright and some things come more easily to him than other kids, like, say, memorizing dates or names, but other things are just hard. Like figuring out what the hell Shakespeare is getting at with all those endless metaphors. Or trying to write an essay on a J. D. Salinger story when the characters never say what they mean, but you're supposed to know anyway.

Now that he's in high school, some of his teachers run their classes like mini college courses, lecturing for the full hour and expecting the kids to take the kind of notes they can later study from—not so easy if you're someone with language-processing issues.

Andrew sailed through elementary school academically. He was an early reader and, as I said, a good memorizer, and none of the work was very challenging for him (social life and navigating free time were a different story). Middle school academics were definitely more complicated: different teachers meant different teaching styles. He thrived with the teachers who broke down everything into simple facts and struggled with the ones who were confusing or long-winded. Rob and I didn't always have the time, patience, or knowledge to help him figure things out, so we engaged a tutor and still use one today.

We look at Andrew's tutor as a sort of interpreter. She's able to restate the ideas and information that he doesn't always absorb during the fast-moving, fast-talking class lecture or discussion. She'll also read through any literature assignments with him and, again, help to interpret—you could almost call it translating—the complicated world of metaphor, innuendo, and nuance that is so incredibly difficult for my very literal son to absorb.

With and without the tutor, Andrew works unbelievably hard. I rarely pass by him on a school night without seeing him typing away on a paper or trying to figure out a math problem. He really wants to do well. Sometimes he does. Sometimes he doesn't. Either way, I always tell him how proud I am of him for putting in so much effort. And I am. I'm not just saying that because you're supposed to praise your kid for working hard— I'm awed and humbled by my son's work ethic.

Not long ago, I quizzed him on some study guide questions for his global studies class. He had memorized every bit of information on all five closely typed pages. I told him he was going to do great on the test, and I really thought he would. He got a 60 on it (the teacher wasn't interested in memorized facts; she wanted the kids to talk about the bigger, thematic issues). When he told me about his grade, head hanging low, I was able to say with absolute honesty, "I saw how hard you studied and I'm really proud of you. As far as I'm concerned, you did great." "Really?" he said, perking up. "Really," I said.

I'm still kind of amazed to hear myself say stuff like that—I was the sort of student who was ready to throw herself off a building if she got below an A minus, and I really thought I might be that kind of mother. It's kind of a relief to find out I've grown up since then.

DR. KOEGEL

How to Be an Involved Parent

As I have mentioned, your child still needs your support once she reaches middle school and beyond—you just have to give it to her from a farther distance than you used to. Here are some ways to still be there for your middle or high schooler, while giving her room to grow.

Keep an Eye on Things

Try to find out what's going on at your kid's school without driving her crazy. Call her teachers or counselor on a regular basis. Some schools encourage e-mailing as a simple way for parents and teachers to communicate, while others discourage it. Find out what the policy is at your child's school. Ask the lunch-duty teacher about the kids your child hangs out with. Good teachers who care about their students appreciate having any concerns brought to their attention and want to help. They may even help facilitate social interaction.

And if you want and have the time, find ways to lurk around the school. Be creative about it. I sometimes waited until lunchtime to bring that important permission slip to school so I could see how free-time socializing was going. Or if one of my daughters forgot her lunch, I would hang out until she had a break and hand deliver it—observing her in class the whole time. Forgotten homework papers and items always provide a good opportunity to drop by school. There are also other ways to keep an eye on your kid without his being aware of it or feeling burdened by your attention.

Go watch your child play sports, see him in the school play, cheer him on at the spelling bee. And do it regularly. Even if your child protests, make it a rule. Middle and high schoolers are OK with rules and if you simply say, "Most of the parents go to the games and I'm going too," that usually suffices. Think of ways to make yourself liked by your child's peers. For example, you and your child can bring a case of cold water to a ball game or other sports event. You can take pictures of the kids and have your child hand deliver them. You and your child can make armbands with the school colors that he can give the kids to wear to the school games. Or bake cookies for the school plays (and let your kid sneak a few to good friends ahead of time). In other words, try to set it up so the other kids are saying you're really a cool parent.

One quick note: a cool parent is *still a parent*. Don't go for just the cool part and forget about the parent part. Middle- and high-school-age kids do not want their mothers to dress or act as if she's their age. They want parents the other kids can respect and talk to, not one who's competing for Cutest Girl in the Class.

If you can't often go to the school yourself, you can also help your child by sending in things that facilitate social communication, like cool sports car magazines, a great new CD, or just some special snacks to share. These will be great conversation starters—and sharing at the middle school ages *does* help to make a kid popular.

Spending Even More Time at School

Children on the spectrum may need more on-hand parental support than their typical peers in middle school. Try to volunteer at school if you can or start up a new club, so you have a useful reason to be around. Another possible way to get involved is by tutoring. Kids will appreciate some extra help with algebra, writing, or whatever else you're good at.

One girl we worked with was having difficulty getting to know other kids at her middle school—she had quite a few repetitive and idiosyncratic behaviors and the kids just weren't including her socially. Angelina's mom was a talented amateur photographer, so she decided to teach a group of kids how to compose, shoot, and print photos. They took photos every week at school and also went on weekend and afternoon outings to take some landscape pictures. At the end of the semester, she helped them turn their photos into beautiful albums. The kids enjoyed Angelina's mom so much that she provided an instant group of kids for her daughter to spend time with.

Like Angelina's mother, try to figure out something you can do with your child's peers that they'll enjoy and that your child likes. Here's one easy idea that works for us every time: kids love to make desserts, so you could conduct an after-school baking session or have kids come over to cook at your house.

Having more adults present decreases bullying and teasing, so even if you don't have a specific activity to do at school, volunteer to walk the halls one lunch a week (and be sure to greet the kids cheerfully when you do it). Carefully planned involvement can help your child on the spectrum and all the other children who are having trouble adjusting at this age.

Be Involved—But Don't Encourage Dependence

Having said all that, if your child is overly dependent, you will need to gradually and systematically phase out your presence in his school life. I've worked with a few parents who simply couldn't let go when it was time to do so.

As much as we enjoy being around our children and want to be helpful to them, especially if they're on the spectrum, we can't do this to the point of hindering their peer socialization. So if your child is overly dependent on you, make a concerted effort to transfer the fulfilling of her needs to her peers. If she forgets her lunch, ask a nice peer to hand deliver it when you drop it off. If she is by herself at lunch, make sure she joins a club—even if you're not the one who runs it. If she's always at home hanging out with you on weekends and after school, make sure that you have other families over with children her age.

In short, you need to carefully analyze your teenager's responses to you and figure out a comfortable level of involvement that allows you to supervise your child without compromising his burgeoning (and necessary) independence.

Help Your Child Meet Other Students Ahead of Time

Once you know which middle or high school your child will be attending, it's time to make sure she gets to know some of her classmates ahead of time. Summertime is a great time to set up some get-togethers. Even if your child is continuing on with many of the same kids, if she's been having social difficulties, take this chance to introduce her to some new peers or reintroduce her to those she never got close to but who you think have the potential to be good friends. If you want to throw a get-together for a bunch of kids, see our advice in Section II, Chapter 4 on how to throw a successful party.

You can also find out what types of activities, camps, and school events are going on in the summer and get your child involved in those that are likely to have a lot of his future classmates in attendance.

Supporting Their Efforts to Make Friends at School
There is some research that suggests that typical peers often feel that individuals on the spectrum aren't as giving as others. If this is true of your child, make sure to prompt him to give a high five to his buddy when he does something well, or e-mail a compliment when a friend gets a good grade, or make a cute cupcake or bring a Baggie full of cookies for a pal on her birthday. Sharing and giving are great ways to improve your child's friendships, and she or he will be learning about ways to develop and maintain good relationships all through life.

See Section II for more ways to make and maintain friendships at school and in the community.

Encourage Your Child to Join a Sports Team
Team sports are a huge part of middle and high school life. When I talk with my children about their social lives in middle and high school, they both talk about how much sports helped socially. Everything from hip-hop classes to organized school sports provided my children with an instant group of friends.

In elementary school, kids who participate in team sports often do them at a recreation center or park. But once they're in middle school, kids can play on their school team, and it can be a huge bonding experience. Sometimes it takes a few tries before you hit on the sport that's a good match for your child. One of my daughters loved basketball and volleyball but, unfortunately, she inherited my gene for (short) height and couldn't really compete with some of the almost six-foot-tall girls. It was heartbreaking seeing her sitting on the bench during the games, but all the other kids absolutely loved her because she was a good sport and always cheered them on. I can't tell you how many awards she got as Most Spirited Team Member and Most Enthusiastic Team Member. We did finally find a sport that she became really good at (tennis), so don't give up if you don't find something that fits right away.

As my daughter's basketball experience shows, even if your child isn't the greatest athlete, he can still be the team's greatest supporter. Teach your child to cheer on other team members and give them high fives when they score. This will help with team spirit and make your kid very popular among the crowd. Remind him that simply being available for practice and cheering on his teammates at games makes him a valuable part of the team.

Here might be a good time to mention the importance of making sure the activities are age appropriate. Don't encourage your child to play dodgeball, hopscotch, or T-ball if only elementary schoolers play those games. Since a huge part of getting your child involved in sports is for social reasons, you want to have kids who are the same age playing with him.

One other thought: I've known really caring coaches who'll give less athletic kids a boost by "hiring" them as their "assistants." For those kids who find playing on a team too challenging and frustrating, having a different kind of role to play can make them feel really important and help get the other kids to look up to them. Of course, you'd have to talk to the coach privately about this and see how he or she feels—not every school can arrange this. But I know one little boy who got a real social and emotional boost when he got to carry a clipboard and whistle as the "assistant coach."

CLAIRE

The middle school that Andrew went to had a no-cuts athletic policy. Andrew had never played a team sport before he got to middle school (we tried some out, but a ball heading toward him made him flinch and cower when he was young). In sixth grade, at a brand-new school, he suddenly decided he wanted to be on all the teams. You can imagine what his skills were compared to the other kids'.

But his school had an "everyone plays" policy and very kind coaches, so onto the teams he went. And, overall, it was a positive experience. His biggest contribution was keeping the benches nice and warm, but he was so enthusiastic and so obviously admiring of the others' abilities that his teammates seemed to get a kick out of him. We tried supplementing the coaching he got at school with some one-on-one instruction at home, and I think the coaches appreciated the extra effort. He did improve quite a bit, although he started at such a disadvantage that he never caught up.

I will admit that the games were agonizing for me to watch, so I delegated the job of cheerleader to anyone I could: my father, when he was in town; Rob, when he was available; our babysitter, when the timing worked out . . . I felt guilty not being there myself, but the truth was that the games alternated between being incredibly boring, because Andrew wasn't playing, or absolutely terrifying because he was. I was desperate for him to get through the few minutes he was allowed to play without any huge disaster that might annoy the other kids, like fumbling the ball or stumbling against a teammate. I never cared what the final score was or whether his team won or lost—only whether Andrew felt OK about himself at the end or not.

Andrew's willingness to put himself out there and try to do something that difficult in public was inspiring. My son has always been willing to face challenges I would have run away from like the coward I am. He's the bravest person I know.

DR. KOEGEL

Look for a Job Your Child Might Be Able to Do in the School Community

Everyone likes to feel valued and important. Giving responsibility to a child with social difficulties can really boost her morale. We worked with one child who had difficulty interacting socially but was extremely bright and a great reader. The junior high school counselor suggested that he work at an elementary school, tutoring low-income children in an after-school program. The program was so successful that pretty soon the principal was asking for more volunteers. About eight other children joined up and all the kids carpooled together, which gave them more opportunities to interact. Discussing the progress of the children they tutored gave them plenty of topics of conversation. Abe now had a social life!

Explain the Situation to Her Classmates (If You're Comfortable Doing So)

If your child has some unusual behaviors, and the other kids are noticing, you may want to meet the issue head-on and have a frank heart-to-heart talk with her classmates. Obviously this is an immensely personal family decision, but I have found that, in general, knowledge and understanding tend to promote goodwill. (See Section I, Chapter 2 for detailed instructions on how to conduct the conversation to make sure it's successful.) We've had several families do this with great success, including Melissa's.

Melissa had been complaining that the kids at her charter school weren't being nice to her, so her dad felt that it was time to take action and ask the whole class to be more supportive and explain why. Read on for Juergen's first-person account of the speech he made to her class and its successful outcome.

JUERGEN

There is a weekly gathering at the school where my seventh-grade daughter Melissa goes. Melissa had increasingly complained about her peers teasing and making fun of her. This was a serious distraction for her in class and affected her work, so I decided to talk with her classmates. Melissa didn't attend the gathering.

As Dr. Koegel had suggested, I began by talking in very general terms about how everyone is different, has a different personality, genetic makeup, and so on. I asked the students if they knew anyone with physical disabilities. Many hands went up. I pointed out how we would normally be aware of someone's physical disability (such as being in a wheelchair) but that this is not always the case with someone who has a neurological disability, as Melissa does.

I then asked the students if they could tell me how Melissa was the same as everyone else, and how she was different. Many students spoke up. "Melissa has excellent retention"; "She gets angry and frustrated, hits the computer keyboard, throws books down on the floor"; "She's sweet"; "She's smart"; "She seems a lot younger, she's short in stature and plays with toys, animals"; "She tattles on other students"; "I've seen her in class looking into books she seems very interested in" were some of the things mentioned by the students. Next, I talked about the symptoms of autism, with examples relating to Melissa, such as her meltdowns or aggression.

Toward the end, I said to the students, "Just ask yourself how you would feel if you could not express yourself very well, or could not easily ask for something, did not have many friends, or were unable to pick up on social cues." I asked some kids to tell me how many good friends they felt they had, and most mentioned some number around three. Then I said, "Well, Melissa feels she has no friends in this school."

I welcomed them to help Melissa, and several students came up to me afterward, including a student who had seen Melissa on the bus. He asked how he could help and has, in fact, since taken Melissa from one class to another whenever possible.

But by far the biggest reward of my one-hour talk came later, at the end of the school day, when Melissa called me and said, "Dad, ever since you gave your speech, everyone has been nice to me including my worst enemies." Her work at school has improved enormously since then, as all the teasing that she endured was, in fact, a huge distraction for her.

ANDREW

I think that the biggest difference between middle school and high school is that in high school, you have more

freedom. In middle school, you do not have free periods and cannot go off campus during breaks, but in high school, you can. In high school, you also have more electives and can choose some core classes that you would like to take (such as in science).

For me, it is really tough to decide whether I like middle school or high school better. In high school, you get more freedom, but in middle school, you get less homework and it is not as challenging. Kids have probably been nicer to me in high school, even though there are still some kids who are jerks. My middle school was so small that everybody would just talk to one another and I was the one kid who could not really relate to other kids. In high school, I have more close friends and I can relate to the kids more than I could in middle school.

I think that school is hard in some ways but easier in other ways. Work and tests can sometimes be hard in school, but my finals are actually not too hard, but still stressful because you need to dedicate your time to them. What I would say helps me most in school is my tutor, who has been a huge help with my academic work (with organization and the actual work). My parents have also been a huge help because they have really helped me study for quizzes by quizzing me on the subject that I am studying and also by editing certain papers I've had.

The most helpful thing in school is taking notes in classes so that I could refer to them later for assignments or tests. I like teachers at my school who are extremely nice and helpful, ensure that my class knows the material, and who write information down on the board so that I can understand it more easily. I do not like teachers (who I tend to find too hard) who go through the material too fast, who assign too much stressful homework, and who talk too fast without writing information down on the board. I am more of a visual learner than an auditory learner.

My favorite subjects are probably foreign languages,

science, visual art, and PE. Foreign languages are easy for me because you really only need to memorize words and conjugations in order to nail them down. I kind of like science as well because you can do fun experiments and it can be interesting to see the way things in the world work. I like visual art because I am a person who likes to draw and create things, and in art, you have the chance to do both of those things. PE is a nice break from academic classes and instead of sitting down, you can get good exercise from running and playing physical games.

My least favorite subjects are probably English and math. English is tough for me because my reading comprehension is not great; it is harder for me to write thorough analytical essays (essays that represent an argument), and I also do not have a great vocabulary. Math is also hard for me, because you need to solve complex problems and take a lot of steps to solve (such as proofs in geometry).

I am happy that I am getting close to going to college and living independently, but I do not want to have to go through the tough process of getting into college. I am really looking forward to being able to major in something that I want to do later for my career. I am also looking forward to being able to wake up whenever I want to make it to class in time. I am a little scared about having to pay expensive bills and not being able to afford a lot of things that I will need for school.

I think college will be very stressful in some ways because of work but also a great experience being completely on my own. I would definitely like to live with roommates who are nice and welcoming, but I would not like to live with roommates who are rude and make me miserable. My ideal college would probably be a college on the East Coast (like in Florida or New York) that has a great graphic design and animation program and that has mostly nice kids and professors. I want to major in Web site building, game making, or animation, so I would like my college to have good computer design programs. I am definitely worried about the application process, mainly because I am not familiar with it. I hope my parents and my college counselor at my school will be really helpful to me when I am applying to colleges. I am also worried about my grades in the future and just hope to work really hard throughout the rest of my high school year. Even though I had decent grades in ninth and tenth grade, I want to work even harder in eleventh and twelfth grades.

Frequently Asked Questions

The teachers at my son's middle school like to have kids partner up for projects or even work in small teams. This is always agonizing for us. First of all, the other kids partner up really quickly, so my son, who's on the spectrum, usually ends up with someone who has behavioral problems whom no one else wants to be with. Second, his partners usually take advantage of him, because he's a real innocent: they'll tell him he has to do most or all of the work, and he'll just go ahead and do it, often with a lot of difficulty. When I said to him once, "You shouldn't be doing it all—you should divide it equally," he said, "I'm just trying to be a good friend." Any suggestions for dealing with this in the future?

This is a difficult issue that you really need to discuss with the school staff. The reason I say this is because there is some research that suggests that if the teachers randomly pair up the kids, they don't enjoy the activity as much as when they're allowed to work with kids they choose. So in a sense, when the teachers let them choose their own work groups, they are doing what they should. On the other hand, it's important that your child not be taken advantage of or constantly be paired up with a partner who's not a good role model. I suggest that you talk to your son's teachers directly and make two suggestions to them. First, the teacher should ask students to write down on a piece of paper the name of the person they want to be with so she can honor their requests but also include the kids who are less likely to be requested. If possible, she should make it clear what your son's strengths are to the rest of his group or his partner, so they can appreciate having him included. She also needs to make sure that all participants play an equal role in group activities. We all remember group assignments where we ended up doing most or all of the work. The teachers can alleviate this problem by dividing the assignment in such a way to ensure that each child does equal work or is required to note which sections he did. Group projects are a good idea but do have to be carefully planned with many things considered.

Again, kids do better if they can choose their own work groups or partners, so if your child's teacher is willing to make this happen, he may have a whole classroom full of happier students. There will be kids in the class who'll work well with your son—the teacher needs to find those kids and make sure they're part of your child's future teams.

My daughter is being left out socially—she eats lunch alone every day. I feel that we should appeal to her classmates directly for support, but my husband is adamantly opposed to it. He says that if we tell everyone she has autism, then she'll always be "that autistic girl" and no one will ever accept her as just another kid. I know what he means and the last thing I want to do is make socializing harder for her, but the way things stand now, she's completely isolated. Do you have any advice?

It's important that she be active socially, and if your husband doesn't want her to be labeled, that's understandable. However, I have done social groups without labeling the students. In fact, I set up one for a middle schooler, and the students asked me what was wrong with the child, but because his parents had been adamantly opposed to having the other children know he had autism, I simply said he had some difficulty making friends. They were fine with that. The important thing is that you get a support team and program in place so that she isn't alone every day. That needs to happen right away before she gets even further behind socially.

My son failed a couple of his courses and now the school is saying he should be in special ed. But I've seen the special ed classes and those kids aren't learning much of anything other than how to bake cakes and wipe off tables. I want more for my son, but how do I get the school to keep him fully included?

If your son is failing, the school needs to make some curricular revisions. This can be done in a variety of ways. He can be required to complete only part of the work, or the problems can be simplified for him so that they are the same problems the other kids get but are at his level. They might also be able to give him more time to complete his work or prime him beforehand. There are many, many ways to revise the curriculum to help a child experience success in the regular education classes. My guess is that they haven't taken the time and energy to explore all the curricular options that can help him be successful.

Back in elementary school, class trips were a day-long visit to a local museum. But now that my son is in middle school, I'm getting all this info about the "seventh-grade class retreat"—there'll be one every year from now on! Frankly, I'm terrified. My son will have to share a room with other kids, be responsible for his own belongings and hygiene, participate in a ton of group activities, and eat whatever they serve him. I'm not sure he's ready to do any of that. But I'm worried that if I keep him home, he'll miss out on a chance to connect with the other kids and it will only add to his feeling different from the others. Please advise!

There are a number of things you can do on these overnight trips. The most common one is to volunteer to go yourself, as a parent chaperone. The schools usually request support from parents and you may want to volunteer. If you can't go, consider asking a relative or close family friend. If you just can't find anyone who wants to go, or if the school refuses to allow parents to go at all, you can prime your child for the upcoming experiences. If he can read, send notes reminding him of what's expected of him at any given point in the trip. Make sure that the teachers pay extra attention to him, both in picking compatible roommates and throughout the trip. Thanks to cell phones, you can keep in constant touch these days as long as it's not a really remote location—and if it is, get the landline number there, and make sure there's an adult whom you can contact regularly to offer advice and give assurance. And remember, these trips usually last only a few days. If his hygiene isn't perfect or he doesn't change his socks, he'll still survive.

3. College

I can't believe my son is going off to college! His high school grades have been really strong and he has some friends. Even though he's doing great in so many ways, he still has some social difficulties and finds change hard to deal with. How can I help make the transition to college successful without hovering and smothering him?

CLAIRE

On the list of things I'm thankful for, the fact that my son is still two years shy of heading to college is way up there. It's not that I don't want him to go—and it's certainly not that he doesn't want to go, because he can't wait—it's more that I'm terrified. There are too many unknowns at college. He'll be spending time with people I haven't met, walking in neighborhoods I haven't been to, going places I don't even know he's going to, and experiencing emotional swings I won't be able to monitor and help him through. I want him to go to college and I want him to succeed there. But part of me also wants to keep him safe at my side. We have a good community college within a couple of miles and sometimes I drive by it and wistfully think, "Couldn't he just go here and live at home with us for another year or two?" That's not what Andrew wants, though, and I'm *glad. I want him to experience college the way I experienced it: leaving home and living with other kids my age. But even for me, it was fraught with social and academic challenges beyond anything I'd known before. How is he going to navigate all that? How much support can I offer him from far away—and how much should I offer him?*

DR. KOEGEL

Things have changed significantly in the last few years in the area of higher education. The great news is that many kids with autism are responding so well to intervention that they are able to go to college and develop a career. It also means that this is new territory for all of us.

In the past, we've had a handful of kids on the spectrum who completed four-year degrees, or even graduate school, but they were few and far between. Now, however, we're experiencing a geometric increase in the number of students on the spectrum who are enrolling at a university. We're just beginning to develop programs to address their academic and social needs. Unfortunately, there are many areas to be addressed that still lack research and experience, such as rooming, getting a support staff in place, picking the right college, and so on. But we *are* having some success and can discuss the things that are working.

Just remember: college is scary. Kids think it's going to be great living on their own with a whole bunch of other eighteen- to twenty-two-year-olds, but I've had two daughters successfully survive college and I *know* it's hard. It's kind of like a feast-or-famine thing. When they're home with all the rules, restrictions, and responsibilities, they think college is going to be the key to independence: no curfews, no bedtimes, no having to clean their rooms, no hounding mom—complete freedom. And it's true. But the flip side is that suddenly they have to handle *everything* themselves, from managing their time to laundering their clothes to budgeting their money to fighting their own battles with unfair teachers and unfriendly roommates. Complete freedom isn't a vacation—it's a long and arduous lifetime undertaking.

Meanwhile, we parents have our own anxiety to deal with. We've done everything we can for our kids on a day-in-and-day-out basis, and all of a sudden they're gone. We worry about whether they'll make friends, get passing grades, wander into trouble with all that freedom—basically we worry that they won't be able to survive without our support.

And of course the anxiety is worse for parents of kids on the spectrum. They already know their kids have had a tough time learning to socialize, and now they'll have to be social *all* the time, even back in their dorm rooms. Will they be able to succeed in courses that aren't in their particular area of interest or will they completely lose focus? What about their social life? How will they do at school parties? Will they be more susceptible to peer pressure far away from home? Will they be lonely?

Well, fortunately, we are beginning to help more and more kids on the spectrum succeed in college. And it's best not to leave it up to chance. Here are some ways to help your child have the best possible college experience.

Helping Your Child Prepare for College

SAT Prep

Oh, the dreaded SAT! It's geared for the mainstream kid and not for those who excel in one specific area or the child who has communication difficulties, so it's no wonder it can strike fear into the heart of the parent of a kid on the spectrum. Here are some things that may help your child:

First, there's the PSAT that children as young as seventh-graders can take, although it's primarily geared toward sophomores and juniors. This early exam gives students a chance to practice under real-life circumstances, and if their scores stand out, schools will often recruit them. The PSAT will help you and your child learn which areas he needs more practice and tutoring in. This way you can address your child's weaknesses and strengths and figure out what kinds of scores you can anticipate on the SAT. Second, you can help your child strengthen areas of weakness by having him study SAT preparation books. SAT prep courses and tutoring can be helpful too. Many colleges have SAT prep courses during the summer (my daughter had a great time one summer when she took an SAT prep course and an art class at Yale University), and that's a great way to have your child get a taste of college life. A little extra practice may boost his score enough to push him over the edge at some schools.

There are dozens of study programs to help prepare your child for the SAT, and there are some accommodations for students with disabilities that you can request on the actual SAT.

SAT Accommodations

If you feel your child needs extra support in the actual taking of the test, certain accommodations can be arranged. You and your child's school will have to fill out some forms documenting the disability and requesting the desired accommodations from the testing agency. Your school is probably familiar with these requests and will be able to help you out, but make sure you start the process well in advance of the time your child will take the test. Requests have to be in several months before the testing dates so the testing company can review them.

Here are some of the more common accommodations that can be helpful for kids on the spectrum:

- **Altering the test format.** If your child has trouble with written tests, the testing agencies will make adjustments so that there are fewer items on each page. They can also use a larger font and different colored paper. In some cases, you can have the instructions and the test items read out loud to your child. These accommodations will simplify and decrease any confusion your child may have with the actual test.

- **Altering the way the responses must be made.** Many of our students have difficulty with filling in the little answer bubbles and also handwriting an essay. You can request that your child be allowed to respond verbally and have the answers transcribed. If handwriting is a problem, your child may be allowed to use a computer for writing essays (although grammar and spell-checkers are not allowed). He may also be allowed to dictate answers into a tape recorder or use a larger block answer sheet. These types of accommodations may make responding easier for your child.

- **Altering the timing and scheduling.** Many children with autism have sleep disorders, and if your child just can't respond well at eight o'clock in the morning, you may be able to request the time of day your child takes the test or ask to have the test given over a few days. Your child can also be provided with extra time (usually time and a half) to complete the test. Or if your child needs more frequent breaks, that can be arranged too.

- **Altering the environment.** Some kids just can't work with distractions. In fact, I remember that when I was an undergraduate student and spending the bulk of my waking hours in the library, if someone at the cubicle next to me started talking or tapping a pencil, I always found it impossible to concentrate. If your child is distracted by other people in the room, you can request that she take the test in a smaller group setting or private room. Special lighting, acoustics, or screens to block out the distractions are also possible. So the bottom line is that you can have your child take the test anywhere she will do her best, whether it be at the front of the room or in a different room altogether.

CLAIRE

We haven't had to deal with the SAT yet, but Andrew had to take the Independent School Entrance Examination (ISEE) twice, once to apply to sixth grade and once to apply to ninth grade.

It did not go well either time.

The first time, we requested and received an accommodation: Andrew took an untimed test in a special location, with only a few other kids who had requested the same accommodation. Unfortunately, the "untimed" part was a bit too literally true: there was no definite end time, and when Andrew finally stumbled out of the test many, many hours later, he was a wreck (as were we, because we had been waiting for him with no way to communicate). With no one telling him when to stop, he had mulled over the test for far too long, agonizing over the answers he couldn't get, wondering if he was supposed to stay even longer, uncertain what was expected of him. The extra time only prolonged the torture, and the accommodation meant he took the test in an unfamiliar place surrounded by strangers, rather than at his own school with his friends.

The second time, thinking we had learned our lesson, we had him take the regular test at a regularly scheduled time and location—no special accommodations (I am, by the way, well aware of the irony of our turning down accommodations for our kid who's been diagnosed with autism, while helicopter parents all over Los Angeles are desperately inventing "learning disabilities" for their NT kids in the hopes of getting them more time on the SAT and therefore a leg up in the college battle). Once again, he stumbled miserably out of the exam, but this time it was because the poor kid was burning up with a fever. He had come down with the flu in the three hours it took to take the test. Our subsequent attempts to explain away his low scores by saying that he "really was sick" to various school admissions staff were met with exactly the kind of raised eyebrows and skepticism you'd expect.

In all honesty, I'm not sure the fever made that big a difference in the outcome anyway. He's since taken the PSAT under normal low-pressure conditions (his high school has the students do it every year for practice) and . . . well, let's just say that standardized tests don't play to his strengths. They also don't correspond at all to the grades he gets, which are consistently pretty strong because he's such a hard and dedicated worker.

With the PSAT and SAT looming ahead of us and no luck with either accommodations or no accommodations, what conclusion have we reached to help Andrew do the best he can?

None whatsoever. Good thing Dr. Koegel is around to give us all advice.

DR. KOEGEL

The Diversity Category

If your child still isn't too great at all that verbal and writing stuff on the SAT (or even the math), don't panic. There is still one other option. Many universities have a diversity category for students who have overcome extreme hardships in their lives or who have excellent skills in some areas but not all. This category is similar to the allowances that are made for outstanding athletes at a great number of universities. Many universities understand the extreme challenge your child has had to overcome just by having a severe disability. If scores for sections of the test are very high, or if your child has some very strong skill areas, admissions officers will often overlook a weaker section. And even if your child's scores were little lower than the school averages on *all* the sections, many universities will still allow your child to participate, because most strive for a diverse population.

But always encourage your child to keep his grades up. Colleges consider many sources of information about your child when deciding admissions, including the SAT, your child's high school grade point average, and the effort put into the application. Encourage your child to do as well as she can in her areas of strength so the standardized tests can be put in perspective.

Precollege Programs

We are now seeing a number of precollege programs popping up around the country. These programs help prepare kids for college, teaching time management, socialization skills, study skills, vocational exploration, and even actual academics. They are not specifically

designed for students on the spectrum, but they can give you an indi-
cation of areas that may be challenging, and it's a great idea to get
started in these areas prior to college.

These days, many colleges offer programs where high schoolers
can spend a few weeks in the summer taking courses in their area of
interest, and as I mentioned above, practicing for the SAT. These
types of programs are especially helpful when there is a program with
staff who can support a child with autism or Asperger's. Again, you'll
need to do your homework to make sure that the school has support
staff who can help your child if he needs it.

Choosing a College

I would *not* recommend sending your child to a program that doesn't
provide some support for kids on the spectrum, so you're going to
need to do your homework and figure out ahead of time which schools
can meet her unique academic and social needs. I have seen too
many bright young individuals with Asperger's or autism who have
been miserable in college or even dropped out because they didn't get
the support they needed.

Of course, this isn't to say that every child needs the same amount
of support. There are many students who know they have a diagnosis
on the spectrum and still choose not to take advantage of any services. They do well in school, they date, and they don't seem to have
any problems surviving college. And there are those who wouldn't
make it past their first week without support. There's a third group
too—those who can survive without help but who (wisely) do seek
out some support in social areas.

Junior College Programs
If you feel your child isn't ready yet for a four-year college program,
you can find a range of programs at junior colleges. Some are very
specialized and designed just to give some help to special-needs
students—their goal is to help the students gain basic job skills
rather than an academic degree. Usually these aren't really inclusive
and will group all the students with disabilities together. These pro-

grams vary. Most are day programs, but some include living accommodations. The student on the spectrum may live with other disabled students. These programs often teach daily living skills so that the students can learn how to shop, cook, clean, do laundry, and take care of themselves in the future.

Other junior college programs focus more on helping students complete an associate of arts degree or the necessary units to move on to a four-year college. Students enrolling in the degree programs are usually offered academic and sometimes financial assistance through a disabilities office or state fund.

Four-Year College Programs

Many universities, now realizing that individuals on the spectrum are often very gifted in specific areas, are more likely to accept them these days. You'll have to decide whether your child is ready to go directly to a four-year college or whether transferring from a junior college would best meet his needs.

I would suggest keeping several things in mind when trying to make that decision. First, can your child take care of himself independently? This includes getting up in the morning; maintaining a healthy level of hygiene and grooming (although, admittedly, I see a lot of college kids on campus who look as if they just rolled out of bed!); getting out the door on time; buying books, food, and supplies; and doing his own laundry, studying independently, socializing, and finding activities to stay engaged and busy.

If she's going to stay in her room all day, miss classes, and become even more socially isolated, you may want to consider having her attend a junior college close to your home for the first few years. There will be lower academic expectations and you can gradually teach her the skills she needs to succeed socially and personally. But always remember that it may not be in the best interest of your child to keep her *too* sheltered. Eventually, no matter how scary it is for parents, our children need to spread their wings and fly off on their own. They have to fail sometimes and succeed sometimes and on the way figure out what life is all about, all while learning to be self-sufficient. That's the goal for everyone and it should be the goal for your child.

Applications

The actual application process is tedious and time-consuming and a pain for everyone. Your child's high school college counselor should be able to help with the application, but you will undoubtedly have to edit the essays. Most parents do. In fact, I remember editing essays for my kids *and* all their friends. I knew how many essays the admission officers have to read and I knew that if the first line really drew them in, they might read the entire essay, so most of my editing involved turning those essays into compositions the readers would want to finish. Obviously, colleges want to get an idea of *your child's* writing, not yours, so don't write it for him. That would be cheating. But helping him go through draft after draft (whether it's you or your child's school's college counselor) should be helpful and will also be a good learning experience for him. And since many colleges strive for diversity, it might be helpful for your child to write candidly about his disability and the challenges he's had to overcome.

Getting Ready to Go

Once you start getting those letters of acceptance, you breathe a big sigh of relief, then rejoice, celebrate, and . . . panic! You may even be a bit more panicked than the parent of a typical child because you have spent your life fighting for your child's rights—advocating, protecting, and overseeing—and now you're giving up the hands-on control you've always had. But you need to take a moment to celebrate this huge accomplishment and everything you've done for your child to get where she is.

Your child is going off to college. He's an adult now, and he's going to be on his own. But of course you still want to do anything and everything in your power to make the transition as smooth as possible for him.

Now that we've had a number of college students come through our clinic—some of whom went on to complete graduate degrees—we have a good idea which areas we need to focus on to make our students' life at college successful. Read on.

Make the Freshman Comfortable Beforehand

Your child will have a number of opportunities to visit the college she will attend prior to the start of school. Take advantage of them! The more times you can visit and familiarize her with her future home, the easier it will be for her when the time comes to move. Check out activities and organizations in the area—not just at the college, but out in the community as well. Find the places where students gather: church groups, clubs, restaurants, movie theaters, and so on.

We know one mother who brought her son to the UCSB campus at least a dozen times during the summer before he started there as a freshman. These weekly visits helped him learn where to eat, where to get money from an instant teller, where to buy books, and where his classes would be. She was able to introduce him to support staff and faculty on campus whom he could call on when he needed help. This made a huge difference for him.

If geographic or time constraints make it hard for you to get to the campus ahead of time, take advantage of the Internet: download maps of the campus and search the school's Web site with your child so you can figure out together which buildings are which and where she can go to meet people. Contact other families with kids going to the same school and see if you can arrange an early meeting. The school may not be able to give you this information because of confidentiality, but you may be able to get information about students who are going to the college from your local high schools. Also, you can contact professors and find out if they might be willing to "mentor" your child (many are enthusiastic about this) and have them help your child connect with other students.

Finally, your child will most likely get the names of his roommates sometime during the summer. Make sure that he's in contact with them so that he can learn ahead of time about their interests, habits, and preferences. You can then prime him on appropriate ways to engage with his roommates about topics and activities that they'll enjoy. Again, anything you do beforehand can make a difference in the success your child experiences while at college. Also, talk to him about conflict resolution. Any group of people living together for a year will have conflicts. Discuss how to resolve them appropriately, how to compromise, and when to give in.

Take Classes Ahead of Time

Many colleges offer summer programs for high school students, both for the summer before your child applies to college and the one after she's admitted. Summer programs often offer a residential option so your child can get used to dorm life. If the school your child is interested in offers summer classes, it will give her a chance to experience dorm life and get a real feel for the school—while alerting you to any potential challenges.

And if your child is already enrolled there for the fall, a college's summer program can give him a useful head start on his course work. As an incoming college freshman, your child can earn course credit and be enrolled as a regular student. Our daughter did this the summer before she started UCLA and it was great for her to get the "lay of the land" and seek out opportunities to work more intimately with faculty in this large school before there were massive numbers of students on the campus during the regular school year.

Academic Life at College

How Much Parental Involvement Should There Be at School?

There's a huge difference between how much parents are involved in their kids' college lives today compared to the past. When I was a college student, my parents sent me off, and I was on my own. The only time they found out about my grades, major, social life, or any other college-related information was when I volunteered it. That isn't the case anymore. Overly involved parents of college-aged kids have been dubbed the millennial parents, and they are dreaded by college professors, staff, and administrators because they want to micromanage their adult kids' lives. They complain about their child's roommates and what they believe (from afar) is unfair grading, and they don't hesitate to call professors about changing test dates or to challenge the grades their child has received in a class.

I have mixed feelings about this, because kids on the spectrum don't usually have great educational programs *unless* the parents are actively involved, so we encourage parental involvement in general. We even require parents to come to parent education sessions to learn the procedures for working with their child—their involvement means their child's success.

But college is a more complicated issue. On a practical level, some students, even those who are already being highly pressured by their parents, refuse to sign a waiver for college staff to talk with their parents about them. We're still able to talk to their parents about general information, but without permission, we can't talk with them about any specifics. Fortunately, most of our students on the spectrum are willing to sign the confidentiality waiver, so we can talk freely to their parents. I find this helpful, but not essential.

Parental involvement is most valuable when the student is first enrolling in college. As we described above, parents can and should help their kids get set up and familiar with the services, facilities, staff, and buildings at their new school. Many programs have specialists in the disabilities office who can oversee the student's program, and provide a real person for the student to contact for support and aid. These specialists usually ask the students to come in regularly and to contact them *before* there's a serious problem. Unfortunately, the students don't always do this. We've known many who have waited until they were on academic probation to let anyone else know there was a problem. The disabilities offices don't receive the student's grades, so the bulk of the responsibility is on the student's shoulders to seek out assistance when necessary.

While they might try to contact the student if they hear that she's skipping class or having some extreme problems, ultimately it isn't the responsibility of the staff at the disabilities center. College students are adults and are expected to take responsibility for their own educational success. So if you feel that your student needs more intensive monitoring than the disabilities office is set up to provide, you may have to arrange that yourself by finding a fellow student, classmate, or staff member to help out.

College is about giving our kids choices and opportunities and helping them develop their strengths through higher education, but for all that to happen, it has to be successful, and unless you do some advance work, there's a very real chance it won't be. *You need to prepare the school your child will attend.* Go to the disabilities office. If they don't have a lot of experience with kids on the spectrum, educate them. Have them keep track of your child while he's there and provide the support he needs. If you feel it will help, have them contact your child's professors and politely explain what support he may need to be successful.

Some of our students require more monitoring than others. We've had a couple of college students who simply stopped getting up in the morning and going to class. So you need to have someone checking up on your child. To find someone who can do this, ask first at the disabilities office or any specialized counseling or autism center the school might offer, but if you can't find anyone through them, you may need to hire a student to help out. Students are always looking for work, and something that doesn't require a car and can be done on campus fits the job requirements of many.

Finally, most colleges have career and counseling centers. In addition to the general college offices, some departments (such as psychology) have practicum clinics where supervised students can have hands-on experience. The students at these clinics can help with behavioral, psychological, or social challenges your child may have.

Again, when picking the college for your child, you should research these services and help your child become well aware of them during orientation and prior to the start of school.

The short of it is *don't* leave your child's success at college to chance or hope. Make sure a supportive system is in place before problems arise.

In the months before your child leaves home to go to college, you need to work with her on the strategies she'll need to stay academically afloat in the years to come. Remember: you won't be there to manage her time, her studying, or her relationship with her teachers *for* her. Take advantage of the time you still have together to help her figure out strategies for ultimately navigating all those things on her own. Some of these skills will come in handy during high school, others she won't need until she's actually at college—but at least you'll have made her aware of what lies ahead.

Time Management

The whole college experience is *so* different from high school. The kids go from thirty hours a week in school and twelve hours a week of studying to twelve hours a week in classes and thirty hours a week studying. This is a huge adjustment for most kids—there just isn't the same kind of structure to their days. Many have trouble the first year of school because they just don't know how to manage their time, no one is checking on them, and it's human nature to procrastinate.

After all the work of getting into a major university, you don't want your kid flunking out because he didn't make it to class or finish an assignment. In addition to having a support system in place (see previous pages), you should work with him on the skills he'll need to stay afloat.

The most important piece of advice? *Get him to use a calendar.* Many parents of kids on the spectrum are so used to hauling their kids from here to there and keeping track of every appointment that they haven't taught their kids to keep a calendar for themselves. This is a critical skill for college life and the sooner you teach your child to keep her own calendar, the better. It can be paper or electronic—whichever kind she's more likely to maintain and look at every day. Get her started doing this *before* college so it's a habit by the time she goes.

Once he's using a calendar, have him learn to schedule study time into it. College requires discipline and a lot of work outside the classroom. Your child will need to schedule *daily* study time. Again, this is a habit you can get him started with ahead of time, while he's still in high school. He's much more likely to realize that he can't meet friends on a Sunday evening for dinner because he has a test Monday morning if he's already written down "study for test" on Sunday's schedule.

Study Skills

Again, most of the work you do in college takes place outside the classroom without a teacher hovering and making certain you're getting it done. It's easy to lose your bearings in this kind of situation.

We recommend that all of our students do some review *right after class*. This can be done by simply taking time to read through the material, rewrite and organize the notes they've taken, discuss the lecture with classmates, and maybe even memorize some of the information they have just learned. Too many students, both typical and disabled, try to cram, and that just isn't the best strategy in college. It's important to stay on top of things. Remember how you taught your child to give herself a certain amount of time to complete the work back in middle school? That will come in handy now because she has no one to check in to make sure she's getting it all done. Remind her, whenever you have an opportunity, to budget her time, find study groups, get tutoring, go to office hours, and take advantage of any other academic support the college offers before she gets into trouble.

Tailoring the Course Load

Our students have different levels of needs. Some need a lot of help studying and others don't need any help at all. Some can take on a full course load but others need to go more slowly because it takes them longer to complete assignments than most typical learners. Your child may need to experiment to settle on the right number of units for him to take each quarter or semester. Most universities will allow as much extra time as is necessary for a disabled student to complete college, so even if it takes an extra year or two, that's fine—he'll still get a college degree. Years ago I saw a T-shirt in our college bookstore that read "College—the best ~~four~~ five years of my life!" Well, now it isn't a joke. Many students take five years to complete college—our daughter who's in med school did, and her accomplishments in that extra year provided an excellent background for her career choice.

The good news is that the percentage of disabled students who graduate is about the same as the number of students without disabilities—but getting the right services and accommodations is essential.

Classroom Strategies

These days, most professors post their PowerPoint presentations on the Internet, which is great. They can be printed—and reviewed—

after class, which removes a lot of the burden of taking good notes during the lecture.

But even if the professor doesn't do that, there are other solutions for the student who has trouble taking notes. She can sign up in the disabilities office and get a copy of another student's notes. These days all colleges (junior colleges and four-year colleges) have various programs for disabled students.

We had one young man who would get so anxious about note-taking that he started hyperventilating in class when the professor went too fast. This attracted plenty of unwanted attention from the other students. To decrease his anxiety, we told him to simply stop taking notes when he felt overwhelmed and leave the page blank. Later, we got the class notes from the disabilities office, and he filled in any gaps. This created a partial-participation situation: he still learned how to take notes in a large lecture course, but with a lot less anxiety about missing information.

Seating is also important. If a student gets distracted easily, it's a good idea to have him always get to class early and sit toward the front of the class.

Electronic Devices

Many courses now have electronic devices that students use in class so that the instructors can be sure that they're participating and learning the information. The students' answers on these devices are often included as part of the overall grade. The electronic devices are purchased at the bookstore and are programmed with the students' school identification numbers. The devices help the instructor monitor the progress of the class. If she asks a question about material that was just presented, and only half the class answers correctly, she knows that she needs to cover that material in more detail.

Electronic devices are a mixed blessing for kids on the spectrum. For some of our students they're fantastic. They eliminate the need to raise a hand and be called on publicly, which can be excruciatingly painful for kids on the spectrum. On the downside, some of our students can't process verbal information very quickly and just aren't ready to respond when the teacher asks the students to use the electronic devices. In such cases, we usually talk with the professor and arrange for some other type of testing procedure.

Taking Tests

As we discussed in the section on the SAT above, many students with disabilities have difficulties taking tests in a standardized way. Schools are usually quite sympathetic to this problem, and there are many options, ranging from taking the test in a quiet room to getting extra time. We have found that many faculty members are amazingly helpful with our students when approached directly. One anthropology professor even volunteered to give the test orally to a student, on his own time, when he learned that the student had trouble writing essays.

These and other accommodations can be arranged ahead of time at the disabilities office, so the student can demonstrate what she has learned in the class without distractions that may put her at a disadvantage. The exact way that campus offices deal with students may differ somewhat, but most of the time the responsibility is on the student to follow through with getting assistance.

Finally

Remember, your role as the parent of a college student is to support and plan for success. Because your child is on the spectrum, you can't just send him off without a second thought: you need to prepare him for the upcoming changes, help him develop an academic study plan he can follow with minimal supervision, and make sure there's a support system in place that can swing into action if problems arise. At the same time, remember that the goal here is independence. The more your child can manage by himself, the more he'll be ready to live a fulfilling adult life when he leaves college. Don't hover or interfere if you don't need to—and if you've done all that advance preparation, you very well may not need to.

Social Life at College

Socializing is the area where we have to intervene the most with our college students. It's absolutely crucial to their collegiate success that they are able to make and keep friends. But when kids go to college, their whole social network changes. They no longer have the constant support of a family who's there from the time they get up in the morning to the time they go to bed at night. Back at home, if they were lonely or hurt, their parents were there to comfort them. And most of them had a group of friends they could hang out with. College changes everything. But the good news is that *all* the kids are going through a period of adjustment, and everyone's looking for new friends.

Here are some of the life changes and choices your child will face when she gets to college, and some strategies you can use to help her navigate this socially challenging time.

Living Arrangements

Some students opt to live at home the first year or two of college. Others prefer to live in an apartment with at least one support person living in. In these situations, usually the parents or a state agency will help pay the costs of room and board for the support person, who can even be another college student.

Other students live in the dorms the first year or two of college, although the dorm option is available for all four years if your child is finding that setting a successful place to live.

If your child applies to live in the dorm, the school will send him a questionnaire so that he can be matched with compatible roommates. He will be asked questions ranging from what time he likes to go to bed to how much quiet he likes, from how he feels about alcohol to whether he's messy or neat, and so on. Then the school will try to match him with other students based on his profile.

If you look at the satisfaction surveys, most students find that larger setups with more roommates—say, three on each side with a bathroom in the middle—are the most successful, probably because it gives them more opportunity to mix and match. But your child may prefer a single. This is something you'll have to give a lot of thought to.

If your child is rooming with others and has social difficulties, you'll have to prepare her (and yourself) for the possibility that her roommate(s) may request a change. At most schools, any child can request a change of roommates within the first few weeks without any questions asked. After that initial period, it's much more difficult to change.

Many colleges now have floors that are devoted to specific qualities that may appeal more or less to your child. For example, there's often a substance-free floor, a rainbow floor (for gays and lesbians), a male-identity-issues floor, an environmental floor, a multicultural floor, a wellness floor, and so on. If your school has a special-interest floor that fits in with your child's concerns, it may provide him with a similar peer group.

If possible, you should talk with the staff at the dorms. Most are trained to offer support for any challenges the students might face and can lend a hand in helping your child get involved in social activities—or simply do a little extra checking up on your child on your behalf. Some college programs even have mentors, usually older students, who can also provide some extra social and emotional support to your child.

A lot of college social life revolves around just hanging out. This may be difficult for your child. Finding out what's going on, getting invited or inviting friends out, and having success on outings are often challenging to kids on the spectrum.

CLAIRE

When I think back to my college years, the first thing that comes to mind is how I could sit at the dining hall tables for hours just talking to friends. I don't even know what we talked about—classes, I guess, and professors and philosophies and hometowns and crushes and so on. Same thing in my dorm room: my roommates and I could start talking at nine at night and not finish our conversation until one or two a.m. In many ways, it was the best part of the college experience.

Unfortunately, that's kind of a scary thing to realize when you have a kid on the spectrum who finds making social conversation unremittingly difficult. In high school, Andrew's definitely able to shoot the breeze with his pals for the forty minutes or so of lunchtime—but in college, where conversation stretches on for hours and encompasses everything from politics to religion to the best ice cream in the city, will he be able to keep up? Will he find it so enervating he'll crawl to his room in a state of exhausted anxiety? Will he grow more and more silent and just sit there feeling left out because he can't keep up verbally?

Maybe times have changed, but when I went to college, you hardly ever went to the movies or planned some other specific activity with friends—you just congregated and chatted. And it was glorious. But the one thing I've learned as Andrew's mother is that he does his best socializing while participating in specific activities. But how do you find those kinds of activities in a college setting? And how do I help him survive—and maybe even enjoy—all the endless hanging out and chatting?

DR. KOEGEL

Setting Up Social Success

The first thing we usually recommend is to help your child with his social conversation skills (see Section II, Chapter 2). Sometimes one little thing he does, like fidgeting or not looking another person in the eye or correcting someone on a minor point, may be putting people off right from the start. The last thing we want to do is to have one of our students make the effort to invite someone to hang out, only to be turned down or have it be a disaster! So we try to eliminate these potential pitfalls ahead of time to ensure our students' success.

As we've discussed earlier, if your child can find a club or class that speaks to her area of interest, she can find an instantaneous peer group. Study groups are great too—the structured activity of studying gives the student on the spectrum something concrete to focus on while still being social.

The bulleted paragraphs that follow list the things college students on the spectrum must learn to do if they want to have friends and dates. It's your responsibility to make sure your child knows what to do to *help himself* once he's alone at school. The following advice is helpful for high school students as well, so you might as well start working with your child on all these things before he goes off to college, and then all you'll have to do is remind and encourage him once you're not available to do more.

- **Work on changing behaviors.** Most individuals on the spectrum are motivated to improve, but we have had a small percentage of students who really resist any kind of change. It's hard to help someone who doesn't want help. Your child needs to understand that relationships require constant adjustment and flexibility and that following the advice of professionals and peers who have his best interests at heart will really make a difference in his life.

- **Check in.** It's painful sometimes, but it is necessary for your child to learn to check with her friends to see if she has any habits that might need to be changed. Simple questions like "Are you sleeping okay at night? I know I stay up late," or "I have a hard time throwing out old newspapers; are there getting to be too many for you?" can go a long way toward improving social relationships. Of course, if the answer is "It's a problem," your child needs to make an effort to change any behavior that's objectionable. Married folks have to do this all the time and that's why their relationships work. You can help from a distance by encouraging your child to ask questions about habits you suspect might be irritating to others.

- **Initiate.** The best way to make friends is to get out there. Encourage your child to introduce himself and ask questions, to join clubs and study groups, to smile at strangers and just keep putting himself out there. And remember, Internet friendships *don't* count as friends. Your child needs to be able to make friends in real life.

- **Look for clubs.** College is all about clubs, groups, teams, and organizations. Someone out there is offering something your child is bound to like. Look for sign ups and opportunities when you're first bringing your child to school, and remind her to keep her eye open for the right fit once you're gone and she's on her own.

- **Be considerate.** Tell your child to think about the people he's met and liked and to try to do things that will make them happy. He can buy a friend coffee or hot chocolate on his birthday. If his roommate doesn't like messes, he can clean up the place. He could help a friend study. If he's aware he has habits that aren't socially appropriate, he should try to find alternative behaviors. Being considerate will help him make and maintain friendships and relationships throughout his life.

- **Take advantage of strengths.** If your child is good at a subject, encourage her to try tutoring someone who isn't, or if she has a talent, volunteering her skills. We have a student who is great at computers and always fixes them for other students, which makes him especially valued when computers are getting extra use during midterms and finals, when they tend to crash. A good artist can help make invitations for a friend's birthday. You get the idea. Your child should learn to help out in situations where her strengths will be valued.

- **Ask for help.** Many college campuses are equipped with services to help not only in academic situations, but also in social and emotional circumstances. If your child is having problems making friends, he can get professional help from counseling services to learn why he isn't making friends and how to fix the problem. Again, your role is to be aware and to encourage action on your child's part.

Dating in College

Dating is something that is often neglected with kids on the spectrum. They may not have dated much, if at all, in middle and high school, so many are starting from scratch. Fortunately, college is the perfect environment in which to start dating. There are many members of the opposite sex who are all also looking for partners.

We usually like to start with some practice dates and support. Again, at this point, because you are no longer with your child on a regular basis, you or she will need to arrange for this through one of the campus clinics. Once our students have learned how to engage in good social conversation, we work on getting them interacting with other students their age. First we have them go places with someone their age who works at our center and who can introduce them to other peers. They've gone to movies, malls, sports events, parties, bowling alleys, restaurants, and a whole bunch of other places with a support person.

For more specific information on dating and nurturing romantic relationships, please see Section III, Chapter 2.

Jake's College Experience

Jake's parents brought him to the Center last summer. He's a brilliant student with Asperger's syndrome who got a perfect—yes *perfect*—score on the SAT. He was accepted at a top-tier school, but once there, he had no support. He didn't make friends and was soon miserable, and he eventually made his way to UCSB. We started working with him on social conversation, using video modeling, and after only four sessions, Jake was able to carry on a perfect and interesting conversation. Since then he's found a group of friends who greatly enjoy his fantastic sense of humor, sweet personality, and intelligence. With just a little support, Jake has become a wildly popular student.

One of the reasons Jake's program has been so successful is his willingness to accept feedback and change accordingly. Because of this, his intelligence, and great personality, I know he will make the most wonderful husband for some lucky woman, who probably won't ever know that he has been diagnosed with Asperger's syndrome unless he tells her.

JAKE

Meeting new people has always been difficult for me. For most of my life, I have actively avoided conversing with people I do not know. The anxiety I felt whenever I considered chatting with a stranger was absolutely crippling. Should such a conversation take place, the awkwardness that typically ensued only served to reinforce my fears.

Although one might expect this issue to lead to a childhood of isolation, such was not the case for me. I went to Poly, a small school that ran from prekindergarten through high school. I started there in third grade and had little trouble making friends. My theory is that the small size of the class forced me to get to know the other kids despite my initial reticence. Likewise, the prospect of a new friend in such a close-knit environment probably inspired the other kids to persevere past any oddness on my part. I quickly developed a small group of friends that I was very comfortable with.

Middle school added another twenty-five kids to the class, bringing the total to approximately seventy. While it was somewhat disconcerting to have so many new people walking around, the fact that I had my own group of friends made it much easier. The new kids felt obligated to come to us and integrate themselves into our established social groups. Thus, there was little pressure on me. Because a few of the new students hung out with my group more and more, I eventually attained a level of ease that allowed me to feel comfortable interacting with them. Soon enough, the new students were fully integrated into our little clique. Indeed, two of the new students would eventually become my best friends.

High school brought a few more students to our class, bringing the total to eighty-five, but my circle of friends was effectively complete by eighth grade. Throughout the entirety of high school, the only new friends I made came when I joined a new swim team in my senior year. However, this was a very similar situation to when I came to Poly in the third grade. It was a small team and there were only two other guys my age. Thus, they were willing to overlook my awkwardness and we became friends.

At this point, there were about ten guys whom I considered very close, which is a very healthy, acceptable number, in my opinion. Around these ten fellas, I was typically lively, gregarious, and funny. However, whenever we were hanging out with people from outside our posse, I would clam up and become almost an entirely different person as my issues and fears came to the surface. Although I didn't realize it at the time, I think that I had analyzed each one of my friends and mentally broken down their personalities. I knew what they liked and didn't like, what they found funny, and so on, to a degree of accuracy that can only come from knowing people for years. Whenever an "outsider" infiltrated our group, I didn't know how he/she would react to me and would slip into my shell as a result. I didn't make the connection at the time, but this was a terrible sign for my immediate future as a college student.

As our first post–high school summer came to a close, we all prepared to go to college. I had chosen to attend Duke University, the only person in my graduating class to do so. When I look back now, it is remarkable how little anxiety I felt at that time. I was headed to the other side of the country to a place where I knew no one, and yet I felt strangely calm about the whole thing. When I met my roommate, he seemed like a good, friendly guy, a seemingly positive sign. For the first few days, everything seemed to be going swimmingly. However, it was not to last.

As the first week passed, I noticed that friendships were forming around me, but I couldn't bring myself to talk to anyone. Indeed, without my high school buddies around me, my fear of interacting with strangers became distressingly intense. When I missed my first chemistry lab because I couldn't find the room, I was too terrified to seek out the professor or the teaching assistant. In fact, I was too anxious even to go to the second lab because the thought of explaining what had happened was petrifying. I couldn't bring myself to chat with anyone in the dining hall, even though I understood intellectually that just about anyone would be open to making a new friend. I had no experience with the social dynamics in such an environment and felt completely incapable of finding my way.

Depression, which has always been an issue for me, often overshadowing any of the problems caused by Asperger's, hit me full force. I stopped going to class. I began spending most of my time in my room alone, leaving only for food. Talking to my roommate became my only real social interaction. To be honest, I don't remember much about this period. It was such an unhappy time that I seem to have blocked it out of my mind. All I remember is that when my parents received word that I was failing all of my classes and came to bring me home, I couldn't even muster up the will to tell my roommate what was going on. I moved my things out in the dead of night, a cryptic note on the dresser the only evidence that I had ever been there.

Back home, I slipped further and further into the depths of despair. As all of my friends from high school had scattered hither and yon to attend college, my isolation continued unabated. I enrolled in a few courses at the local city college, putting little effort into any of them. However, since this was at a city college, even minimal effort was more than enough for me to pass with decent grades. On the occasions when I actually went to class, I would sit in the back, never speaking to anyone, leaving the moment the class was over. During this period, I even cut off communication with my friends from high school, further compounding the situation.

Summer eventually came, allowing me to see all of my old friends again, which helped alleviate my depression to some extent. Hindsight being twenty-twenty, I probably should have focused more on the "friends=less severe depression" equality. All the therapists and medication in the world were not helping me, but having a few friends around instantly bumped up my mood several notches. Since I battled depression throughout high school, it's fairly clear that having friends present is not a cure-all. However, I feel confident in saying that having a few buddies moderates my depression and helps to keep it from being debilitating. Nevertheless, at the time, my improvement was largely attributed to the medication and therapy taking effect.

My parents and I made the decision to move to North Carolina as a family while I gave Duke a second shot. The thinking was that I would be able to succeed with a solid support structure around me. And for a time, this proved to be true. In fact, I made the dean's list during the fall 2005 semester. Nevertheless, my social issues still loomed large. I still could not muster the courage to talk to anyone, leading to the same sort of isolation I had experienced during my first stint at Duke. While I love my parents very much, having them be the entire extent of my social interaction was not particularly satisfying. Friendless and alone once again, my mood slipped, my effort slipped, and my grades slipped. I kept it together enough to pass all my classes during spring semester, but my A's and B's had turned into B's and C's, so it was clear to all involved that something was not right.

Come fall 2006, the wheels came flying off once again. I was again in the throes of a depressive episode likely triggered by my isolated state. A further problem was that I had signed up for two math courses that were effectively at the master's level. In no way was I ready to take these courses, but there were no safeguards in place to prevent me from doing so. At the beginning of the semester, I managed to stay afloat, despite my inadequate mathematical background, by working relatively hard. However, once my depression intensified and my effort dipped, I quickly went into an unrecoverable tailspin. Once again, my parents got the call that I was on the brink of failing most of my classes, forcing me to withdraw.

It was at this point that I sank into the deepest depths I have ever experienced. I had just failed at school for the second time, I had no friends within a thousand miles, and there seemed to be little hope that things would get better. Suicide seemed to be a fairly attractive option. It was then that I discovered the game World of Warcraft. Although WoW has a fairly negative reputation in some circles due to its addictiveness, I firmly believe that it helped me during this period. It served two primary functions. First of all, it allowed me to escape the negative, terrible thoughts that were constantly running through my mind. Playing WoW was the only thing that allowed me to shut my brain off. While I certainly wouldn't say that I was happy while I was playing, losing myself in WoW at least allowed me to feel less sad, which was incredibly significant at the time. Second, WoW provided a social outlet for me. Through text chat, and eventually voice chat, I was able to get to know my guild mates and have some social interaction outside of that with my parents. Although using voice chat was difficult for me, because the anxiety I feel when talking to a new person only increases when I can't actually see the person, the fact that it was a necessity for some of the more complex encounters in the game gave me motivation to overcome my fear and insecurity. Looking back, I feel somewhat embarrassed by the fact that my life became devoted to a computer game for months, but at the time, it was really all I had.

Eventually, my family and I decided to move back to California. My parents decided on Santa Barbara, and we moved there in the spring of 2007. The initial plan was for me to take some time off from school and work for a while. At this point, I was feeling pretty good, especially compared to where I had been four or five months earlier. I started doing martial arts at a local studio, which gave me an opportunity to both exercise and socialize. Although I still felt very uncomfortable meeting everyone at the studio, the fact that we were all there to do the same activity helped to smooth the road somewhat. I decided to forgo all therapy and medication, having come to the conclusion that they had been of little or no help up to this point. It was surprisingly difficult to find a job, but eventually I found an administrative position at a local company through a temp agency.

After a few weeks doing mind-numbing data entry work, I realized that I really needed to go back to school and get my degree. My parents were somewhat less than enthused because college hadn't worked out particularly well for me up to that point, but I was determined. I worked out a deal that they would allow me to go back to school if I paid my own tuition. So off I went to Santa Barbara City College (SBCC) for the fall 2007 semester.

Once again, I completely failed on the social front. However, this time I was determined to make the academics work, irrespective of how I was feeling and whether or not I had any friends. Experiencing the job market without a college degree was a fairly sobering experience, one that provided me with all the motivation I needed. While taking courses, I decided to apply for winter 2008 transfer admission to UCSB. Despite my calamitous experiences at Duke, I had withdrawn from all of the classes I was failing, so my transcript didn't actually look that bad. That fact, combined with excellent test scores, led to my being admitted.

As I was finishing up my semester at SBCC and preparing to start at UCSB, my mother heard about the Koegel Center. More specifically, she heard that they were working on developing treatment and support mechanisms for college students with Asperger's. I was actually somewhat reluctant because I felt that therapy had done little for me up to this point, but I decided to give it a shot. I must say, I'm quite glad I did. The work I have done at the Koegel Center has been extremely helpful, and I believe that I have made a great amount of progress in a relatively short period of time.

I think that the focus on specific methods and techniques is what has made my time at the Koegel Center so beneficial. In the past, I would routinely have conversations with psychologists that followed this general outline:

THERAPIST: Do you feel anxious in social situations?
ME: Yes.
THERAPIST: Why do you think that is?
ME: Um, I'm not really sure. I'm hoping you can help me with that.

THERAPIST: What about socializing makes you anxious?

ME: I don't know . . . I just feel uncomfortable and do my best to avoid such situations whenever possible.

THERAPIST: Where do you think these anxious feelings come from?

ME: . . .

And so it would go . . .

At the Koegel Center, instead of trying to probe my feelings about my issues, the focus has been "Here's what you have been doing when you talk to someone you've just met; this is what you should be doing instead." Simple tips from my clinician, Whitney, such as "If the person seems interested in the topic they're talking about, try to come up with a follow-up question" have been more helpful than a hundred conversations about my feelings and insecurities. Each week, it was arranged that I would talk to someone I did not know, or barely knew, which ensured that I practiced talking to new people. Had I just been told to go out on my own and talk to random strangers to gain experience, I probably would never have gone past square one. Instead, I practiced my conversation skills week in and week out, whether I felt like it or not, which undoubtedly helped me progress as an interlocutor.

Another extremely valuable aspect of the treatment was seeing each of my conversations on videotape. Although I never really got comfortable seeing myself on tape, it allowed me to gain numerous insights as to what worked and what didn't. In fact, between trying to integrate the tips Whitney had given me and watching myself on film, I came to realize that social conversation can be broken down and analyzed much as an academic problem can be. That is, I began to think about how I should respond to various situations, to consider a person's potential reaction if I were to respond in a certain way, and to ponder what I should say next given the current topic and flow of conversation. Basically, I started thinking several moves ahead, almost as if the conversation were a game of chess or Go. I'm not certain whether this approach is typical or not, but it has certainly helped me greatly in my quest to be a normal, engaging converser. I must say, it was a rather gratifying moment when my partner in one of my final videotaped conversations said, "I thought that I was going to be talking to someone with social issues," and then chuckled when I lightheartedly suggested that I might in fact have more issues than she realized.

I also think that having the same clinician the entire time has been very helpful. Talking with Whitney each week has allowed me to obtain a high level of comfort with her that has likely facilitated my progress. Indeed, things have progressed to the point where we're friends beyond the confines of the clinic, which is something I couldn't have imagined at the beginning.

Now, having "graduated" from the staged, videotaped conversations, I am trying different activities in order to integrate myself into the campus community. Whitney helps me find potentially interesting activities and provides subtle reminders about what to say, what to do, and what not to do. Although I still feel anxious before talking to someone I don't know, my anxiety is usually at a manageable level because I know that I've successfully negotiated similar situations before. Certainly there are still times when I lock up and become abnormally quiet, particularly if my mind is elsewhere and I am not actively focusing on the conversation at hand. However, these instances have become far less common than they once were. In short, while I will never be the proverbial social butterfly, I have gained the ability to interact in a relatively natural way with people I do not know. Though making new friends still is not easy for me, I have managed to make a few in the past couple months, a vast improvement over my experiences at Duke, Pasadena City College, and SBCC.

The next leap I am looking to make is into the final frontier, otherwise known as the world of dating. As I've joked to Whitney, "If you thought that I needed a lot of help with basic conversation, you haven't seen anything yet." Having never been on a second date, a romantic relationship is truly the great unknown for me. That said, as I write this, I have recently returned from a walk on the beach with a girl I chatted up in a bookstore, a sequence of events that would have been absolutely unfathomable six months ago. Things went well enough that my consecutive first date streak may be broken soon enough. I'm sure that there will be a number of tragically hilarious missteps on my part along the road to a meaningful amorous relationship, but the mere fact that I am putting myself out there and committing those missteps is a victory in and of itself.

In conclusion, the skills I have gained at the Koegel Center have been of immense value. Is it possible that I would have succeeded at Duke if such a program of treatment had been in place? I'm not really sure. In hindsight, there is a good chance that I was simply not ready to attend an elite university at the age of eighteen, irrespective of the support I had around me. However, now that I am focused and determined to succeed as a college student, the work I have done at the Koegel Center has served as the final piece of the puzzle in many ways. The social skills I have gained are helping me get closer to the elusive goal of being a "normal" twenty-one-year-old. My hope is that one day I'll look back and laugh at the times when I couldn't carry a conversation with a bucket. Although that day is still a ways off, it seems much, much closer than it once did.

DR. KOEGEL

Paul's College Experience

I met Paul when he was in elementary school in a special education classroom. We gradually moved him into full inclusion, arranging support for him so he could succeed in the regular education classrooms. We also started some lunch groups so that he would have friends to socialize with during his free times.

Paul maintained good grades in all of his high school classes and applied to UCSB. He was accepted and is just completing his first year. We have focused primarily on academics during his first year and we will target social areas starting in the summer. This is his story (so far!).

PAUL

When I went to high school I knew I wanted to go to college. I applied to just one four-year college, the University of California, Santa Barbara (UCSB), that was close to my house (about an hour away), and I knew they had an autism clinic that could help me. I worked with people from the UCSB clinic in the past, and they encouraged me to apply. If I didn't get in to UCSB, I decided I would go to a junior college for a year, then transfer over. When I first visited UCSB it was overwhelming because the campus seemed so big with big classes and that made me feel a little nervous.

After I decided to go to college, I had to take the SAT. It was a big pain in the butt. I have a few choice words about the SAT because it was hard to study for it in addition to all my classes. I got extra time on the test, but I kind of wished I hadn't because I had to go in to take the test on two days, including a Sunday, instead of one day like the rest of the students. I think I could have done it in one day. Someone also read the questions to me, but I felt like they were talking down to me and assuming that I wasn't that smart. It felt like they were reading a script instead of reading the questions and answers that were printed on the test. I think I could have done just as well if I had read it myself.

The application process was a little difficult because I didn't know what to say about myself. I wrote essays on my strengths and weaknesses, and I wrote what it was like being on the spectrum for one of my essays.

When I got accepted into college at first I was nervous. I wondered how I was going to navigate the mazes. I had the same nervous feelings when I transferred from elementary school to middle school, except on a larger scale. But then it was cool. It was pretty cool because I realized that everyone was going to be there to help me and it was pretty impressive to tell people that I was accepted into a good college.

I decided to live at home the first year of college, which was sort of difficult to deal with because of the traffic, but it hasn't been that difficult. I was planning on moving near campus the second quarter but that didn't happen, partly because I like being at home. I am hoping to live on campus my second year, but I really don't want to be away from all the stuff I like, like my bed, my TV, my models that decorate my room, and all that stuff that just feels familiar. I don't think I could have taken all that stuff to my dorm room. Next year I am thinking about living in an apartment but I may stay at home because we have a housekeeper and stuff, and I'm not that good at cleaning and making my bed and that sort of leads to an element of discomfort.

School is going well. I have had some professors that are really great, some are okay, and some I haven't appreciated that much. Of the ones I like, one's name was Dr. Mohamed Spocter, and he was always very nice to me. For the essay part of the final he came in and discussed the questions with me. He also came to my twenty-first birthday party. He talked with me a lot about other stuff besides school, like South Africa, where he is from. There were about three hundred students in his class but he still took out a lot of time to help me. Another professor, Dr. Peter Huk, was really accommodating and helped me learn college writing. Then I had a few who were not as understanding of a situation. Like in second quarter, one of my professors of economics tried to help in every way he could, like unlimited time during tests, but he wasn't understanding at all. It was very hard to approach him after class. He gave short answers and was inflexible about everything. He had ways of doing things, and PowerPoints he followed exactly, and wasn't willing to give any extra help on any of the lectures or assignments. It would have helped me if he had been friendlier, explained things better, had written more detailed notes, and stuff like that.

In general, I have some accommodations on tests. I get extended time, a proctor who brings me the test and stays there while I take it, and I take my tests in a separate room. Doctor Spocter came to the separate room to give me my essays in person. That was really nice of him. I also get some other help. In class, I have a girl who works with me. She helps take notes and goes over the notes with me right after class. I also have Gus, who helps me go over notes on days that I am not on campus. He helps me study and helps me write my papers. I study about three to five hours each day besides the time that I'm in class. Gus helps me during most of the hours I study, but every night I review the class notes on my own. I think I am going to major in economics because I want to go into business.

Socially, I have met one friend and there is this girl who knows me in my geology class, and I know one other girl that went to high school with me, and another girl, Brittany. Most of them came to my twenty-first birthday party, which was at a pizza parlor in the college town right by campus. I bought pizza, beer, and sodas for everyone. Most of my friends are girls. I guess I get along better with girls.

The way I meet girls is that I usually try to pair up with teams in class and I always introduce myself to other kids in class. Usually I say, "Hi, I'm Paul. What's your name?" I don't do a lot with my friends from the university outside of school, but on the weekends I get together with my friends from high school, since it's about an hour drive to my house.

So far, I've gotten a B average. I got one C in a history class. But it's going pretty well. I like the college experience. It's sort of hard to meet other kids because they are always with their friends and doing their own thing and I am doing my own thing trying to stay on top of my work. In the next few years of college I'm hoping I can make more friends, do well, graduate, and have a successful life.

DR. KOEGEL

Jeff's Roommate Experience

As a freshman, Jeff was assigned a roommate with Asperger's syndrome, Jimmy. Jimmy, while brilliant in the area of computer sciences,

had no support system. His family didn't visit him—not even once—
he rarely left his room and had no social life whatsoever, aside from
Jeff's daily interactions with him. Well into his second quarter, Jeff
noticed that Jimmy wasn't leaving his room at all. After repeatedly asking him if he was missing class, and Jimmy repeatedly assuring him
that he wasn't, Jeff found out that his roommate hadn't even *registered* for classes. Below, Jeff discusses his challenges and his thoughts
as the college roommate of a student with Asperger's syndrome.

JEFFREY MORRIS

My freshman-year UCLA roommate never really showered. California droughts and a liberal campus—I guess this made sense. Unfortunately, he never seemed to have a friend or family member around
to give him feedback on his body odor. At the time, I knew little
about AS and diagnosed Jimmy's condition only after stumbling
upon an Asperger's self-help book when I was browsing through the
bookstore one day. His quirks and social particularities gradually
made sense, and I came to understand why Jimmy never left our
shoebox of a room.

A perfect SAT score and a knack for the trumpet had landed
Jimmy at UCLA. His parents remained in northern California, in a
city that was, as Jimmy casually proclaimed, 318 miles away. He
marched in UCLA's marching band—the Solid Gold Sound—and performed in-head calculations that surpassed my own abilities with a
TI-89 calculator. He was, quite literally, a genius. A few days into my
freshman year, Jimmy revealed that he was actually a sophomore.

Sadly, via a monotone administrative letter, the school silenced
Jimmy's beloved trumpet. His freshman year academic record had
failed to reflect the high school computer science heroics, and effective immediately, Jimmy's band eligibility perished. He became a
member of a new group: the Academic Probationers.

Minus his Solid Gold Sound, Jimmy retreated into a virtual en-
clave known as World of Warcraft. The multiplayer online role-playing
game hosts over ten million adventure seekers hoping to slay monsters

and goblins. Although I invited him to come to events and go on outings with me, he always declined. The game serviced Jimmy's social
aspirations and, by taking up all his time, rendered unlikely any prospect of academic recovery. He ascended the virtual WoW rankings,
seizing control of an online clan that practiced every day for twelve
to eighteen hours. He often commanded the army for days without
sleep—I had to admire his attention span and stamina, even if I
wasn't so crazy about his choice of activity.

Jimmy's reputation for strategic innovation and wartime practical-
ity made him a legend within the virtual world. His real-life heroics
became fables too: he once walked six miles to Best Buy for a computer microphone that became his conductor's baton. Jimmy shouted
"advance" and "retreat" to online ensembles with an efficacy that
never synchronized with my sleeping habits. In fact, it seemed that
Jimmy never slept. All night long he played and played. After time, his
virtual promiscuity frustrated me, and after much thought, I allied
with the Internet cord beneath my bed. In the wee hours of the morning, when we both needed sleep, I began unplugging the broadband
cord, killing our Internet connection and Jimmy's ability to command.
Jimmy never discovered my status as the secret operative responsible
for the assassination of our broadband connection. During these new
off-line hours, Jimmy and I began to talk more, which was refreshing—I
was the only human he was having any contact with. At first, I talked,
and Jimmy listened. Eventually, Jimmy did the talking, and his chosen
topics exposed the interests of a typical UCLA student. Coed girls
intrigued Jimmy, and quotations from *Top Gun* and *The Big Lebowski*
were typically followed by "goddamns" to USC. Sometime around
May, with classes winding down and finals approaching, I unplugged
the Internet cord and shut my eyes, ready to get a good night's sleep.
To my surprise, Jimmy responded differently this time. He began
pounding his microphone against the keyboard, his forearm moving
like a carpenter with a defective hammer and a broken will. I had no
idea what to do—Jimmy had never reacted this way. His desperation
turned into a melancholy and a discernible loneliness. Even so, I
didn't revive our Internet connection; Jimmy needed to live in the real
world, I thought.

And then I heard something new—a box opening and a low pitch attempting to find higher tones. I opened my eyes to see Jimmy playing his trumpet. I listened intently for hours as the melodies grew optimistic with the night.

The concert explained everything: Jimmy, like all of us, just needed a companion to follow and sometimes conduct—his just happened not to be another person.

DR. KOEGEL

In Summary

College can be a great experience and it can also be a nightmare, whether or not your child is on the spectrum. But when your child *is* on the spectrum, he's starting out at a disadvantage.

As you've experienced throughout your child's schooling, techniques and programs that help her academically are much further along, better researched, and more abundant than programs that can help her socially. It's critical—not just a luxury but *critical*—that your child have a comprehensive program that addresses any needs she may have academically, behaviorally, *and* socially. Have this all in place before saying good-bye, so that you're ready to address any potential problems well before they blow out of proportion. Make sure there's support *in place* at the college before she starts her freshman year. Do everything you can to make the college experience a happy and positive experience for your child, her roommates, and her circle of friends.

Frequently Asked Questions

My daughter doesn't want to have any roommates, but that's not a possibility for freshman year at the school she's going to. Given that, is she better off having one *roommate (less noise, maybe less stress) or several (the burden wouldn't always fall on her to interact)?*

Most larger schools have floors that group similar students (based on the forms they initially submit). For example, there's usually a floor devoted to quiet. This floor is for the more studious student and may be a good match with your daughter's desire not to have to socialize as much. The school will also try to match her with a compatible roommate by having her fill out a profile. In the profile, she can indicate that she likes to go to bed early, likes quiet, and maybe has other behaviors that are less likely to be associated with very social students. This should help her end up with roommates who aren't likely to be loud and intrusive.

There are pros and cons to the number of roommates. If she has one roommate, it will certainly be quieter than with two. However, if this one roommate isn't compatible with your daughter, they will have to either switch immediately or be together the remainder of the year. In contrast, if she has two roommates, she may get along better with one, or the other two may get along well and socialize, leaving her more time to be alone in the room. Either way, it will be important to help her get intervention so that she learns social interaction skills that will help her throughout her college days and career.

The university my son goes to has asked that parents refrain from contacting faculty members, and I understand that policy in general. But I think it would really help my child if his instructors knew a little bit about him. Do you think it's okay for me to contact them?

I would recommend first talking with the disabilities office and any specialized counseling clinic (or any specific program center for kids with autism or Asperger's) that may exist on your campus. Having the professor learn about your child probably would be very helpful, but many busy faculty members find it difficult to deal with students' parents. Additionally, if you interfere too much, you may change the relationship between the professor and your child. The best gift you may be able to give your child is to teach him to advocate for himself. Teach him to go to his professors during office hours and discuss his personal situation. Believe it or not, if there isn't an imminent midterm or final, many professors don't have any visitors at all during their office hours and have plenty of time to offer support.

Being comfortable approaching the teacher on his own might have many other benefits for your child. I've discovered, from having college kids of my own, that a professor will sometimes change a grade if the student makes a real case for doing so. One of my daughters e-mailed an English professor that she thought her paper was A quality, but she had been given a B. The professor reread her paper and changed the grade without even meeting with her! Again, teaching your child to advocate for himself may be the best way to get the appropriate considerations, along with any accommodations provided by the disabilities office, of course.

I'm not happy with the limited disabilities support at my daughter's college. If she's living in another state to go to school, is she eligible for any services there?

Yes. You will want to check for local autism resources that may provide some support to her that supplements what she'll be receiving through the college. Many states, such as California (which has Regional Centers), have specialized programs that can help with socialization, leisure activities, and any self-help areas your child may need. These services are nice because they can fill in any potential nonacademic gaps the college isn't able to help with.

What types of college programs are available to my child and how do I make sure my child accesses them?

All colleges have disabilities programs and any enrolled student is eligible for the services. Some may have better programs than others and some may have a variety of programs in different departments. For example, many universities have a disabilities office that's separate from their counseling and career services. Some may have a clinic in the psychology program and other services within departments. Study the options thoroughly before your child starts. Now, having said that, I need to emphasize that many students who are eligible don't take advantage of the disabilities office. They may not pick up notes and may not show up to work with the staff. Because they're adults, it's their choice. The disabilities office may not get notification that they're failing in school because that's confidential information provided to the student. Often a parent doesn't even know that his child isn't going to class or is on academic probation or has flunked out (until he gets a refund on the tuition). But as I mentioned above, the percentage of kids with disabilities who flunk out is about the same as the percentage of typical kids who flunk out, so it may have more to do with motivation than the disability per se.

Beyond the College Years

1. Introduction

My son is only in high school but I spend a lot of time thinking about what the future holds for him. Right now he needs so much support that I can't imagine that need will simply end when he graduates from high school or turns twenty-one. I can keep him at home with me, but I know I won't live forever, so

having him just as dependent on me when he's forty as he is now hardly seems like a solution. But I'm not sure what the alternatives are.

CLAIRE

The future looks pretty good to us these days, but it didn't always. When Andrew's first speech therapist let us know he had some serious "processing issues" and was probably on the spectrum (she was being careful because she didn't feel qualified to diagnose), she tried to allay our fears by saying cheerfully, "You don't know what the future holds. Why, I had a kid just like him whom I worked with for years and he went to college!"

It wasn't all that reassuring. It hadn't occurred to us yet that Andrew's speech problems meant he might not go to college. But from that point on we realized that nothing was a given with this child of ours, not college, not marriage, not children of his own, not a career—none of the things that we took for granted in our own lives would we ever be able to take for granted in his.

The good news is that after years of interventions, we're pretty hopeful about the future. We'll never take anything for granted, but we're not ruling anything out either. A current big topic of conversation in our family is which colleges Andrew should look at, even though he doesn't have to apply for another year.

We know we're lucky. For many years, I wondered what would happen to our little boy when we died, and whether his siblings' lives would be burdened by his needs. The stories I was hearing about adults with autism at that point weren't consoling ones. I may not have to worry about those things anymore, but I think there's been so much improvement in interventions, awareness, and information that everyone's future—not just Andrew's—is brighter than it might have been a decade ago.

DR. KOEGEL

With any child, you never know what the future holds. We all try to do the best we can with the one chance we have to raise our kids, but in an unfortunate circumstance or an unexpected instant, everything can change the lives and futures of our precious children. You don't want to be crippled by fears of what might happen, but it's important to remember that the future isn't predetermined for anyone.

If you have an older child on the spectrum, and have survived and navigated the diagnosis, the early years, the IEPs, the bad teachers, the untrained aides, and experienced the good—your child's accomplishments, the supportive teachers, the specialists who encouraged her, the friends and family who were there for you—you know that anything is possible. As we discussed earlier, each year the intervention gets better, and each year more individuals with autism are included in community, work, school, and recreational settings.

But now that your child is grown up, we have other things to think about.

The future needs to take into consideration all aspects of the person on the spectrum. Is he living in a physical facility and location he likes? Does he have friends? Does he have recreational activities? Does he live with people he enjoys? Does he have a job he gets pleasure from?

If the answer to any of these questions is no, then we need to do more. I'm hopeful that the rest of this section will help you get to a place where the answer to many of these questions will ultimately be a resounding *yes*.

As always, when it comes to being a parent of a kid on the spectrum, nothing is easy or taken for granted. But with some effort, you can help to ensure that your child is happy, fulfilled, taken care of, and comfortable with her life as an adult.

2. Jobs

I wouldn't say that I skip to work every day, but I like what I do and I'm good at it. I want my daughter, who's on the spectrum, to know what it's like to feel fulfilled at the workplace, but I'm worried that her social issues and unusual mannerisms will make it hard for her to land an interesting job, ultimately forcing her into a more menial occupation. How can I help her find her way to a job she enjoys? Is that too much to ask?

CLAIRE

When Andrew was fifteen, he decided he should have a summer job. A few of his friends were earning their own money and he had an expensive enchilada and frappuccino habit that his allowance wasn't up to. He expressed interest in working at a local restaurant (one which happened to make really good enchiladas—I'm sure he was picturing the fringe benefits) and when my husband first contacted them, they said they could use a part-time busboy and he should come in to interview.

We made some mistakes with that interview. We did a little priming but probably not enough. Neither of us was available to drive Andrew there, so he rode the bus and arrived very early and very hot and sweaty. Not sure what to do with the extra time, he hovered anxiously in front of the restaurant, so he was a bit of a wreck by the time he went in for the interview. I don't know exactly what went down, only that the interview was very short and ultimately unfruitful. Andrew didn't seem very happy with the whole experience, and no one ever called him back from the restaurant.

We realized we had to be less ambitious, start smaller, prepare more carefully. Fortunately, a much better opportunity presented itself. His best friend worked for a company run by close family friends—people who already had met Andrew socially. They said they could use another pair of hands in both their warehouse and the office. Although the job was pretty much guaranteed, we talked to Daren, Andrew's incredibly nice employer-to-be, and we all agreed that it would be best for Andrew to go through the interview process.

This time, we primed him thoroughly, going through all the potential questions we could think an employer might ask and letting him come up with the right answers. We insisted he dress nicely in a button-down shirt with khakis (he looked so handsome!) and I drove him to the appointment and walked him in.

It was an amazing experience. Both Andrew and Daren took the interview very seriously, but it was all geared toward success this time. They talked for a long time, and Daren assured me afterward that Andrew had done a good job in the interview. He told Andrew he was hired.

Andrew worked hard there all summer. Not only did he do a lot of different things at the office (and in their warehouse) but he had to get himself there and back by bus every day he worked, and if you've ever tried to use public transportation in LA, you know that couldn't have been easy. Daren told me that Andrew was dedicated and hardworking and willing to try his hand at anything they needed him to do, and he must have done okay because they said he could come back and work there again this summer. And Andrew made enough money to buy himself a whole lot of enchiladas.

Lately Andrew's been thinking about his future career and,

to my great delight, has moved from some fairly unrealistic dreams (theme park owner?) to something he can actually work toward. He loves playing around with flash animation and recently said to me that he hopes he can find a job working with it someday. We just signed him up for a college extension flash animation course to hone those skills. He doesn't need to have a career picked out yet—few of us do at the age of sixteen—but the fact that he's thinking seriously and realistically about the choices he makes toward that end fills me with optimism.

DR. KOEGEL

As researchers, we think in numbers. We carefully measure everything and remeasure over and over again to make sure our interventions are working. We've published articles about such things as using physical exercise, self-management, video modeling, and priming to reduce repetitive and other undesired behaviors. These programs work, but when we say "work" we often mean "help." Physical exercise may cut repetitive behaviors in half, but if someone is going on a job interview and engages in, let's say just five seconds of repetitive behavior, he probably won't get the job. And then, on top of the repetitive behaviors, there may be some subtle social cues your child doesn't pick up on, so job interviews—especially without some support—may be difficult for individuals on the spectrum.

There are many *many* areas that are sorely subadequate for people on the spectrum and with other disabilities. One relates to jobs. While there are civil rights laws that prohibit discrimination against people with disabilities, check any survey and you'll see that many kids on the spectrum are unemployed. This is an area that has begun to come to the attention of organizations dedicated to developing meaningful employment opportunities for individuals on the spectrum. But, to be direct, your child may need help finding and keeping meaningful employment.

First you need to help your child find a job he loves and will want to get up for every day. Whether this is in the arts, writing, math, or whatever else really interests him, you need to help him make that type of job happen.

People with disabilities are too often forced into employment training programs that don't take into consideration their interests, strengths, or desires. Time after time, you'll see high school classes herd a whole group of adolescents into a restaurant where they'll set the tables, fill up the salt and pepper containers, mop the floor, and so on. This direction needs to change. Just as *we* wouldn't want to be told what to do with our lives, we need to explore the wide variety of career opportunities for kids on the spectrum.

Although we're seeing more kids on the spectrum being included in preschool and elementary school, we still aren't doing such a great job of including older kids on the spectrum in regular education classes, community homes, work settings, and recreational activities. In fact, I was in a high school recently where the children with special needs were picking up the trash during lunch for the other students. I couldn't believe it—I still can't believe it—but it was really happening—part of their "educational" program was to walk around the grounds picking up the trash during lunch! I was appalled. In fact, the reason I was visiting the school was because the administrators there wanted to put a child with autism into that very special education class, and the parent didn't want her to be there. After we visited, the mother quite understandably said that she didn't want her daughter picking up trash. The school's response? "Then she can wrap sandwiches in the cafeteria." And this is a child who can carry on a full conversation, who reads, does prealgebra, and loves to socialize. This was theoretically preparing her for life on her own after high school, but instead of widening her future choices and career possibilities—which is, of course, the *point* of education—the school was narrowing them, as if a job performing menial tasks was the only possible future for this girl. Fortunately, this child's mother didn't let it happen. Every child on the spectrum—or with any disability, for that matter—should be able to work at a job she enjoys.

There are some steps you can take to make your child's future better, the first and most important being *to keep him fully included at school,* or at least included as much as possible (the more included the better). Don't let your school force you to put your child into some kind of special ed program like the one I described above—your child needs to be learning the same things his peers are so he can figure out what he's good at and enjoys doing, and so he can continue learning what it's like to function as an integral part of society. Years of picking up trash will make him good at doing one thing: picking up trash. If you want something different for your child, keep his options open by keeping him included with typical peers, socially and academically, through peer social groups, partial participation, priming, and so on, all the way through the school years.

First Jobs

Of course, your child's first jobs are going to be for you, her parent. As we discuss in Section VI, Chapter 3, on managing behavior, doing small jobs around the house is an important part of achieving independence and self-reliance. From the time your child is old enough to follow directions, give her age-appropriate chores to do and increase her responsibilities as she grows older and more capable.

Different families have different rules about rewarding their kids for household chores. Some view an allowance as payment for chores performed, some think chores should simply be part of a child's responsibility as a member of the family, some pay separately for each and every chore, and still others pay above and beyond the allowance for what they see as "extra" jobs (such as washing the car or running an errand) and not for the regular, daily chores such as setting the table. You can choose what feels right for your family, but it might be a good idea to occasionally relate the performance of a job well done to payment, so your child gets the idea of working for money and the subsequent pleasure of spending that money freely. And don't forget to take your child out to spend his hard-earned money. We worked with one family who started paying their son for chores but never took him to buy anything. Needless to say, he eventually stopped doing his chores. But a simple trip to the store to buy a desired item changed everything so that he was *asking* for more chores.

Praise is also important: if your child listens to directions and follows them carefully and completes the job fully, then she deserves your full and heartfelt praise and thanks. If she doesn't, then this is your chance to impress on her the importance of doing all those things, before it becomes a real-life, out-in-the-world situation. Jobs begun must be completed. Instructions must be followed. And *you* shouldn't forget to pay her promptly. If you keep forgetting to stop by the bank on the scheduled pay dates, you'll probably have a much less enthusiastic worker. All these things will help prepare your child for that important first real job.

First Job in the Real World

Again, different families have different feelings about when a child should start earning money out in the world. Some feel it's important to start as early as possible and will encourage their kids to babysit and mow lawns when they're still too young to be hired in the adult world and to look for a real job outside of the home once they're not. Others feel they'd rather have their kids focus on studying and extra-curricular activities and not worry about holding down any kind of a job until after high school or even college.

The decision is yours, but if your child is old enough to apply for a job, and some of his friends are doing so, and he expresses the desire to do it or you feel it would be advantageous, then it's probably worth pursuing. But you do want to make sure that these early forays into the workforce are successful, so take some time to prepare the way.

The ideal thing is to find a close friend or relative who runs a store or office and ask her or him to hire your child for a few hours a week. Don't feel awkward about this—most jobs are acquired that way. Make it clear to your child that even if she knows the owner, she's expected to work hard and be respectful at all times. Have her dress appropriately for the job and always arrive on time. Stay in touch, and if any problems arise, do what you can to manage them, such as using self-management techniques (see Section I, Chapter 2), so your child can monitor her own performance. If you hear from her boss that she's not performing to expectations, it's time to have a serious talk with your child to let her know that employers won't tolerate any-one who doesn't try. And if she's doing good things, celebrate! When she gets her first paycheck, make a big deal out of depositing and/or cashing it and praise her like crazy.

In this protected environment, your child is likely to succeed—and if he doesn't, at least you'll have learned where any future problems are likely to lie, and you can work on fixing them right away.

If you don't have any friends or relatives who can help you out, there are other ways to set up a protected first-job environment. One mother I know discovered that a local camp director was more than happy to "hire" young teenagers as assistant counselors (their salary actually came from their parents, but they didn't know that). We have hired many people on the spectrum at our Center—some assist with our summer camp and others work in the office.

Even if you can't find a paid job, volunteer job experience can be helpful. Some camps accept CITs (counselors in training), and if they do well, they are hired as counselors the following summer. Volunteer jobs can get a child used to showing up on time at a job and helping out—in a safe environment without any risk of failing.

High schools sometimes run summer programs for younger kids that their students can help out in, for pay or community service hours. And I've known kids on the spectrum who have been hired by the clinicians who work with them to help younger kids on the spec-trum with *their* programs.

So ask everyone you know, and you'll probably find that perfect first job.

Future Jobs and Careers

Obviously, unless your family owns a business that can employ your child right out of college, you can't supply your child with jobs forever, and you wouldn't want to. First jobs are supposed to be about learning to work hard and being paid for it. But the jobs young people seek out when they're all done with their schooling ideally help to set them on a path toward a career they'll find fulfilling.

We know one young man on the spectrum who got a master's

degree in psychology and now works with kids with disabilities. Another works in the library—his absolutely favorite place in the whole wide world—and he's very good at asking people to "quiet down please" if they're too noisy! Another college student we know works with all his friends at a local hamburger joint near the college that almost exclusively employs students. He loves the job, and as a "starving student," enjoys the free hamburgers he gets every day. A young adult we worked with loves the outdoors and landed a job with the Forest Service. Finally, one adult with limited verbal skills, who always loved taking Jacuzzis, actually got a job cleaning them for a company that lets him jump in after he finishes his work each day.

All of these jobs were carefully selected with the individual on the spectrum in mind. Some were self-selected, and for those with fewer verbal abilities, their team carefully selected jobs that would be enjoyable, incorporate their interests, and maintain their dignity.

And as I mentioned earlier, your child's education has a lot to do with the career choices he's likely to have as a young adult. That alone is a good reason to help your child achieve the highest level of education possible. (See Section IV, Chapter 3 on ensuring a successful college experience.) Kids often find something they're passionate about during their college years and start to specialize in it at school. If that goes well, it may lead directly to some very specific career choices.

Of course, even if your child knows what job he'd *like* to have, that doesn't mean he'll get it. There are several steps you can take that might help him obtain that dream job—if not immediately, then down the road.

- **Keep it realistic.** One problem I've encountered with some young adults on the spectrum is a propensity to believe in things that just aren't very likely. If your daughter has a tendency to speak grandiloquently about how she wants to own a movie studio one day, or your son says he's going to be a famous pitcher (well past the age when most kids have given up *that* dream) or own a fleet of private planes, you need to kindly but firmly bring reality back into the picture. She can't go out and buy a movie studio—but maybe she can get a job working at one. He's not likely to be a world famous pitcher—but maybe the local newspaper would be interested in an assistant who has as many sports statistics memorized as your son has. Owning a fleet of private planes may not be realistic, but being a pilot or even a business major may get her nearer that goal.

- **Help sort through the options and find some concrete possibilities.** You might even make some discreet inquiring phone calls on your own. Even though your child is an adult and will ultimately have to prove herself on the job without your help, there's no reason not to step in and help her during the job search. Find a menu of possibilities you can discuss with her. Gauge her reaction, provide more details, maybe even expose her to the workplace. The goal here, basically, is to feel out what interests your child and might make her happy.

- **Assist with the application.** Read through and make suggestions. You would be surprised at how many challenges some of our students have with applications (and time sheets). We've had adults write the job title under "Name" and put in information that's completely irrelevant under "Previous Experience." Job applications can be a great learning opportunity. Make sure that your child understands about tailoring the application to the specific job desired.

- **Prepare him for the interview.** Make sure he's dressed appropriately and looks neat for that first impression. Review the questions an interviewer is likely to ask and make sure his answers are what they should be. If they're not, suggest some better responses and then practice them with him. This is critical. If appropriate, have him e-mail after the interview with a thank-you in which he lets the potential employer know how much he enjoyed the interview and how much he would enjoy working at that company. And if your child doesn't get a job he applied for, encourage him to e-mail or call the interviewer (or you can do this) to find out in what ways he could have done better.

- **Set up a grooming and preparation checklist for work-days.** Once your child does get hired, make sure she knows what she has to do each and every day to get ready for work. If she has trouble keeping it together, make a self-management chart. Teach her about arriving a few minutes early and leaving a few minutes late, just to make sure her employer knows what a hard worker she is. Teach her about good communication with her employer, and how to ask for more work. Finally, many kids on the spectrum don't understand how important it is to smile and have a good attitude. If your child doesn't, it's a great idea to practice greeting people with a smile, asking them how they're doing, and speaking positively about the job.

- **Check in.** Speak to your child often to see how the job's going. If you sense there are any problems, do what you can to help him overcome them. You want him to be independent, but you should always be willing to offer support. For adults on the spectrum, independence is best maintained with some amount of distant supervision.

Some Career Areas That Work Well for Adults on the Spectrum

Your child may have her own ideas about what she wants to do when she's ready to find a job, but if you feel that she's waiting for your lead, these are some areas you might want to consider steering her toward:

- **Microenterprises.** Most everyone would like to own his own company, and for many years that goal wasn't a possibility for someone on the spectrum. We have seen an increase in microenterprising, where kids with disabilities can actually learn to develop a business within their interests, whether it is computer business, dog grooming, car detailing, accounting, or whatever. There are new agencies that work with people to help them develop enough business skills to be able to start their own businesses and hire employees. (I was able to find several of them simply by doing an online search.)

- **Creative endeavors.** Recently, a number of organizations have supported arts projects for kids on the spectrum. We have seen fabulous movies, books, and art produced by these kids, and the subsequent recognition can lead to useful business connections. Usually these organizations rely on donations and the sale of the kids' artwork, but sometimes they can provide financial assistance for start-up projects.

- **Computer-related jobs.** Several of our students have had good luck in the world of computer design and software development, possibly because so many young adults on the spectrum feel more comfortable on the computer than they do in more socially demanding interactions.

Regardless of the amount of support your child needs to maintain a job, the important thing is that he enjoy what he's doing. If he doesn't have enough communication to express verbally whether he enjoys a job, take a look at him. Does he look happy? Are people nice to him where he works? Does he get up in the morning and leave the house with enthusiasm? If you're answering "no" to these questions, it may be time to explore other job options.

ANDREW

The first real job I had was babysitting for my cousins when I was about thirteen. I got it because at one point, my aunt and uncle were both trying to look for babysitters for my

cousins during the weekends and they realized that I was old enough to watch younger children, so they hired me to watch them. I actually liked that job not only because I was paid a good wage (about seven or eight dollars an hour), but my cousins are also really well-behaved and nice kids, and my aunt and uncle are both really nice. It really was not that hard but I would probably say that the hardest part of it was putting the kids to bed (because they always begged me to stay up later) even though I was good at it and my cousins would go to sleep when I told them to. We would play games and watch movies before my cousins went to sleep.

Last summer, I also did some community service work for my school for my therapist's summer autism program for elementary and middle school. I helped the kids out, telling them what they should be doing in order to participate in the program. I actually liked assisting the younger kids, not only to help them concentrate but also to play games with them (such as softball and capture the flag) whenever we would walk to a nearby park for lunch. The hard parts about my community service were getting kids to participate in games that we played within the program. Some kids would listen to what I would say to advise them, but others would not listen to me and would yell to me, "You are not the boss!" The easier parts were just playing games with the kids and having nice conversations with them during lunch.

I have another job now, working for a dermatology company as a paid assistant. I really like my dermatology company assistant job mainly because everyone else who works there is really nice, but it also uses computers, which I like to work with. For this job, I have also organized folders, scanned papers, and put labels on CDs. The only frustrating thing about this job was scanning papers. On my first day of scanning, I had to scan about two or three hundred old bills the company had. The scanner there has always been hard to work with and is complex, so on the first day I did everything wrong and the files were not scanned, so I had to start all over again. Because of that problem, I was worried that I would disappoint my employer. I was not worried about losing my job, but I was just worried that my employer would not think that I was good at following directions. The good news was that my employer was not mad and was very nice about it, telling me that everybody has trouble using the scanner. The easiest parts of the job for me were probably burning CDs and DVDs, organizing files and putting labels on the CDs and DVDs. I would definitely do my dermatology company work again (which I already am doing) and I would probably also do the community service again if I need it for school.

I mainly like to do work that involves computers and organizing. When I grow up, I want to make Web sites, animations, or video games for computers. Even now I like to make my own Web sites on Freewebs (a free Web site design program online) and make my own games and animations on Macromedia Flash (a 2D animation program) by following tutorials.

I think that if you are going to find a job, the best thing to do is to find something that interests you. It is good to make a lot of money from your job to help with your financial needs, but if you want to make money, it is best to find something that you want to do and that you will be happy doing for a long time. If I had to choose between a high-paying job I did not like over a low-paying job I did like, I would probably prefer the low-paying job I did like. As I said before, in my opinion, you should definitely find a job you like that you could maintain for a long period of time without quitting.

I would highly recommend that teenagers start working. It is great if teenagers want to have more money to spend and save for the future and it would also help them get a better sense of what the job application/interview process is

like. And also, if you are getting a job, you should be really
responsible and put a lot of effort into doing the interview
and making your résumé.

Frequently Asked Questions

*After some searching, my son finally got hired at a local business.
It's a starter position but there's potential for him to move up
through the ranks over time, and I'm thrilled. The only thing that
worries me now is his expectations. I've overheard him talking to
people and from the way he describes his job, you'd think he was
being hired as CEO! He'll find out soon enough what the actual
work entails, but I'm concerned that he'll lose interest with the job
once he realizes it's not as high-level as he'd hoped. How do I get
him to stick it out and understand that someone with his level of
education and experience has to pay some dues?*

> The great news is that your son has worked hard enough to get the
> job. He may be aggrandizing the job a bit to impress his friends,
> but we've all had jobs that weren't what we expected or were te-
> dious and boring while we were in college or trying to work our way
> up. If he expresses some discomfort that the job isn't what he ex-
> pected, have him first work hard so that his employer knows what
> he's capable of and how much he puts into the job. Then have him
> talk with his boss to find out exactly what the promotion schedule
> is like and what the likelihood is that he'll be able to get promoted.
> If it's optimistic, then it should give your child more of a reason to
> keep working hard. If it doesn't look good, it may be time to search
> for a more compatible job that will give your child advancement
> opportunities.

*My daughter went to a local junior college program where she learned
life skills and some basic menial job training. I want more options for
her, but I don't think she could make it through a four-year college.
Is there any other way to expand her opportunities?*

The first step is to figure out what your child's interests are and where her passions lie. The second step is to get her specialized training in those areas. This can be through extension courses, online courses, or on-the-job training. As mentioned earlier, it is not acceptable for your child to hold a menial job if she doesn't want that type of job. Keep searching for supportive businesses and educational opportunities for her.

My daughter came home from work upset yesterday and went up to her room, where she stayed for the rest of the day. When I asked her if something had happened, she refused to talk about it. Do you think I could call her boss just to check in? Or would that make her look incapable? I want to stay on top of things but she won't tell me anything.

If your child works at her job completely independently, it may not be a good idea to get involved. You may want to wait this one out and see if it passes. We all have bad days now and again at work. However, if it persists, I would try to get involved. You may want to drop in at the job site and see how she's being treated, without letting people know that there may be a problem. In the meantime, try to get your child to communicate with you so that you can help her out. And if more subtle approaches just don't seem to work, you may want to find someone whom she'll confide in. You'll have to weigh the possible negative and positive outcomes before making the decision to check in with coworkers or her employers. And if you do decide to call her employer, you may want to let her know that you're thinking of doing that. Sometimes unhappiness can be totally unrelated to a job. I had a friend whose child was in physical pain but didn't want to talk about it. Eventually the child confessed that he had a serious and painful physical problem, but not before his parents had wrongly guessed just about every other potential problem. Again, communication is the best thing.

What skills should I have my child focus on in high school and college to best prepare him for jobs afterward? I'm not worried about his having a great, fulfilling career—I just want him to be able to earn a little money and maybe one day live by himself.

First and foremost, getting along socially is what can make or break a good job interview and help someone keep a good job. That's most important. Next, your child will have to navigate the world of applications, interviews, and financial planning. Finally, teach your child about going the extra mile. If a company has a financial hardship, they're going to keep the employees who don't watch the clock but who get to work a little early and complete that last job even if it means staying a few extra minutes. They'll also prefer those who get along with others and who keep a positive attitude about work. These are all things you can work on with your child, and they don't require any special aptitude other than a willingness to learn.

3. Living Conditions

*Our son has lived with us his whole life, but now that he's well
into his twenties, it just doesn't feel as if it's in his best interest for
him to live with his parents anymore. We'd like to see him become more independent, especially because there's a world full of
young people his own age out there. But he's not really ready to
live alone. What are our choices?*

CLAIRE

Remember your first apartment? It was probably small, ugly,
and falling apart, but you loved it because it was a symbol of
your independence and burgeoning adulthood.

There are so many things we want for our kids because we
remember how much they meant to us—long-lasting friendships, an exciting romance, the joy of holding your first baby in
your arms, and, of course, a room/apartment/house (ideally in
that order) "of one's own." Unfortunately, a lot of young adults
on the spectrum don't have the skills to move out of their parents' home (or a supervised housing situation) to set up house
by themselves.

We're lucky. I don't doubt for a second that Andrew will be
fully capable of living on his own. At the age of sixteen, he already can drive, cook, clean up his room, answer the phone,

make plans, and do his own laundry. But back when he was a small boy who couldn't even learn to talk and who seemed locked in a separate, isolated world, I remember being struck with the thought that instead of following the natural course of things and moving out of our house when he was a young adult, he might simply stay reliant on us. It was a painful thought, not because I wanted to be rid of him, but because I had always pictured my children hitting the same milestones I had hit as I grew up and became an adult. And there was something so giddily and frighteningly exhilarating about living on my own that first time—I didn't want him to miss out on that whole wild experience. I'm glad he won't have to.

Andrew has been amazingly successful, but there are many young adults on the spectrum out there who simply aren't ready to live a completely independent life. Fortunately, that doesn't mean they have to live with their parents forever. There are other choices, maybe not as many as there should be, but more and more all the time.

DR. KOEGEL

Living conditions vary widely among people on the spectrum. Many live independently, hold a job, marry, and have a family. Others live in their own homes with assistance (varying from live-in help to occasional visits from someone who's paid to check on them) and are able to get out, work, and engage in recreational activities.

However, I'm very sorry to say that many adults on the spectrum live in substandard conditions. Too many live in group homes with eight, ten, fifteen, or even more other individuals with disabilities. I've visited some of these places and, believe me, I couldn't wait to get out. Although their staffs are usually dedicated and supportive, these are facilities I wouldn't want to live in—most have too many people with disabilities living in quarters that are too close, aren't pleasant aesthetically, and don't provide many opportunities for the residents to do anything outside of the settings. I had one dad tell me that every residential setting his daughter was placed in had the same stale and unpleasant odor. And if we don't like even *visiting* these places, I can't imagine how it would be living in one day in and day out. We need better choices for our young adults on the spectrum. To realize that, here are some recent options that are emerging as potential solutions:

- **Staying at home longer.** Too often families would like their child to stay at home longer but just aren't able to take care of them and aren't provided with any resources to do so, so they're faced with an either/or situation: keep them at home with no support or send them away with full support. We need to give families more support *in* their homes. If their children need constant supervision, we need to make sure that there are people available to provide them with that support. And this means helping families pay for these services.

  There are already some options available now. Some services that are generally acquired through a local agency specializing in programs for adults will provide overnight respite if the parents want to take a vacation or have a romantic getaway. Check with your local state agency for disabilities about these options. A couple who own a farm in our area will take kids and young adults on the spectrum for the weekend—it's like a summer camp with animals and activities, and after spending a weekend there, the weekenders beg to go back. Dedicated people who really want to care for adults with disabilities can provide support and comfort for short periods of time. We need many more of these regular but short-term "summer camp" options, where parents can feel good about leaving their adult children for a weekend, a few weeks, or another short-term period of time.

- **Live on their own in a house or apartment.** There are lots of options for adults on the spectrum who live in their own home or apartment. Various levels of support can be provided. Some adults need a lot of support initially, but it can eventually be faded as they get to know the area, the bus schedules, their work schedule, and entertainment options. Other people need regular ongoing support and supervision from people who are paid to assist.

- **Live on their own, with roommates.** Some individuals on the spectrum will also live in their own homes, but with typical peers as roommates. These typical peers are often provided with room, board, and a small stipend to help out. Some families have the resources to provide a home for their child, which is fantastic, but I've also known others who participated in state-paid programs. Those work out well. The ones I've seen have been nice homes with people who care. Different states vary in just how much they contribute, but if you live in a state that helps adults with disabilities, or if you can help set up a home setting with your child's state and federal money, this may be the right setting for your child.

- **Small, well-run community homes.** For many years, I was a board member for a foundation that provided care to individuals with severe disabilities and ran a community home that could service no more than four individuals. We had a backyard, daily outings, gourmet food, hired people who cared, and close family contact so that the adults could spend many weekends and holidays at home. But to create this environment, which wasn't even as integrated as I would have liked, was expensive. We constantly had to have fund-raisers and request donations just to be able to service those four adults.

  There are several reasons for this. First, the state reimbursement rate for staff is very low—as far as the government is concerned, it's basically a minimum wage job to work with people with disabilities. Although we raised funds, they were applied toward bigger items we needed, such as transportation, gardening tools, kitchen appliances, and so on. There wasn't enough to help with staff salaries. Second, we didn't get state money if the residents with disabilities went home for the weekend, even though we felt it was in their best interest to do so. Some of the state payments are based on the number of nights the residents spent there, so if they went home for the weekend—which we encouraged—we didn't get paid for those nights. This is the reason many group homes have residents packed in. In fact, at one point the board had a disagreement over whether to add more residents for the sole reason of cost efficiency. Fortunately, a few of us talked them into quality over quantity.

Also, the government periodically checks to make sure everything is operating within the legal mandates. While their standards are there to protect the patients, the scrutiny occasionally reached absurd limits, especially when there was a temporary problem. One time our hot water monitor broke and the temperature had to be controlled by hand so that it didn't get too hot—we were fined for this. And fined a large amount. This was money we didn't have.

So you can see some of the problems. What we were able to do was have a warm homelike setting with aquariums, nice furniture, good food, great employees (who unfortunately didn't always last long), wonderful recreational opportunities, and great family support. But it was expensive.

Unfortunately, there's usually a long wait list for these types of comfortable community-based homes. In addition, the facilities often are reluctant to take kids on the spectrum who are disruptive, aggressive, inclined to run away, or have other behavioral issues. So adults with autism and challenging behaviors aren't always the first picked.

- **Live with a family.** Many couples or families provide a home and care (or foster care) for a person with disabilities. This can be a short-term or long-term arrangement. The home owners often get some kind of financial compensation, and the person on the spectrum becomes a regular family member.

Although it may seem more like a business arrangement than a familial one if the home owners are being paid, I have met many, many wonderful families who have chosen to have an adult person on the spectrum, who is unable to live alone, move in. Essentially, the desired outcome of your child having a "family" happens with this type of arrangement—they go on outings, celebrate holidays together, and so on. Often, the biological family of the adult on the spectrum will spend weekends and holidays with them, but even if they can't, the adult is in a home environment, surrounded by a real family who cares.

April's Story

April is a student in our PhD program who is just about to complete her dissertation. I had observed her many years ago when she was in high school. A fellow researcher and teacher at her school had started a club aimed at helping students with severe disabilities. One of the students we were working with had autism and was participating in the club. At that time, I didn't know April personally, but I was impressed by the way she and other students (a clique of high school kids who were recruited to have lunch with students with severe disabilities) took Jackson under their wing. They went above and beyond the required lunch periods and took him to sports events, movies, festivals, and just spent a lot of time hanging out with him. Jackson's mother, a diabetic, suffered immensely during his high school years, and eventually (after several amputations and blood transfusions) passed away. His father was unable to care for him because he was partially paralyzed from a stroke he had had while Jackson was a young child. Jackson could no longer live at home, which, unfortunately, led to a few unpleasant years of living in less than acceptable institutional settings.

Unhappy with his situation, Jackson's friends got together and made a change for him. And April spearheaded the movement. I have asked this extraordinary woman to write about her experiences that changed this young man's life.

APRIL REGESTER

When I was in high school, I was labeled an at-risk student because of my lack of involvement in extracurricular activities. At the time, most students had two periods out of six that they were allowed to spend doing any elective they were interested in (cheerleading, student clubs, sports, and so on).

My counselor suggested that I become a peer tutor in the county special education program to fill my electives. I enrolled as a freshman, and during that time I agreed to participate as a subject in a research project on the perceptions typical peers had about students with disabilities. After that, I was recruited to join a club to promote friendships between students with and without disabilities, and I became an active member of the buddy program.

While I participated in these programs I met Jackson, who was a special education student in the county class at my high school. We were the same age. I got to know Jackson and his family, and I realized that his situation at the time was not good. He was in and out of the house with his dad, who had had a stroke and used a wheelchair. While his father enjoyed Jackson, he had a difficult time caring for him on a full-time basis. At the same time, his mom had a terminal illness and was dying. Jackson was placed outside of the home during this difficult time and lived in a variety of institutional settings. After Jackson's mom died, he continued to move around and spent small pockets of time living with his father. This did not work well for either of them and he again was placed outside of the home.

Although he was my friend and we got along well, he was very aggressive toward staff at the institutions where he was living. He was kicked out of two institutions, various group homes, and a state hospital, among other places. I was heartbroken as I watched this take place over the course of five years.

I graduated from high school, and, because of my high school experience with students with disabilities, I became interested in working in the field. I worked as a paraprofessional, vocational assistant, respite care provider, inclusion support person, and in many other related jobs.

In the meantime, I had kept in close touch with Jackson, and shortly after we graduated, a group of his friends and former teachers got together to try to figure out how to help him stay in the area and improve his living conditions. This was a challenge because he had been turned away from every local living situation. We talked about options, and the idea of a supported living arrangement came up. It was a fairly new idea at the time but offered a person the option of living independently, with all the freedoms that go along with that.

My husband and I volunteered to look into it and spent about a year researching programs and visiting homes that were considered to be the best. We, in essence, created a home where Jackson would be provided with twenty-four-hour support. Now, this may have been considered expensive to some, but in comparison to the amount the state was paying for residential care for him, with all his aggression, it actually saved the state money. However, many were skeptical about our intentions. They had a difficult time understanding our motives in wanting to help him simply because we were friends. But by that time, I was deeply involved in his life, understood his likes and dislikes, knew what motivated him, knew how to get him to get out and into the community, and basically felt so close to him that he was like family to me. As we moved forward with the idea, the state agency haggled with us, so we rewrote and redesigned our plan, and presented many versions to the state. Finally, after we had reached our limit, we filed for a fair hearing and later that *very same day* our plan was approved.

A year after we had started the whole process, we celebrated as Jackson moved into his very own apartment. In fact, it was New Year's Day, which made it more eventful.

Our goal was to provide the best life possible and to create a life that Jackson wanted. We had many meetings, and with a core group (including Jackson), discussed what would be the best for him. Jackson had many requests. He did not want to live with someone who had a disability. He wanted to be able to play his trumpet. He did not want stairs in his home. He wanted to have mostly women helping him out. He did not want a lock on the refrigerator. He wanted cable television. And so on. After many interviews, we ended up finding a young (typical) male to room with him who was compatible in age and interests (he also likes music), and who had experience with individuals with autism.

Next, we started hunting for a place for Jackson to live. Money was a huge factor, but we had a large group of people scouring the town for us. We put his name in a lottery for a new low-income apartment complex, which was exactly one minute away from my house. We won the lottery and secured a home that was downstairs and had a pool and other nice amenities. We made sure that *Jackson's* name was on the lease, not *ours*, to be sure that regardless of who his service provider was, he would be able to stay in his home.

At the time that Jackson moved into his own home, he was being heavily drugged due to his aggression and other disruptive behaviors in the institutions where he had been placed (some were dorm-style with hundreds of residents—all with severe disabilities). Fortunately, I was able to secure a grant that paid for a private psychologist to reevaluate the meds he was taking, which was basically a cocktail of Ativan (at high levels), Risperdal, Zoloft, and a variety of others. We worked out a plan to lower the medication levels and increase the behavioral methods to deal with his aggression. Over the course of two years, he was completely taken off most of his medication. Instead, we focused on training the support staff to use positive behavioral supports, antecedents, environmental cues, and natural consequences. There was lots of coaching and his aggression decreased dramatically.

Simultaneously, we reinstated his trumpet lessons, which had been long forgotten in the institutions, took him to regular community events, provided him with a healthy diet, and made sure that he exercised daily.

A combination of state funding, In-Home Supportive Services (IHSS), and Social Security pays for Jackson's personal expenses and bills. While this split in the cost is very tricky, because different agencies pay at different rates, we have worked it out so that all of Jackson's expenses are covered, and each employee's hourly rate is higher than most others in the same field.

During the day, Jackson attends a day program with individuals with disabilities. This is something we would like to change. While he enjoys the program, we would like to see him start a microenterprise to get job experience and become more financially independent.

In the evenings, Jackson cooks, browses Borders bookstore, plays the trumpet, exercises, reads, listens to his music collection, hangs out with friends at events, goes to the movies, and does other fun things. On weekends he spends a lot of time out and about. He is now part of my family and is often busy attending whatever event we have going on: graduations, holiday celebrations, birthdays, and so on. He also has a large group of friends he spends a lot of time with, most of whom do not have a disability.

Jackson has now been living in his own home with the same roommate for nine years. My husband and I never planned on taking on more people like most agencies but just wanted to help out Jackson. A large part of friendship is its reciprocal nature. Although people view what I did as beneficial for Jackson, I definitely got something out of it too. Because of my experiences in high school and beyond, I decided to go into the field of disabilities and am now completing my doctoral dissertation. During the last nine years, I have had two children, and the money we were paid for managing Jackson's home helped me support my family. And while it wasn't a large amount of money, the flexibility of my schedule allowed me to take graduate classes. Further, I was able to take my kids with me whenever I was with Jackson, training his staff, and managing his home. I also learned how to run my own business, train and supervise up to eleven people at a time, consult with other agencies, and in general, learn about the adult residential system.

Jackson and I have continued to remain extremely close through all these years. He is genuinely a part of our family. My son's first word was "Jackson" and we decided to give my daughter the middle name King because it was always one of Jackson's favorite words, and he would repeat it frequently.

Jackson and I have helped each other out in different ways. He is now stable enough to handle changes in his service providers (which used to really upset him). He loves his home and his friends and never, ever is aggressive, as he was regularly in the past. His latest support staff considers him to be very mellow and fun to be with, and can't believe he was ever aggressive and unwanted by many previous residential settings.

I met Jackson when we were both in high school. My group of friends and I spent lunches, weekends, and summers with him. We went to sports events, listened to him play the trumpet, and just hung out. And when his mom died, and his dad was too ill to take care of him, we stood by him. And now, almost a decade later, I look at him in amazement: he has managed to hang on to his core group of friends through all the difficult times he had, in addition to being unsuccessfully relocated from one institution to another. But I firmly believe that all of the early intervention he had as a child through the clinic and school, and the support from his mom, helped him develop some very important tools and skills to be able to connect and communicate with others. And now he is independent, happy, active, and a great guy to be around.

Frequently Asked Questions

We couldn't keep our adolescent son at home because his behavior was too disruptive. He is now living in a residential setting with around fifty other adolescents and adults. I worry that they don't take good care of him. When I visit, his clothes are dirty, he has no pictures on the wall, he rarely leaves the residential setting, and they basically let him watch TV for hours on end. What can I do?

I would suggest looking into a different setting that has more opportunities for your child. I often see children who have disruptive behavior left to themselves in these types of settings because when demands are placed on them, they become disruptive. However, your child won't learn if he's left in front of the television for hours and hours. He needs a real program, one which includes chores, the acquisition of self-help skills, academic goals, and fun leisure activities.

My son is getting older and I'm not sure if he's going to be able to live on his own. He's very smart and does well in school, but I'm very worried about the types of group homes that are available to him. Is there a way I can start working on this now?

The best thing you can do for your son is to make sure he is learning how to live on his own. Have him help you cook, clean up, do his laundry, ride the bus, shop, get up on his own, dress and bathe on his own, and do other activities that will teach him independence. You can start setting up some self-management programs so that you don't have to watch him constantly. All of these areas will help him live more independently when the time comes. And if he has any disruptive behavior whatsoever, make working on that a priority. Disruptive behaviors will cut way back on the community activities your adult child will be able to participate in, and even worse, he's likely to be placed in a living situation that is focused on dealing with behavior problems, with a lower staff-to-patient ratio and, generally, other residents with behavior issues—all of which will mean fewer opportunities and activities, and similar roommates who are not likely to help him to grow and improve.

4. Legal Planning

I've taken care of my daughter her entire life. Despite all we've done, she's still completely dependent on us at the age of thirty-five. She has no siblings. My husband and I were on the older side when we had her, and I'm terrified about what will happen to her after we die.

CLAIRE

I once had a great heart-to-heart talk with a man whose sister was on the spectrum. The whole family was wonderful, which was good because his sister was still quite dependent. She had her own little apartment, but a member of the family checked in on her regularly there, and the parents paid for it. She held down a part-time job, but it was fairly menial and the amount of money she made wasn't close to supporting her—her parents supplied the rest. She couldn't drive, so they all pitched in when they could to drive her places she couldn't walk or ride the bus to. And she was socially fairly isolated, except for a few special clubs and organized outings, so her family provided most of her social life, picking her up and taking her out and arranging family get-togethers whenever possible.

This man loved his sister dearly and was honestly happy to do anything he could to make her life better. But you could still *hear the strain in his voice when he said, "I know that when my parents die, I am going to be completely responsible for her, financially, physically, and emotionally." It was an overwhelming thing for a young man with his own growing family to have to take on. People all around us do it every day, of course: take responsibility for adult children, siblings, parents, grandparents, and others who can't take care of themselves.*

No one can, or should, take the burden of caring about a family member away, but there are things you can do to alleviate the burden of caring for her.

DR. KOEGEL

Of all the concerns I've heard from parents of older kids on the spectrum, the most troubling is that they worry, day in and day out, about what will happen to their children after they die. Parents have been there to care for, advocate for, and abundantly love their children since they were born, but as they get older they realize that they won't be able to do it forever. They worry that, once they're gone, there won't be anyone to take their place and make sure their children continue to have a nice life, are comfortable, are held to their highest potential, and make the right decisions on a daily basis.

If you believe your child will need assistance managing his life, whether it's financially or practically or just in a specific area like vocation, you may want to consider contacting a disabilities attorney to help you arrange for these lifelong needs.

The Social Security Administration has some programs that provide benefits for individuals with disabilities who are unable to work and/or who have limited income and resources because of a disability. This has to be documented by professionals, and I have helped many receive these benefits. Even children who live at home can get regular payments that help with their care. The rules are complicated (as is the paperwork) and the assistance given depends on the child's age (under or over eighteen), employment—even part-time—and any assets that are in his name. So make sure you thoroughly understand your child's options in order to make the most educated long-term plan.

You can also set up health insurance and life insurance plans for your child, but these vary widely, so again, the best way to assure that everything is set up the way you desire is to seek help from a qualified attorney.

The Bad News

Regrettably, as we mentioned in the chapter about living arrangements, there is a lack of high-quality community housing and vocational programs for people with disabilities, and I have seen a number of "work training" programs that I consider to be demeaning and/or unsatisfying for adults on the spectrum. Further, with the growing number of kids diagnosed with autism who are reaching adulthood, we're seeing a growing crisis in this area. Both residential options and work opportunities are limited, and we desperately need more research and intervention in these areas.

Here are some concerns you need to be aware of as you're planning for the future:

- **Many residential care facilities have long wait lists**. Especially the most desired ones. Homes that have few people or even just one person with a disability are in demand. Start looking around *now*. There may be places close to your hometown that offer a nice environment for your child. And if you can't find anything, you may want to consider making plans to develop such a setting. We've had many families who worked with state agencies to set up a situation that they and their child felt good about. Preplanning is essential.

- **Unemployment rates for people with disabilities are high**. I talked about this in the chapter on jobs earlier in this section, but it's something you need to be aware of when considering your child's financial future. Try to get your child involved in some sort of regular job—even if it's a summer job—during adolescence. As it would for any child, it will teach him how to be responsible and follow a schedule, and you can even work with him to understand how to deal with finances when he gets a paycheck.

- **If not done properly, estate planning can actually hurt your child.** In some cases, money you leave for your child can result in government money being cut back, so be sure to have a disabilities attorney explain how to develop a will that allows your money to supplement, *not supplant,* your child's government-paid benefits. Again, you need a professional trained in estate planning for families with special-needs issues.

Fortunately, there are things you can do to make sure that your child will be well taken care of in every way, even after you're gone. Read on for some more general considerations.

Plan, Plan, Plan

Ask yourself if the life your adult child is living is a life *you* would like. I have visited many residential facilities over the years that I couldn't wait to get out of. Some have too many residents packed into dormlike halls with no pictures on the walls, horrible food, and staff who sit around chatting with one another instead of interacting with our kids. Other residential facilities are beautiful, provide lots of recreational opportunities, and have dedicated staff who are eager to work on improving the residents' communication, daily living skills, socializing, and so on—but these types of settings are rarer for one reason: they cost more.

When you plan for your child's future, think about every aspect of her life and what would make her happy, then put effort into setting it up that way. Don't forget about anything: exercise, diet, hygiene, clothing, her likes and dislikes, leisure activities, work, functional activities, compatible roommates, behavior programs, therapies, educational programs, medical care, and so on. And then spread the word so that you can get together with other families, community members, politicians, and whoever will listen to develop these types of settings. The mere fact that parents have to worry about what will happen to their children after they die means that we, as a society, are not doing our part. Parents have enough stress without having to worry about their child's quality of life after their deaths. We should all be working to make sure that every young adult on the spectrum can have not just an okay life but a *fabulous* life throughout her adult and more advanced years.

As I mentioned above, if you don't have a will, and you do have some assets, your child may inherit property that will end up being used to provide care that the government would otherwise provide. You need to consult an attorney to make sure your assets are a help, not a hindrance, to your child.

If you have definite ideas about the living conditions you would like your child to have in the future, make sure you have an attorney help you make them happen. Also, if you're worried about the high price of attorneys but want to donate your assets, many organizations have attorneys on staff or volunteer attorneys who will help you arrange the donation without having to hire your own attorney. I know one family who donated their home with the stipulation that their child, and three others with disabilities, could live there throughout her life. This arrangement provided a home setting, and the government paid for the staff to care for their child and her roommates.

In addition to physical living space, if your child will not be completely independent as an adult, you'll want to choose someone you totally trust to care for him. You may need to go to court to ask that that person be appointed guardian after you and your spouse die or can no longer care for your child. Placing the assets in a special-needs trust (SNT) (see legal section that follows) provides an added layer of protection. The guardian and the person who cares for your child can be different people, which may be better, depending on your child's individual needs and situation. You'll sleep a lot better once you've settled on someone for this responsibility. Most often it's a sibling, but it doesn't have to be if your child with autism doesn't have a sibling whom you trust to do this. I've seen people settle on a close family friend, a cousin, and even a caregiver who had taken care of the child in a way that the family felt was compatible with their values. People often leave assets to the guardian specifically to be used for the person with disabilities, so that money isn't taken out for expenses that the government would pay. However, if you do this, it's very important that you fully trust this person you've designated as the guardian.

Advocate for the Best Living Arrangement

As we mentioned in Chapter 3 in this section, there is a variety of possible living situations for your adult child, so make sure you've really looked around and made yourself familiar with what's available. Care facilities vary so much in regard to number of residents, supervision, amount of interaction between employees and residents, location, options for recreational activities, and so on. You want to find the best possible arrangement for your child while you're still around to make the decision.

It has been my experience that just as with educational programs, the best living conditions are when the parents have advocated for a specific arrangement for their child. We work with adults whose parents have provided them with the opportunity to live completely independently in their own homes, whether they're paid for by the family or by the state. Many states have regional centers or specialized offices that make these arrangements for individuals with disabilities who can't live alone. We work with adults whose families have created state-paid programs where their adult child lives in a beautiful community home, with a private bedroom, and with typical peers. They have daily fun activities, cook with their roommates, and some have part- or full-time jobs. In short, they've arranged for a great life for their children.

Again, a few families I know have given community homes to organizations to set up amazing residential facilities for their child *and* others. While you obviously need to have some resources to do this if it's in addition to the home you live in, some parents will donate their *own* home so that when they pass away, their child can continue to live there in a familiar place. This type of situation can ensure that your child continues to live in a nice family home she's familiar with.

Once you've decided on a care facility, you may want to ask your friends to help support this financially. (As I mentioned in the chapter on living arrangements, most facilities desperately need more funding.) One couple who was celebrating their fiftieth wedding anniversary asked that instead of gifts, donations be made to the facility where their child with autism resided. Most care facilities have a mechanism for accepting donations, and these donations may be used to improve the quality of care and to purchase items needed for the facility.

Don't let your child's future scare or stress you. Start planning what you would consider an ideal life for him. Some of the same things that were important in his younger years are still important—his program and goals need to be coordinated, he needs to have ongoing intervention, he needs to have leisure activities, he needs to have a consistent approach and consistent services (speech, psychological, physical exercise, communication program, and so on), and he needs to have well-trained staff who will follow through on a regular basis. Once all that is in place for now *and* for the future, you'll feel a lot better.

Tim's Legal Tips

None of us want to think about dying, and if your stress level is high just dealing with a child with disabilities, you may be putting off writing a will. But it's something you need to be thinking about, at any age. My friend and colleague Perry A. Zirkel, from Lehigh University, who specializes in educational law for children with disabilities, warned me that educators aren't lawyers, and don't always interpret the laws accurately. He referred us to Timothy E. Williams, an attorney in Tacoma, Washington, to help us understand the laws relating to estate planning. Mr. Williams has worked extensively and tirelessly helping families with disabilities and sits on a number of boards relating to individuals with disabilities. He is nationally recognized for his contributions and assistance with estate planning for parents of children with disabilities. He has generously answered our questions.

TIMOTHY E. WILLIAMS, ATTORNEY AT LAW

When should parents start thinking about a will?

Parents should be thinking about a will and general estate planning as soon they know they have a child with a disability. Many of us, especially when we are young and just starting a family, don't want to think about dying. Regrettably, some people do die young, and when they leave children without having made plans for them, many problems are created that could easily have been avoided.

Let's start with the distribution of your estate. Your estate is all of your "stuff" and, as they say, you can't take it with you. It's going to go someplace. If it is going to benefit your child with a disability, two questions come immediately to mind: Can my child manage these assets? And will the very fact that he'll have these assets affect benefits he might otherwise have received? If you have concerns about either of these things, you should be setting up a special-needs trust (SNT).

Keep in mind that wills, probate, and guardianship law is all state law, and the laws and rules can vary widely from state to state. The information here should be accurate in all states, but you really need to see a lawyer in your own state to be sure.

How important is it for a parent to write a will and are there any alternatives?

If you don't have a will, or if your will leaves a share of your assets outright to your child with a disability, your child will receive a share of your assets when you and your spouse die, regardless of his or her ability to manage it, and regardless of its effect on benefits. Depending on the extent of the disability, it is often possible to at least partially "fix" this lack of planning after the fact, but it is virtually always less expensive and more advantageous for your child if you do it before you die, rather than leaving it for someone else to do at what is usually a most stressful and certainly inconvenient time.

The primary vehicle for dealing with these issues is an SNT. An SNT can solve both of these concerns, and can be quite flexible as long as it satisfies some basic requirements. There are whole books written about SNTs so I won't go into them all now. However, here are some basics:

- An SNT can go into whatever you use for your estate planning, such as a will or a revocable living trust. This will become funded upon your death.

- You can also set up a separate SNT now, rather than putting it in your estate-planning document. You would generally do this if the trust is going to be funded before your death. For example, if you anticipate that someone other than you or your spouse (such as a grandparent) is going to leave an asset to your child.

- You can select the trustee, including successor trustees.

- You can decide who will receive what is left in the trust after the child dies.

Is there a way a parent can make sure her child isn't financially abused and that the money left to the child is used for supplemental services to make his life better?

Properly drafted, the SNT will take care of any concerns about management of the funds, protect her from financial abuse by others, and will shelter the asset from being considered an "available asset" should your child receive benefits from the state, such as Medicaid or Supplemental Security Income (SSI).

This kind of SNT is known as a third-party SNT because it uses assets that come from someplace other than the person with the disability. There is another kind of SNT we use if the person with the disability already has or is about to receive an asset and you have concerns regarding either management or eligibility for benefits. The asset might be from a personal injury award or settlement, or from an inheritance that went directly to the person with the disability, or from some other source. This is known as a first-party trust, and is sometimes referred to as a D4A trust because of the federal statute specifically authorizing such trusts, 42 USC 1396p(d)(4)(A).

This kind of SNT has less flexibility than a third-party trust, but can still be an effective way to maintain state benefits and to address management issues. This kind of trust cannot be in a will, but is set up at the time of, or in anticipation of, receiving the asset.

Rather than setting up the trust yourself, in your will or otherwise, in many states there are pooled trusts available, usually managed by nonprofits such as the ARC or another agency interested in those with disabilities. This can be either a first- or a third-party trust, and is especially helpful if the amounts to be placed in the trust are relatively small.

What money can parents leave their children that won't supplant SSI or other sources?

A properly executed *and* managed SNT will have no effect on SSI, Medicaid (MediCal), or other needs-based benefits.

What about leaving property (homes, jewelry, and so on)?

Anything can be left to a trust.

What should a parent know about an adult child's guardian?

First of all, while your child is a minor, no guardianship is necessary—you are already the legal guardian for your children. You can name the person you want as guardian for your minor children in your will in the event you and your spouse both die while your children are minors.

Guardianships for adult children are a completely different matter. In most states, you cannot designate a guardian for an adult child; a guardian is appointed by the court, usually following a court proceeding. The guardian is not automatically the parent or someone designated by the parent. (In some states a guardian is also referred to as a conservatorship.)

Legally, your child is a fully autonomous adult when he or she turns eighteen. Of course, disabled or not, not everyone is ready to be a fully functioning adult at eighteen! As a basic protection of their rights, those rights cannot be removed without going through some formal legal process. None of us would be comfortable if it were easy to remove our individual rights as adults.

Whether your child has a guardian is always a legal decision requiring court action. It is not a medical decision, and it is not a parental decision. While you as parent will have a significant say in the process, it is the court, not you, who will make the final decision. This is understandably difficult for many parents. If you wish to be the guardian, you will most likely be appointed as the guardian. And the appointed guardian is usually designated with the authority to select a backup guardian if something should happen to her or him. But in most states, selecting a backup guardian is not done through a will, and courts will always retain jurisdiction over the guardianship.

So who gets a guardianship? Many individuals with significant disabilities live their whole lives without a guardian. Others may need the protection provided by a guardianship at eighteen, and will be harmed by delay. Still others may appropriately defer a guardianship for many years, but will ultimately need one. While it may seem counterintuitive, it is often the case that the more severely disabled are less in need of guardianship!

The question to ask is "How vulnerable to abuse is my child?" If she is never out of my care or control, has no money, and needs constant supervision, a guardian may not be necessary because there is little opportunity or motive for abuse. On the other hand, if my child goes places on her own or with friends, is easily influenced, and I have concerns about her judgment, she may be much more vulnerable, despite being much less disabled, and much more in need of a guardianship.

The primary purpose of a guardianship is to protect an otherwise vulnerable adult. It always takes away some of the rights of the person with the disability, and shifts that decision-making power to a guardian or conservator.

One question often *not* asked by the attorneys or courts involved is "How will the loss of autonomy affect the person with the disability?" You need to be asking yourself that question. While some individuals lack the understanding to even be concerned, I have had clients who are truly devastated by the loss of their rights. Sometimes it is hard to predict what effect it will have on your child, but it is important to think about. There is a strong natural tendency to overprotect our most vulnerable children. Recognizing that natural tendency while making the decision about whether to seek a guardianship will help you make a better decision.

The process of guardianship varies widely from state to state, so I cannot definitively talk about procedure. Most states do require some sort of ongoing reporting to the court, often annually. This can be both time-consuming and costly, and you should discuss those issues fully with your attorney.

The most common interactions that lead to questions about guardianship are with schools and health-care professionals. Many appropriately allow you access to information and to participate in decision making for your adult child. Federal education law (IDEA) and health law (HIPAA) specifically authorize a parent to do this. However, some practitioners (and regrettably their attorneys) are misinformed about this area of the law, and will make it difficult to proceed without a guardianship.

Some have argued that providing information to the parents of an adult person is a violation of the privacy and autonomy of the disabled adult. Quite the contrary, this allows the disabled person to avoid a guardianship, and maintain legal autonomy, while ensuring they continue to receive a free appropriate public education (FAPE) and appropriate medical care through the advocacy of their parents.

You should strongly consider a guardianship if your child has or is likely to have contact with the justice system, either as a victim or an alleged perpetrator.

There are alternatives to guardianship. If your child is relatively articulate and understands what it means to designate an agent, having him sign a power of attorney may be helpful and appropriate. While this will not protect him, it will allow you greater ability to advocate for him and to help to manage his assets.

In addition, all states have a process for surrogate decision making, either by common law or by statute. So if your child cannot make an informed medical decision, there is a hierarchy of persons designated to make that decision on her behalf. In most jurisdictions it falls first to a spouse, then adult children, then parents, then siblings. Since our disabled children often do not have spouses or adult children, parents often make medical decisions with full authority, but without legal guardianship.

Guardianships should not be done lightly. While it may be appropriate occasionally to do so solely for the comfort of the parent, as a general rule you should consider a guardianship only if there is truly some need for the guardianship, such as some risk of abuse to the child. Many parents have expressed to me their concern that if they don't become guardian, the state will step in and begin making the decisions. My experience is that the state does not want to do that, and only steps in if there is a real problem. When that happens, even being the legal guardian will not insulate the parent from state action.

What questions should a parent ask a lawyer about special needs in estate planning?

You want to find an attorney who is knowledgeable and comfortable around persons with disabilities. Ask about their experience with those with autism. Ask about their experience with SNTs.

What sources of state/federal funds are available for children with special needs?

The primary source of income for the disabled is Supplemental Security Income or SSI. It has the same qualifications as Medicaid, and requires that your child be incapable of meaningful work. (I know it is much more complex than that and does allow for some work, but essentially this is what it comes down to.) These programs are funded mostly by the federal government, but are administered and supplemented by the states. The states vary widely both in the amounts provided and in the details.

SSI and Medicaid programs require that persons with disabilities have income below a certain level, and that they have just a small amount in assets (usually a few thousand dollars). Certain items are exempt from these limits, including a home, a car, and most personal property.

SSI is meant to be enough to live on. When your child turns eighteen, he may be eligible for SSI. Some may be eligible prior to age eighteen if the family is of limited means.

Because SSI is meant to cover all living expenses, if your child is living at home, you should be charging room and board. You should discuss how much with your attorney, because the regulations vary. If the child is not living at home, and SSI assistance is not enough, Medicaid picks up the difference.

If either parent is disabled, retired, or deceased, your child with a disability may be eligible for disability benefits based on the parents' account. This is known as SSD, and knowing the benefit source for your child is important. The amount from SSD may be greater, sometimes much greater, than SSI. And it does not require that you have limited assets! Keep in mind that if your child also needs Medicaid, the asset and income limits will still apply.

Can you give any tips about finding a lawyer who specializes in this area?

Because guardianship law is also focused toward the elderly, the members of the National Academy of Elder Law Attorneys (NAELA) is a good place to start. You can also ask your local advocacy organization for a referral. Of course other parents are often an excellent source.

Frequently Asked Questions

There's no question that my son will be his sister's guardian after we're gone. There are only the two of them and he's always been very loving toward her. But I don't want that responsibility to be too onerous. How can I arrange things so he can manage and oversee her future needs without allowing those responsibilities to interfere with his life on a daily basis?

It's wonderful that you have someone in your family who is willing and able to care for your child. You should be able to set up the daily arrangements and just have your son oversee the program. If you have any savings, you might want to consider financially compensating your son for doing this, because it will take some time and effort on his part. Also, some states will provide payment for individuals who provide caretaking in their own homes. Talk with your son to determine just how much time he's able to provide, and work around his schedule and within his capability. Remember, the more you arrange ahead of time, the less he'll have to do when you're not around to manage things anymore.

My grown son is on the spectrum and has had occasional violent outbursts that have made group living arrangements difficult. We don't own our house and can't afford to buy one. He lives with us now, but we're getting old and it worries me. Who will take on an adult with violence issues? I don't want him to end up somewhere scary and horrible.

You'll need to address this right away. It should be your top priority. If your child has had disruptive behavior for a long time, it will likely take a long time to eliminate. One of the areas that's challenging is when there are low-frequency/high-intensity disruptive behaviors. This is difficult because they're not predictable. I work with a few young adults who have major tantrums a few times a month, and because they're adults, the police end up being called in if it happens out in the community. For these individuals, I've found that it's helpful to use self-management, but with the goal of accomplishing so many days in a *row* without disruptive behavior. We've started with two days, then three, then four, and so on until the individual can go for a week at a time without disruptive behavior. And don't forget to analyze the cause of the behavior and continue teaching the replacement behaviors.

We have some money to leave to our kids but I'm worried now that if I leave equal amounts, my daughter (who's on the spectrum) will lose all of her share to costs that the state would pay for anyway. But I don't want to leave her penniless while her siblings (who can support themselves anyway) have so much. How do I make sure she has money if she's in desperate need without jeopardizing state funding?

This is a concern and will require some planning with a disabilities attorney. Again, there are ways to leave money to your child to enhance the services she will receive as an adult, but careful planning is necessary. And remember to be fair. Have a heart-to-heart talk with all of your children to determine who is willing, able, and motivated to tend to all the important aspects of your adult child's life.

Improving Daily Life

1. Introduction

So much is going right for us that I feel guilty complaining at all. We've got all the big stuff under control—my son is doing well at school, he has a few friends, he even has a weekend job—but there's still something about him that's not like the other kids. Some of it is how he looks, some of it is how he behaves. I'm worried that it will affect how people view him as he moves out into the world. I don't want to change him in any fundamental way—I'd just like to "fine-tune" him a little. How can I help him get control over his appearance and his behavior?

CLAIRE

Years ago, we wanted to go on a little boat tour while we were in Hawaii. The family boat was full, so they put us on a "sunset cruise," which turned out to be code for "drinking party." My kids were the only people under the age of eighteen on that boat. It could have been disastrous but it was actually incredibly fun—everyone was nice and a school of dolphins cavorted right under the see-through deck in front.

As the only young ones on the boat, our kids got a fair amount of attention. Andrew was probably about eight at that point. He was clinging to me nervously a bit on the boat, but overall doing fine. A lovely older couple kept smiling at us, and in the way that these things happen, pretty soon the wife and I were chatting away. She mentioned that they had a grown son with special needs. I saw that as an opening to tell her that Andrew had autism. "Yes, dear," said the sweet older woman. "We've already figured that out."

I still remember feeling slightly taken aback that strangers, who had barely interacted with my family, could see it so quickly, especially because Andrew seemed worlds away from where he'd been just a couple of years earlier. Now that I think about it, I'm sure it had to do with the depth of their own experience. Those of us with kids who are on the spectrum can spot children with similar behaviors from a mile away. I didn't particularly mind that they knew—I've always been proud of who Andrew is and to me there's no stigma in the diagnosis, just some delays and challenges that need to be overcome—but it did make me realize that he was noticeably different from other kids, even to a casual stranger's eye.

As Andrew has grown older and has expressed the desire to fit in more easily, I've been wondering what it is exactly that identifies a kid as having special needs and how to help him overcome it.

The easiest area to address is the superficial one: appearance. Inattention to hair, clothing, and grooming can all suggest a kid who's not as socially tuned in as others. But behavioral issues are trickier. Although older kids and young adults on the spectrum are less likely to have tantrums or to self-stimulate in public than small children, they may have other behavioral quirks that people notice (like talking about the same subject ad nauseam). We parents work and work on stuff like that, reminding our kids to stay aware of their conversational and social obligations.

It's good to be different when it's a choice you make out of strength. And so much of who Andrew is is better than other kids—he's kinder, more responsible, more obliging, more polite—and I don't want to change any of that. But when he's upset because other kids at school call him "weird," I'll do whatever I can to help him fit in.

DR. KOEGEL

Sometimes it's the little things that make or break a job interview, first date, or new friendship. I was reviewing a paper for a journal recently, and the author had written a full thirty-five pages on all the social difficulties of kids on the spectrum—without any suggestions about how to help them. That one was an easy rejection. We all know that some kids on the spectrum may have lingering social problems. That isn't a surprise. But while there is an abundance of literature on ways to help them succeed academically, how to teach them to communicate, and how to modify behavior, far less is written on how to help them socially. In the grand scheme of things, it's a relatively new area, and even though there are some fantastic researchers out there working to improve socialization in our kids, there isn't as much attention paid to this area. Not just with kids on the spectrum, but with all kids.

We do know, unequivocally, that including kids on the spectrum with typical kids greatly improves their peer interactions, but there are still far too many programs that exclude these youngsters. And I've been to many schools that are great about including kids on the spectrum in regular education classrooms but, unfortunately, they still let them roam the school yard alone at breaks.

Fortunately, we are aware of some strategies to help make your child's daily life easier, more enjoyable, more manageable, while at the same time helping him or her become more sociable. And if you keep working on these areas, there will be a higher likelihood that your child won't develop other issues, like depression, which we often see in adults who don't have a rich social and leisure life.

2. Walking Out the Door Looking Good

My daughter is on the spectrum and at an age when other girls are spending tons of time thinking about what they wear and how they look. I'm not a particularly girly-girl woman, and always thought I'd discourage any daughter of mine from spending

too much thought and money on superficial things. Now I find myself wishing my daughter would pay more attention to keeping her hair clean and her clothing attractive. She doesn't seem to care or notice that she looks unkempt. How do I get her to care?

CLAIRE

Today was the first day of summer and so I planned a shopping expedition with the kids to get the various items we still needed for trips and camps and stuff like that. My three youngest were all excitedly listing the things they were hoping to find and purchase, but when I asked Andrew if there was anything he needed, he shrugged and said, "Nope, I'm fine."

I wouldn't say it was an inaccurate statement, but it was a debatable one. He has enough clothes to get him through the week, and they're not ragged or anything, but he does wear the same few pairs of pants and handful of T-shirts over and over again—and his dad and I picked out almost all of them for him in the first place. He's always let me choose his wardrobe, which is great in a way—I can pick up a pair of pants when I'm out shopping and not worry about whether or not he'll approve of them—but his younger brother has shown us that teenage boys usually demand a say over what they wear in public.

Still, this stuff is easier with a boy, I suspect, than it would be with a girl. Even though we know some sharp-dressing budding metrosexuals, teenage boys in general are a fairly motley crew, and as long as I'm buying clothes that fit, at stores that have reasonably up-to-date styles, Andrew doesn't stand out in any way. But given the way the high school girls make me aware of what a slob I am, as I slouch around in my old jeans and T-shirts, I have to assume it would be much tougher for a girl who wears any old thing to fit in at this age.

As the parent of a kid on the spectrum, I'm always having to *rethink my natural instincts (in this case, being the kind of mom who says, "You don't need to look like the other kids and it's too expensive to keep chasing after each new fashion") and play a different, slightly uncomfortable role ("You know, I've noticed a lot of the other boys are wearing skinny jeans—you want a pair of those?"). The traditional teenage battle when the kid pushes for more stuff that the other kids have, and the parent says no, gets turned topsy-turvy when your kid has autism. There's a wonderful antimaterialistic side to it all—until you show up at a school event and your kid is the only middle schooler wearing Velcro sneakers.*

The odds that you're going to make your kid on the spectrum really invested in clothing or appearance are slender, but that doesn't mean you can't help make him look better. It just—like everything—requires a little extra effort on your part.

DR. KOEGEL

My sister and her husband recently returned from China, where they adopted a beautiful three-and-a-half-year-old girl. Our oldest daughter was fortunate enough to have her finals fall on the right days, so she was able to accompany them on their exciting trip. One of the things she commented on when she returned was the common "squatty potties" they have in China. Instead of sitting, you squat and relieve yourself into a toilet that has a hole at ground level. Some people argue that squat toilets are, in some ways, more hygienic than seated toilets, and others argue that they aren't. My point is that while most cultures understand the importance of good hygiene in decreasing germs and disease, practices vary considerably from culture to culture, home to home, and person to person. Some parents insist on covering the seats each time their child is placed on a toilet, others just wash their child's hands at the end. While I gave my own kids daily baths, I had friends who bathed their children much less frequently. One girlfriend of mine, who was a medical doctor, gave her kids weekly baths. The other days she just washed them off with a sponge. I have a friend who takes at least two showers a day, and sometimes three. I work with students who never put on a bit of makeup and others who look as if they're walking advertisements for Maybelline cosmetics.

And yet, despite all the variation from person to person, there are some basic conventions, and I've noticed that many kids on the spectrum consistently pay a lot less attention to hygiene than their typical peers. They'll often wear the same clothes day after day, shave less frequently than others, bathe less frequently than others, eschew makeup, not bother combing or brushing their hair, and so on. Many college students and young adults on the spectrum tell me that they just like wearing certain comfortable clothes. Whether it's a hygiene issue or comfort issue, many people won't go on a third date with someone who wore the same green T-shirt on the last date. This area may need some work if your child's hygiene habits are not up to par.

An easy way to stick out like a sore thumb, without even having to say anything, is by looking different from the other kids. Children with social delays often aren't as motivated to be stylish or are even aware that what they're wearing isn't what the other kids are wearing. In fact, when a local residential facility for kids with disabilities took the residents for community outings, they were unmistakable with their mismatched socks, odd clothing, no makeup, ruffled hair—you get the picture.

Never forget that your child's appearance is the first thing people notice. Clothing is one aspect of that, but you also need to pay attention to haircuts and issues of personal hygiene.

Although it seems a bit shallow even to be writing about this, the truth is that our society has created a climate in which looks, hair, clothes, shoes, jewelry, and makeup are important. Just wait in any supermarket line and you'll see dozens of magazines shouting for your attention and promising to tell you how to get the latest look. For many teenagers, the images on TV, movies, and the newsstand send out a siren call they find irresistible—for better or for worse. Most children plead with their parents for the latest trendy fashion and there's some justification for their desire to look "right": there is plenty of research showing that children who are good-looking get more favorable attention.

Dressing Right

You don't necessarily have to pick out a whole new wardrobe for your child every other month, but you should ensure that your child isn't isolating herself with clothing that's out of date or too young.

Look at what the other kids are wearing. It may well be wildly different from what we'd like them to wear, but your kid needs to fit in, so be open to new styles and fashions (obviously, you don't need to clothe your child in something you find genuinely objectionable—there are always choices, even in fashion). You can recruit a stylish peer, sibling, cousin, or babysitter to help shop.

Here are some clothing-related problems I have seen with individuals on the spectrum.

One junior high student we worked with was always impeccably dressed in polo shirts, socks that matched his polo, and Top-Siders. Unfortunately, at his school, the other kids usually wore skateboarding T-shirts, white sport socks, and sneakers. He looked more like a member of an exclusive club than a student.

Another student we worked with had a rather beat-up old car, the kind of "first car" most of us started off with. The upholstery on her car was falling apart and she came in every day with little pieces of foam all over her clothes. While this could happen to any of us (or to our kids who usually inherit the almost-dead family car), she never quite seemed to realize that foam was becoming a regular part of her daily attire. Even when she took her clothes off at night, she didn't notice the foam—or just chose to ignore it—until we intervened with some self-management.

At our clinic, we also worked with one girl with Asperger's syndrome who wore leggings all the time, at an age and time when none of the other girls were wearing them. Her mother loved to shop and was always buying her new leggings with matching tops—she had no idea they weren't in style. When we pointed out to Mom that none of the other girls were still wearing leggings, she decided to take another child shopping with her daughter. This girlfriend helped them pick out clothing that was stylish, and the next week her daughter was wearing a pair of jeans and fit right in.

Finally, we worked with one adult with Asperger's syndrome who wore a pair of black sweats with a white T-shirt every day. While he pointed out that he had several of the outfits—exactly the same, so he wasn't wearing dirty clothes—nevertheless he always looked the same, and the truth is, it doesn't matter if you have a dozen pairs of the same pants, no one else who sees you knows that.

So again, encourage your child to look at his peers, check over himself in the mirror, and vary his wardrobe. This will help him to fit in and make a good impression.

Some Solutions:

- **Shop with a friend.** Sometimes kids on the spectrum just don't know what's in style. And while it's a lovely character trait not to be overly concerned with clothes, if the kids look as if they came out of a time warp, people will get a bad first impression. So we've found it helpful to have kids on the spectrum shop with someone their own age.

  If your child doesn't have many friends, perhaps *you* can bring along a friend or relative who has a child your kid's age. Or find a younger, hipper cousin or neighbor who likes going to the local mall. Or you can call your local school and recruit a student who's into fashion design. Then just give them some spending money and let them loose at the mall. And remember, don't be judgmental. If they come home from the mall with a slightly different style than you're used to, remember that this isn't about *your* taste, it's about what kids are wearing, so as long as it isn't going to get your child sent home from school, be open to the change.

- **Look at magazines.** Many kids on the spectrum aren't all that interested in fashion magazines, but they actually provide a great visual aid for improving fashion skills. Areas we've worked on using the magazines include how to match colors, how to pick out popular styles, which clothes work together and which don't (such as not wearing a winter scarf with shorts), and so on.

- **Look at your child's peers.** If you aren't sure that your child is picking out age-appropriate clothes, notice what his peers are wearing. There are always some particular brands and styles that all the kids wear.

- **Look online.** It's easy to punch in "fashion" and "style" and come up with the latest shows in Paris and news stories of the latest trends. Browsing these will give you and your child great ideas from the latest fashion trends.

- **Watch TV and movies.** TV shows and movies often have stylish clothes. When your child is watching, point out what types of clothes the actors are wearing. If your child idolizes an actor—who knows?—he may want to dress like him.

- **Go to a fashion mall or restaurant.** Go people watching. Look at what everyone's wearing and discuss the outfits you see. This may help your child in more than one way. Many kids on the spectrum don't really pay attention to what's happening around them and therefore don't imitate what others are doing. Having your child spend some time being aware of others may help with what she's wearing—and also with what she's doing.

- **Go through the closet.** Do the spring cleaning. Talk with your child about which styles are in and which are out. Talk about what goes together and how to match colors. And then have him figure out what matches on his own. It may be fun and will certainly help the tidiness of your house or apartment.

- **Sort through your child's wardrobe regularly.** Kids will often continue to put on the tried-and-true clothes that show up on top of the pile after the laundry's done each week, even if the clothes have become too tight, too unstylish, too babyish, or too torn and stained to look good anymore. I know one mom who noticed that certain items didn't fit when her son wore them and tried to point it out to him, but he insisted they were fine. So she simply made them "disappear" the next time she did the laundry. At the same time, she put some other items—newer, more stylish ones—at the top of the drawer piles and he was soon wearing those just as regularly.

- **Mount a daily checklist to make sure everything matches and is put on properly.** See the section on hygiene in this chapter for more on this.

Hair

In most ways, hair styling is comparable to the issues of clothing and you should be able to use some of the solutions we've just outlined. Just as you don't want your child to be wearing clothes that are out of date or dirty or unkempt, you don't want to send your teenager out in the world with a haircut that is clearly a mess or so inappropriate for her age that it's going to raise eyebrows.

For example, one middle school boy we worked with always wore his hair in an unstylish bowl cut. When our clinician trimmed it a bit and taught him how to gel up his hair he looked adorable—and much more like other boys his age. It was an easy fix, but it made a world of difference in how the other kids viewed him.

Hair is of course an easier thing to deal with than clothing, because you can give your child a simple, classic cut on a regular basis and be done with it. At any age, a girl can go out with clean, brushed long hair or a ponytail and look fine. (For help with the "clean" part, see the hygiene section on page 317.) And as long as you can drag your son to the barbershop once every couple of months, you can probably keep him looking fairly decent. Plenty of teenage boys do have overgrown, slightly wild hair these days, so even that's OK. What's not OK is the babyish cut, as the boy had in the example we gave above, or noticeably greasy, flaky hair.

If your child hates having his hair cut, you may want to consider a desensitization program, which we describe how to implement in Section I, Chapter 2.

Makeup

Girls in middle and high school wear a lot of makeup these days—more even than college students or young adults. There are always exceptions, of course—it's hardly a requirement—but you may want to talk to your daughter about wearing a little for special occasions, like school parties or commencement. We worked with a college student who never wore makeup and didn't seem to care about it at all. Years later she visited to say hello and had a dozen or so long and unattractive whiskers on her chin and still no makeup. Another high schooler we worked with never wore makeup. One day before a school performance her mom spent hours helping her apply makeup, but when she got to school she immediately ran to the bathroom and washed it all off. When her mother got to school she was horrified to find that her daughter now looked like a raccoon, with dark mascara smeared all around her eyes.

Again, teaching your child to use a little strategically applied makeup can help her fit in and look like her peers.

Putting this into action might be another opportunity for a fun outing or get-together with a peer: invite a potential or current girlfriend to go with you and your daughter to a department store to play makeover at the cosmetics counter. Or you could have the friend come over to your house, where you've set up an appointment with one of those women who sell cosmetic products directly to the customer. You can turn either event into a game of makeover and, afterward, buy both your daughter and her friend little gifts of cosmetics—your daughter will then have something you can urge her to use for special occasions. She'll have a chance to make a connection with a peer and be more prepared for those special events.

Hygiene

We once worked with a college student who refused to shave or wash his hair. Although he was very nice looking, his grubbiness really turned off the college girls. It took us a while to get him to understand how others might view him, but as he became better at socializing (we worked with him using many of the interventions described in Section II), he came to realize the impression his poor hygiene was making on others and began to change his habits.

Unfortunately, this isn't an uncommon problem for teens and young adults on the spectrum. Their social delays, general absence of self-consciousness, and maybe just a lack of interest lead to a real obliviousness when it comes to the area of hygiene. While they're still young enough for their parents to dictate and watch over their daily regimens, there's no problem, but once those same kids are getting up and ready for school by themselves, or eventually, getting ready to go to work, that obliviousness can cause real social problems. No one wants to work in the cubicle next to someone who forgot to use deodorant, and any potential romantic interest will be turned off by someone who shows up for a date ungroomed and poorly dressed.

Fortunately, it doesn't take a lot of effort to turn things around in this area. Here are some suggestions:

Checklists
Checklists have been a great help for our older kids and adults who have been neglecting their daily hygiene. With checklists, you can target the individual problems. If your child just forgets to wash her hair, but is pretty responsible about other hygiene areas like brushing her teeth and washing her face, you can target just that area by

making sure she checks off "wash hair" every morning (or evening, depending upon the routine you want to establish).

If your child is more forgetful and often doesn't even remember to change clothes on a daily basis, let alone follow through on each morning's many grooming steps, you can create a much more extensive checklist. For example, you could make the following list and have your son check off each item on a daily basis before going out the door:

o Shower
o Shave
o Put on a new shirt
o Put on different, clean pants
o Make sure your socks are clean and match
o Take one last look in the mirror to make sure there's nothing on your face and your clothing looks clean

Depending on your child's level of self-reliance, age, and living conditions, you could either check the list for completion before he leaves in the morning or have him self-manage by checking it himself. If you are checking it on a daily basis, try to fade that support by checking only every other day after a while and then every third day, and so on, until he's completely self-managing. If it helps the self-management, he could give himself a reward after a certain number of days of remembering to do everything before leaving.

We find it helpful to keep these lists somewhere near where the habits should take place, like a bathroom mirror or on the inside of the front door so our clients can check it on their way out.

We worked with one girl who wore her pants so high that her classmates made fun of her. We wrote out a checklist that reminded her to look in the mirror and orient her pants correctly. We also included other tasks she was likely to forget, like looking in the mirror after breakfast to make sure she didn't have any remaining food on her face (more than one time she went to school with egg on her face, and I mean that literally). This successfully helped her to pay attention to small neglected hygiene areas on a daily basis. As you can see, using the checklist allowed us to individualize the program to her specific areas of forgetfulness. While you will probably need to help create the initial list, your goal is to have your child ultimately keep track of the things she needs to do before leaving the house, all by herself.

ANDREW

I actually worry a lot about the way I look. I worry about the way I look because I feel that if I look bad, people would make fun of me and not want to hang out with me much. When putting on my clothing, I do not really care about what I wear each day and just choose what I will wear randomly. When I am searching for clothing, I am normally with my parents. I like to search for clothing that other kids my age would wear every day, like ones with skateboard or surfing logos or ones that represent movies I like. I also care about if it fits, because I really feel uncomfortable in small clothing (especially tight pants), but I also do not want my shirt to look like a dress if it's too big. I really care about looking good every day and want people to like what I am wearing, unless it is just ripped pants.

I also care about how my hair looks every day. I have curly hair and comb it after I shower because I do not want it to look like an Afro (a Jewfro as a nickname). Whenever I am getting a haircut, I really care about how it looks. I do not like to get haircuts that people would think are too dorky. Whenever I want a haircut, I like to search for barbershops where workers are nice and let me decide what kind of haircut I want without bossing me around about how it should look. I also absolutely hate it whenever my parents like to jump in and help me decide what haircut I should

get, because I want it to be only my decision. Whenever I have to decide what haircut I should get, I always like to look at other people from my school or from Internet pictures to see what kinds of cool haircuts other people have. I tend to like to get haircuts that are slightly long, but that change the way my hair looks (such as a surfer hairdo, or like some guy from a rock band, and so forth). I also like to look at other people's shirts and admire them and think that I might want to have them.

I am the kind of guy who really wants to look good every day and have good hygiene. I really do not want to get germs from other people and want to stay healthy. I feel that I cannot go about my day unless I shower and shave at least once every day and wash my hands at least ten or fifteen times a day. I almost never wear dirty clothing and hate wearing it, but whenever I do not have enough clean clothes, I have to wear dirty clothing out of my hamper. Not to be rude or anything, but I absolutely do not like to be around other people who smell bad and who do not take showers every day. It really doesn't bother me when I see that people's clothing is a bit dirty, but it is much worse when they smell bad. Nobody really judges me on the way that I look, but I am still really obsessive about it. I feel insecure whenever I do not shower and then go to school, so then I shower when I get home later.

Frequently Asked Questions

My daughter is going on a class trip and I'm really worried about her maintaining the right level of hygiene—I'm convinced I'm going to see all her packed clothing come back untouched because she just wore the same dirty clothes over and over again. It's what she'd do if I weren't at home to make her stop every morning and go through her checklist. Do you think I could ask a roommate to remind her or would that be stigmatizing?

If your child would respond to a checklist, that would probably be the least intrusive way to help in this situation. If you don't think she'll follow the checklist, you may want to have a counselor help out. And if she has friends who really care about her, and won't make fun of her, asking them is also a good option—but only if both those conditions are true. One last thought: one parent I knew packed an outfit in separate baggies labeled for each day, and this ensured that her son changed his clothes and matched each day of his field trip.

My son screams when I try to run a comb through his hair. He claims it really hurts. Do you think it's possible his scalp is really that sensitive? I keep having to send him to school with it looking like a bird made a nest in there. I'm tempted to buzz it, but I'm worried that it will just make him stand out more. Any other solutions?

It may really hurt. If it is a bird's nest, it is likely that it does really hurt when you comb it. Choices always work better than force. Don't ask your son *if* he wants his hair combed—combing has to get done—but do ask him if he wants to comb his hair *himself* or if he wants you to comb it (spray on a little detangler first!). If you can teach him to comb it himself, he'll be able to stop when it starts hurting—and it's also a good lesson in creating independence.

My daughter showers fairly regularly, but I'm not convinced she's doing a good job: she often has dried shampoo flakes in her hair, soap scum in her ears, and her face never looks any cleaner when she comes out. I can't exactly climb into the shower with her—she would never let me. Any advice for getting the shower to do what it's supposed to?

It may be easier to target one thing at a time and apply some rules to help her remember. You can suggest a certain number to count to while she's rinsing, or teach her how to feel her hair so that she can learn how it feels when the soap is washed out. Targeting one step at time may make it easier for both of you and lead to more rewards for a job accomplished successfully than if you try to work on everything at once.

3. Managing Behavior

My daughter has always fallen apart when frustrated—sometimes she gets weepy, sometimes furious. When she was little, we tried to ignore it, but now that she's older, it's almost impossible to ignore: she's five foot seven and weighs 140 pounds! Just yesterday, she was having trouble finishing her math homework and threw the book across the room and broke something. The worst is that her teachers have said she gets upset at school when the work is too hard for her and the kids are all noticing her meltdowns. How can I teach her to control herself in public, if not in private?

CLAIRE

I knew a babysitter once who worked with a little girl who was on the spectrum and who would fall apart, screaming and flailing, whenever she wasn't allowed to do whatever she wanted (like linger forever at a favorite spot). There was no behavioral program in place at home to help her learn to control these behaviors, and the babysitter had no training in working with kids on the spectrum. For a few years, she struggled to keep the girl safe by restraining her physically when necessary, but as time passed, her charge grew bigger and bigger until she was bigger than her babysitter. At that point, the babysitter simply wasn't

*strong enough to restrain her anymore and was so wracked with
anxiety that the girl might hurt herself, the babysitter, a member of her family—or an innocent bystander—that she found
another job. It grieved her to abandon someone she cared about,
but without the proper interventions being put in place by the
family, she just didn't have the resources to solve the problem all
by herself.*

*If kids aren't taught to control their own behavior when
they're young, they'll still be out of control when they're older.
And how do you deal with a 170-pound adult who's physically
aggressive? The consequences are likely to be truly tragic.*

DR. KOEGEL

Big kids have the same issues as little kids. If they want something—or
want to get out of something—they're probably going to find a way to
let you know. If throwing a tantrum or being aggressive works—and
it usually does with big kids—they'll keep on doing it. I've had a
number of adolescents and adults throw huge tantrums and aggress.
And when they're big, their physical aggression can really do
damage.

We had one young adult, who was almost six feet tall, run down
the middle of a busy street because his interventionist wouldn't let
him buy something he wanted at the store. Another man threw such
a fit in a store because he couldn't buy candy that the owner called
the police, who handcuffed him and hauled him off.

Clearly it's important to get control of these behaviors. If you're
dealing with out-of-control behaviors, you're going to have to do a
functional analysis and figure out the *function* of the problem behavior, then teach a *replacement* behavior.

For example, if your older or adult child is throwing fits because he
isn't getting something immediately, you will have to teach him to
tolerate a delay. Right before you give him something, say "Just a minute" or "Hold on for a second" and wait that moment before giving it

to him. Start with a very small increment of time and then work up so he learns that if he doesn't get something immediately, he will get it eventually.

If your adult child is noncompliant a lot of the time and rarely follows directions, you may want to start with rewarding her for following *any* directions—even those that lead to a desired goal for her. For example, we worked with an adolescent boy who broke items in his home and aggressed toward his mother every time she asked him to do something he didn't want to do. So we had her ask him to do desired things, such as turn on the TV or put the dessert on the table, and then say "Thank you for listening." Eventually, he got used to her giving him instructions, and he didn't associate them with anything negative. It also empowered *her* to feel that he really could comply with some of her instructions. At that point, we started interspersing, very gradually, instructions that were about less desired activities.

There are many other ways to work with problem behaviors, and if your adolescent or adult is engaging in them, please seek assistance from a qualified and skillful person. Aggression that has been going on a long time usually takes a long time to get rid of. But you need to get rid of it. It can seriously keep your child from enjoying many community activities and can stand in the way of his social and worldly success if it isn't curtailed.

Other behaviors may arise with this age group that weren't as much of an issue when your child was little. Read on.

Distinguishing Between Public and Private Behaviors

People don't freak out if a little kid takes his pants off in public or takes a leak because he couldn't wait or sticks his hand down his pants—they may not approve, but they're not going to call the cops either. The parents can simply tell the child to stop and then explain that it's not okay and he mustn't do it in the future. I remember once when I was driving on the freeway, cars started honking and people were pointing at us. I looked in my rearview mirror and saw that my toddler had climbed out of her car seat, completely taken off her clothes, and was peacefully sunbathing on the back window ledge of the car. We still get a chuckle out of that story, but just think about what would happen if an adult did that—someone who didn't fully understand it wasn't appropriate.

Adults and adolescents on the spectrum may have trouble understanding which behaviors may only be done in private and which ones are OK in public. If your child is doing things in public that are unacceptable, you need to step in immediately and make it clear he can't do such things there. If your child is too shy to ask for a restroom and is urinating in public, take the time to teach him how to ask someone where the restroom is and make sure he knows he needs to ask that question before the need grows too dire. Or put him on a schedule so he uses the restroom regularly, before he gets to the point of having to go in public.

Masturbation is another private behavior that needs to be curbed in public; for more on that, see Section III, Chapter 3 on sexuality.

Improving Behavior by Teaching Independence

There comes a time when, whether we like it or not, our kids become independent. The human drive toward independence becomes clear during a child's second year of life, when she can get around and go after objects on her own, firmly (and frequently) declare "No," throw a tantrum when things aren't going exactly as she would like, and use some combination of words or actions that translate to "I can do it by myself."

As the years go by, our kids keep getting more independent, doing more and more things for themselves that we used to do for them (like feeding, bathing, transporting them, and so on), until we sit back and ask ourselves when we're sending them off to college or to live on their own, "What happened to that helpless infant?"

But kids on the spectrum usually need additional help and monitoring to reach that desired (and, for the parents, bittersweet) independence. Just recently I was on a trip to Cape Cod and something about a particular family there caught my eye (and I'm sure the eyes of others too): an adult with autism was holding hands in public places with her mother. My sister (who is also in the field of disabilities) and I were talking about how no one would have guessed that the adult had autism if it hadn't been for the mom's holding hands. In that case, the mother needed to be aware that as lovely as it might have been to be holding hands with her daughter, it wasn't socially appropriate and made her child look different from the other young adults. She needed to gently insist that her daughter walk independently, which is a fitting metaphor for what we all need to do for our kids.

Here are some ways to encourage a healthy kind of independence in your child, without pushing him too quickly into areas he's not yet comfortable with:

Teach Self-Reliance

One of my close friends, whose daughter is diagnosed with Asperger's, told me that he had the most challenging time getting her up and out of the house in the mornings, but when he bought her an alarm clock (which she got to choose herself), she started bugging *him* to get up and out of the house! Teenagers want and need to feel that they can take care of things by themselves, so help them to feel good about themselves by finding positive ways to let them be independent.

One way to encourage growth toward independence is for you to give your child jobs that will help him learn to be responsible, such as walking to the corner market for an ingredient for dinner, helping to plan the family vacation, carrying luggage or grocery bags, or anything else that makes him feel valued, important, and as if you're treating him like an adult. You'll be amazed at how much help your child really can be—and that gives you another opportunity for praise (we're always looking for those!).

It's vital to develop a sense of responsibility in your child, whatever her level—it will keep her from engaging in undesired behaviors and help her develop independence. Obviously, you don't want to load your child with responsibilities that are too much for her—you want her to be successful with whatever she takes on. So tailor the responsibilities to the child and increase them as she grows and proves her ability to rise to the occasion. Do this gradually, making sure your child is safe and is making the right judgments when she's on her own.

CLAIRE

Okay, here's the part where I brag about my son. (Again.) If we're running errands, he grabs the bags from me and carries them the whole time. If we're on a trip, he'll take charge of the heaviest bags and pull every suitcase off the baggage carousel in the airport, then load them up on the cart and push the cart for us. If I fall and hurt myself, he races for ice or whatever else I might need. And his father calls on him regularly to help bring up the trash cans and assist him in any strenuous tasks around the house.

Andrew loves that when we ask him to help out, we're appealing to him adult to adult. The very fact that we're more likely to ask him to do something onerous than his younger siblings makes him want to say yes. He gets that these increased responsibilities reflect his greater maturity and that our reliance on him goes hand in hand with our acknowledgment that he's no longer a little kid, that he's as dependable and hard-working as any adult. And we make sure he gets that message by emphasizing it every time, telling him that the job requires an adult and then thanking him effusively once he's done it. As my mother-in-law once said, "It's nice to be thanked."

DR. KOEGEL

Use a Chore Chart

When he was in middle school, Evan couldn't cook, couldn't clean, and basically didn't help with any of the family chores. So we developed a chore chart for him (see below for how to do this). We began with just one chore (feeding the dog), and gradually added on more and more of them. He had to start his chores before dinner, and his last chore of the day was setting the table, which worked nicely into the natural reward of a great meal.

Chore charts can be accomplished for children of any level. Simply draw up a little grid with the chores on one side and the days of the week up above so she can check them off daily. If your child has difficulty reading words, you can use pictures to prompt her to do her chores. If you want, you can have her check off the chores as she finishes them, or you can put them on Velcro strips and she can pull them off and put them in an envelope when she's finished. Regardless of the number of supports you provide, taking care of the chores and checking them off teach your child to be responsible.

Driving

Every teenager wants to drive, but at the same time, having a teen who drives is really stressful for parents. My own kids and most of my friends' kids have had a fender bender or two during the first year of driving.

Interestingly, very few of the kids I know who are on the spectrum have had accidents. Perhaps they're more careful, perhaps they follow the rules better, or maybe they're just lucky. Here's some advice for you when you're ready to bite that bullet and encourage your child to begin driving:

- **Start the whole process later.** If it isn't absolutely necessary for your child to start driving at sixteen, wait a few years. This will give him a chance to mature a bit before getting a license. But if he's dying to drive, and having a car will help him socially, then go for it.

- **More driver's training.** Kids today have to take driving lessons privately, and they're expensive. If you can afford a few extra classes, it's well worth the investment. Good driving is partly a matter of practice, and it's a lot less stressful to get the practice from a professional than from Mom or Dad.

- **Make specific, clear rules to help with problem areas.** One thing I have done is have the parents figure out problem areas, then establish some rules to keep their kids safe. For example, we work with a twenty-two-year-old who changes lanes without looking over his shoulder. He has had a number of close calls, so we made a no-lane-switching rule. He has to drive in the slow lane no matter what. While he hates it when he's behind a slow car, he just has to live with it if he wants driving privileges.

- **Start close to home.** You don't need to send your child off on the freeway or highway as soon as she gets her license. Start with short local drives to the store or other neighborhood locations, then gradually work up to longer drives.

- **Follow your child.** If your child has only driven with an adult, you may want to follow behind him in another car the first few times he drives alone. If anything looks risky, you can toot your horn.

And remember, praise your child for good driving. It's a huge accomplishment and will provide her with another step toward independence.

CLAIRE

Man, I hate driving. I have four kids and live in LA, so I don't have a choice in the matter, but I've always said that if we were rich enough, I'd just hire a full-time driver and never have to drop off a kid at a playdate or pick one up from an after-school activity again. Because Andrew has always had friends who live fairly far away and has grown tired of trying to make plans with a mother who groans every time he asks her to get him across town ("In Friday afternoon traffic? You've got to be kidding me!"), he was pretty eager to get his driver's license as early as possible.

Now, having watched my son play team sports, I had some concerns about his ability to respond quickly to unexpected movements, so the idea of putting him behind the wheel of a very fast, very heavy machine was nerve-racking. On the other hand, I was just as eager as he was to see him getting himself around town. I remembered that at an autism conference I went to with Dr. Koegel, one mother of a young adult had reminisced about how her son had learned to drive: "I just sent him off with a driving instructor and basically said, 'Bring him back when he's a good driver.' It cost a fortune, but it was worth it." It was the kind of thing that sticks in your head when your kid is about to be that age.

It does cost a lot to hire a good driving instructor. We asked for recommendations from friends who had older kids on the spectrum and when one family highly recommended someone, Rob got in touch with that instructor. His hourly fees were staggering. But . . . what was more important than making Andrew a lifelong safe driver? Not much.

Our driving instructor, Robert, told us a lot of very smart, insightful things about teaching kids who are on the spectrum. He said that, in his experience, they took longer than typical kids to master the skills they needed to be good drivers. They also needed extra hours on the road because they had trouble generalizing from one experience to another, so it was important to expose them to as many different driving scenarios as possible while they still had an instructor to talk them through it.

The example he gave me was that while he could teach a student on the spectrum what to do when a car had broken down and was blocking a lane, that same student would be completely thrown if, say, a tree had fallen and was blocking *a lane. She wouldn't necessarily generalize from the first situation to the second because she would read them as completely different scenarios—even though the driving tactics would be the same. So Robert said we should make sure Andrew had as many hours on the road as we could possibly arrange, first just with him, and later, once Andrew was comfortable behind the wheel, with other instructors and with us.*

The good news from Robert was that while kids on the spectrum might take longer to master driving than typical kids, they tend to be much safer drivers in the long run. Their meticulous rule following and general rigidity turn out to be positive traits when it comes to driving. He said these kids rarely fool around or speed or take stupid chances on the road. So as long as we were willing to take a long-term view, we could be hopeful Andrew would one day be a safe and skilled driver—it just wasn't going to happen overnight (so little does, have you noticed?).

Thus began many months of Andrew's on-the-road training. And he learned. Slowly but steadily.

Half a year later, when we felt our savings account had been adequately depleted by the cost of the driving lessons, we scheduled the road test. I hadn't learned to drive until I came to LA as a young adult, and managed to fail my first driver's license test just a few miles from where we live now. I knew how devastated Andrew would be if that happened to him, but I also knew the odds of passing the first time around weren't good—tons of kids fail their first test.

Long story short: Andrew passed on that very first try.

He's been driving himself around since then, which has improved my life tremendously. (His too, I hope.) Driving doesn't seem to stress him out the way it does me, which is terrific. He has a respectful, realistic attitude about it—he recognizes that being able to drive is one more step toward independence and that driving gets you where you need to go. I hope my other kids are as cautious and as willing to work hard on their skills as he is.

Frequently Asked Questions

On the one hand, my son wants to help out around the house and that's great. On the other, he doesn't listen carefully enough to all my instructions so usually makes some kind of mistake that makes me wish I hadn't asked him in the first place. How do I get him to follow instructions better?

First you'll need to figure out if he can accomplish the task but just isn't listening, or if he really isn't able to perform the task. If he just doesn't listen, have him repeat the instructions before he starts, and make a list for him to follow or give him shorter instructions. If he isn't proficient at the task, you'll need to break down the behaviors into smaller steps and figure out which steps he can complete and which he can't. Then gradually add on the more difficult steps.

My daughter spaces out so much that I think she'd walk out of the house naked, unfed, and backpackless every morning if I didn't constantly remind her to get ready for school. I'd like to get her less reliant on me—especially since she'll be going to college in a couple of years. I think she basically waits to do anything until I start losing my temper. Any suggestions for getting her more motivated on her own?

If she's college bound, her communication and academics are probably pretty good, so you may want to start her on some self-management. And don't forget to reward her for little steps. Don't wait until you lose your temper to get her into action. That just won't work in the long run. Finally, try to see if she's avoiding anything—that is, using these behaviors to get out of doing something she doesn't like. If she hates first period, for example, she may consciously or unconsciously be engaging in these behaviors as a way of avoiding. Making sure that there is something motivating at school when she arrives may make a difference in her spaciness in the mornings. This can be anything she enjoys, like visiting a favorite teacher, watching a favorite video, getting a special treat to eat, or anything else you can think of that will give her pleasure.

My daughter has this little piece of fabric she keeps in her pocket and rubs and pulls at when she gets upset. Most of the time no one sees, but when something really upsets her, she pulls it out and starts playing with it. It would be fine if she were four years old, but she's fifteen! If I tell her to leave it at home, she gets incredibly agitated. Should I just let her have it? Kids have teased her about it in the past and probably will again.

This might be a good time to teach some replacement behaviors. If something is upsetting her, and it's reasonable, she may need to learn how to express herself to deal with the problem more directly. However, if it's something she shouldn't be upset about, you may want to consider teaching her some self-management procedures.

My son is now able to drive himself around town, which is great—except that I'm terrified that someday he'll be pulled over by a policeman for some violation or another (it happens to everyone at some point) and that he'll say and do the wrong things, and the policeman, not knowing he has autism, will think he's being rude or is on drugs or something like that. How can I prepare him for something like this so he acts appropriately and doesn't make a stressful situation much, much worse?

A few months ago I got a call from a mom whose child I had diagnosed with Asperger's syndrome many years ago while he was in high school. He had been driving and, like many teens, was speeding. Unfortunately, the red lights and siren started up behind him. He panicked, and instead of pulling over and stopping, he started to drive faster. He didn't pull over until several miles later, by which point a number of other police cars were also following him. Then, to make matters worse, he began arguing with the policemen. Well, that landed him in jail.

As a result of a series of letters I wrote, and the testimony of others explaining that kids on the spectrum may not fully understand the gravity of the situation, he got off with a relatively light sentence.

In retrospect, he felt bad about the whole incident, but I truly believe that at the moment when the siren started, and during the minutes afterward, he didn't fully understand that what he was doing was problematic.

There are a few things you can do to make sure that your child doesn't have a similar experience. First you'll need to prime him. Teach him how to interact with people during the unfortunate situation of inadvertently breaking the law. Help him understand that many people get pulled over and get tickets, and while we aren't happy about it, the goal is to keep people safe.

The other important area to target is the police. Many organizations have begun to train law enforcement officers in the symptoms of autism spectrum disorders. Police officers are often called when a child runs away. In fact, a police officer found an adolescent in our area by the side of the highway engaging in repetitive behaviors and handcuffed and arrested him—very unnecessary but the policeman thought the child had taken drugs and didn't understand that it was a communication delay. Police officers need to be taught how to engage with individuals on the spectrum.

It would also be helpful to have something on your child's driver's license to indicate he has a disability. This could simply be a note asking the officer to call a parent in case of any problems, or even a sticker that explains that your child has autism. Your child would have to be comfortable with having something like that on his license, and its usefulness would ultimately depend on how receptive any individual officer is.

Finally, you may want to make a visit to your local police

department, introduce your child, and have someone talk to your child one-on-one about the whole ticketing process. People on the spectrum are often excessively honest, and that may not go over well with a cop, so they should have some sense of how they need to be respectful and polite in a ticketing situation.

4. Managing Modern Technology

My son spends hours each day in front of the computer. I check now and then to see what he's doing there and it's nothing alarming—mostly games, no porn sites or anything like that—but when I encourage him to call a kid from school to come over or go somewhere, he always makes up an excuse and ends up right back at the computer table. I don't want him to live his life

virtually but I can see how relaxed he is at the computer and how tense he gets when he's in a social situation. How can I deny him something that makes life so much easier for him (and for me too)?

CLAIRE

It feels as if we're constantly fighting the technobattle. We're forever coming up with new rules to limit how much time all our kids spend at the computer—that is, when Rob and I can tear ourselves away from our own computers long enough to talk to the kids about how they need to spend less time on theirs.

Of course, when Rob and I are on our laptops, we're working.

Except when we're not.

Time has a way of blurring when you're on the computer, and tasks get strung out into something else entirely—for both kids and adults. Homework turns into YouTube viewing, an instant message or chat about a class project (acceptable) turns into an exchange about annoying teachers (not acceptable), research gets detoured by an interesting tangent (I've always wondered how they got those ships in those bottles . . .). All of my kids spend too much time on the computer. I spend too much time on the computer.

Still, there's a noticeable difference between Andrew and our other kids when it comes to electronics. They all feel the draw of the computer—no question about that—but our younger kids also feel a draw toward a lot of other things, like reading and playing games and doing art projects. If Andrew is home and doesn't have anything scheduled, he's at his computer. Nothing else engages him so entirely.

An even bigger difference shows up when we're all out in the world. The rest of the kids leave technology at home. If we're visiting friends or new places, they're running around, exploring, talking to people, buying things, whatever. But if Andrew's not home, and there isn't a specific, scheduled activity, then he's probably sitting in some corner playing with his cell phone or iPod touch (which allows him Internet access anywhere there's Wi-Fi). If we tell him to stop, he will, but his default activity is always to retreat into staring at the small screen. I don't know why—it's easier, I guess, and predictable, and some of the things that enchant the rest of the family, like wildlife and scenery and meeting new people, just don't appeal to him in the same way.

The Web sites that Andrew gravitates toward aren't bad ones. He loves theme parks and constantly checks on the progress of any new rides that are being built. He likes to go to IMDb and glean information about famous people (information he retains like no one else could—he knows the age and birth year of virtually every celebrity). He works on his own Web pages and has even been known to create Wikipedia pages for members of his family (check out mine—it only exists thanks to him). Lately he's been teaching himself flash animation. So it's all pretty innocent and arguably even productive.

I have no objections to what he's doing online—just to how much time he spends doing it. He likes getting together with friends, but it's easier to stay at home and play on the computer, and that's what wins out most of the time. I'd like to see him find other more active and social things to do with his free time.

DR. KOEGEL

For better (mostly) or worse, our kids have grown up with technology that seems to expand exponentially each year. Kids communicate through instant messages, text messages, e-mail, and social networking sites. They play competitive games on the Internet, create blogs, and voice their opinions in chat rooms. This can be a good thing, even a great thing, but it also has negatives.

The trend of increasing accessibility of information is great if you just want a little education on some esoteric subject, but it comes with obvious risks, because the source may not be as reliable as we think.

I recently read in a medical training journal that the Internet is changing the way doctors practice medicine. That's because patients now look up their symptoms on the Internet and arrive at their doctor's with a fair amount of information, unlike the old days when they waited for their doctors to provide all the answers. The article discussed how doctors now have to be trained to engage in a detailed discussion about a patient's illness and potential therapies and outcomes rather than just unilaterally decide on a course of action. The truth is that while the greater knowledge patients have access to is usually a good thing—it means they're better informed and more likely to ask important questions at a doctor's appointment—it can also cause huge problems if people misdiagnose themselves or skip going to the doctor when they really need to. So here is our electronic age in a nutshell: so much out there is good—but only if it's used wisely.

New and popular technologies allow people to maintain friendships they might not have continued otherwise. My kids have kept in touch with a whole bunch of elementary, middle, and high school acquaintances through social networking sites. In fact, kids are so tech savvy these days that they could easily go through life without much *real* conversation. They can text friends and family to make plans, buy everything from groceries to clothes to movies on the Internet, and get any information they want by Googling it. They can also entertain themselves endlessly with competitive games and chat rooms dedicated to their specific area of interest.

The Bad News

A lot of this is good, but for many kids on the spectrum, it's so much easier to interact through the Internet or via text messaging than it is to socialize with people face-to-face that they stop being willing to do the latter. And that's a problem. Their skill and comfort with technology *can* act as an opening into greater social interactions (for example, cybercamps or clubs), but if your child is using technology to withdraw, be unrealistic about what is really happening, or simply to replace almost every other activity, you'll need to intervene.

Other problems can arise when there are strangers involved. About a third of teens report that they've been contacted by uninvited strangers over the Internet, and if your child is gullible, there's a really scary possibility she might agree to meet in person someone she thinks she "knows" but doesn't really.

Another big problem is cyberbullying. Mean kids spread rumors about other kids, personal and private text messages are forwarded to prying eyes, and embarrassing pictures have been known to pop up for the public to view.

The Steps You Need to Take to Deal with the Internet in Your Home

As you'll see from the case studies later in the chapter, you really don't want to leave things to chance when it comes to your child and how he uses the Internet. The risks are real and if you wait until there's a problem, you could have too big a problem to handle after the fact. You need to stay on top of the situation from the very beginning. Here are the steps I recommend you follow to do so:

- **First, decide if it's helpful.** All the parents I know have mixed feelings about video games, but they can provide an opportunity for socialization. (This is much truer for boys than girls.) Obviously, you don't want your kid sitting at home alone all day playing, but many of the games can be played with others, turning them into a social experience. Also, many cities have video arcades where middle and high schoolers hang out. Kids can have a lot of fun playing well-supervised video games (please don't get the ones with too much violence), and again, it gives them something to do and talk about. I've known parents who, after listening in on the conversation in the lunchroom, have gone out and bought the popular computer or video game that all the boys were talking about and then taught their child on the spectrum to play it, just to give him an entrée into the conversation.

- **Make rules.** Have clear, specific household rules, including a limit to the time spent on the computer. Figure out what an appropriate amount of time is for your child to spend on the computer (it can be a daily or weekly number and you can check around with friends and experts to see what most kids are doing) and then make it clear that the computer will be turned off after that. Also be specific about what your child is and isn't allowed to do while on the computer. In many households, kids aren't allowed to use the computer for anything other than homework until all homework is done. Other families allow games and recreational use only on the weekends. Figure out what you're comfortable with and then set those rules for your family. Post them somewhere near the computer so your child can always check them.

- **Monitor.** The only way you're going to know if your child is following your rules is if you check on him. There are different ways to do that. Some families keep the computer in a public area so they can see when their kids are online and what they're looking at. Others install programs on the parents' computers that show them what their kids are doing online at any given moment. Some families have a rule that Mom and Dad can check the computer's online history whenever they choose to see what sites their kids were on and how long they were there. Whatever method you choose, it's vital that you be honest with your child that he's being monitored and in what way. You don't want him to feel spied on—you want the monitoring to be an open and natural understanding, part of the "Going online is a privilege, not a right" contract.

- **Step in if there's a problem.** It may be that no matter how hard you try to keep your child's computer time restricted, she won't be able to stay away from it. Or maybe she's figured out how to hide the Web sites she's visiting from you (and because our kids are more computer savvy than we are, she can probably do it). Don't just ignore the early warning signs—take action before a potential problem spirals out of control.

- **Analyze the situation.** As always in a situation where there's a behavioral issue, you need to do a functional analysis to figure out *why* your child is doing what he's doing. Only by understanding the underlying motivation or reinforcement can you counter it with appropriate alternative activities. So, for example, if your child keeps going back to the computer despite your attempts to make him cut back on his time, you need to stop and think about why he's doing it. For many of our kids, the cause is fairly simple to figure out: it's easier to be social and make friends online than in person. If your teenager is actively seeking out porn, then you need to think about his changing hormonal needs and how to address them. (See Section III, Chapter 3 for more information on helping your physically maturing child.)

- **Find alternative activities.** The alternative activities you decide to provide for your child depend on what you've figured out in your analysis. If your child is using the computer as a way to escape the challenges of interacting with real people in the real world, then you need to start her on a program that will make real-life socializing easier and more successful. (See stories that follow of those we have helped.) If your child is able to connect online with people with the same interests in a way he hasn't been able to with people in your community, look for a club or group that's based around that interest. (Or maybe allow him extra time online for this pursuit if you think it's ultimately a positive thing.) If your child is surreptitiously looking at porn, talk to him frankly about his developing body and make it clear to him that some pornography is illegal to download and that even porn that *isn't* illegal can give him misleading and inaccurate ideas about the opposite sex. Make sure you read our chapter on sexuality so you can help him deal with these urges appropriately.

Adam's Internet Relationship

Adam was a college student with Asperger's syndrome who was brilliant, physically fit (he worked out every day), and doing well in his classes until his only friend decided to transfer to another college. This put him into a severe depression. He stopped going to classes and stayed in his dorm room all day long. As he began failing his courses, the school made some efforts to contact him but he didn't respond. Eventually he moved back home with his parents, who lived about forty-five minutes from our Center. They brought him in for treatment, but by this time he had socially secluded himself to such a great extent that he never left his room—or his computer. He was spending all day sequestered in his room surfing the Internet, entering chat rooms, and playing video games. He also admitted that he had gotten to "know" a girl online who had Asperger's syndrome too, and that their relationship had brought him out of his depression. Their communications had been going back and forth for many months, and Adam honestly believed that it was a real relationship, even though they had never met face-to-face.

What We Did

Adam's Internet girlfriend was the only thing that made him happy. He wanted to have a girlfriend so desperately that he clung to the hope that Savannah was the perfect mate for him.

Her acceptance gave him the false impression that he didn't have to work on a major social problem that was preventing him from making other peer relationships, namely, his need to correct others. Adam was very smart and constantly researched different subjects. For most people, this would have resulted in the ability to carry on an interesting conversation but, unfortunately, Adam used his greater knowledge very pedantically, showing off his superior knowledge of subjects rather than engaging other people in acceptable dialogue.

We needed him to see that showing interest in another person—instead of just showing off how much he knew—would improve his social life, and that engaging friends without constantly and rudely correcting them might actually get him some real dates instead of a virtual relationship.

Our first step was to give him feedback about what was appropriate conversation and what was inappropriate by using video modeling (see Section I, Chapter 2 for more details on a video-modeling program). Once he was able to sustain a conversation without turning off his conversational partner, we were ready to take him out into the real world. We asked him to rate potential social situations and outings according to how comfortable he would feel entering them. With that as our guide, we started to take him out, slowly and gradually moving from the most comfortable situation to the least, and enlisting another college student to accompany and provide support for him.

Eventually, over a year-long period, Adam began leaving his room on his own, meeting new people, and successfully interacting with other young people. At this point, he doesn't have a steady girlfriend, but he has a lot of opportunities to meet people his own age. While he continues to correspond with Savannah, they still haven't met in person (and I doubt they ever will). But I'm very hopeful he'll have a real-life girlfriend one day fairly soon.

Sam's Crisis

We all know that kids can be cruel and, sadly, kids on the spectrum often end up being the butt of the joke.

Sam was a small, slim high school student who had always had social problems and had never received the help he needed. While the girls at his school actually found him interesting, other students, particularly the boys, tended to be mean to him, sometimes even physically shoving or hitting him. One boy continued to harass him throughout the school year and even started forcefully pushing him as if he were going to pick a fight, so Sam eventually left. He went home fuming and just couldn't get over the incident. He went online, where he felt more comfortable opening up to others and described the incident on a bunch of chat lines. Eventually an unknown person told him there were ways he could get revenge on the boy who had mistreated him and proceeded to describe some of them. Unfortunately, the idea that Sam seized upon involved calling the person and threatening him. His parents were stunned when Sam was arrested!

While most kids have some type of social support network to help them blow off steam and receive appropriate sympathy when someone is mean, Sam didn't, and his attempt to find solace in the Internet led him down a dangerous path.

What We Did

Sam, like many kids on the spectrum, doesn't have a mean bone in his body. He just didn't understand the fine line between appropriate and inappropriate.

The first thing his parents did was to take away his computer privileges so he couldn't get into any more trouble with it. Meanwhile, we began working on his social skills by using video modeling.

It became instantly clear that, like many kids on the spectrum, Sam didn't know how to maintain a social conversation. He wasn't asking many questions. In addition, he inadvertently interrupted frequently, giving the impression that he wasn't really listening (mostly, though, he was just eager to say something).

Using many of the interventions described in Section II, Chapter 2 on social conversation, we've been improving Sam's conversational skills. We're also specifically teaching him how to deal with kids who bring up the incident by shrugging and saying, "Yeah, that was a stupid thing to do," rather than getting into a discussion that often makes him lose his temper.

His parents have agreed to gradually let him back on the computer, but only under supervised conditions, and they have placed him in a number of community activities so that he can meet a new group of peers. Sam totally understands that what he did was wrong, and as he develops more appropriate social skills, it's easier for him to make new friends and deal with challenging situations.

Joel's Facebook Picture

Joel was a college student who was on the spectrum. He kept in touch with his friends through a social network site where they arranged most of their outings, informed one another about upcoming social events, and simply kept in daily communication.

Joel had joined a fraternity, and one weekend one of his "brothers" (I put this in quotes because a real brother would never do such a thing) decided it would be funny to have Joel pretend that he was having sex with one of his brother's dogs. To make matters worse, he got Joel to post the picture on his social network site. Joel really didn't have a clue that this was a bad idea. He was being egged on and like many kids on the spectrum, he didn't know where to draw the line. It wasn't a terrible picture, but it was bad enough that his small group of friends (online and real) virtually disappeared.

What We Did

First, we made Joel remove the picture immediately. Second, we primed him to explain to his friends that he had been "put up" to posting the photo and now realized it was inappropriate and he regretted it. This helped with one or two friends, but the damage had been done and there were more who still refused to be a friend on his site.

Most students clearly don't understand what university professors have access to. I can't tell you how many pictures I've seen on the Internet and on social networking sites (people can see what's on a site even if they haven't been invited to be "friends") of students half naked, in inappropriate sexual poses, drinking, and doing a myriad of other embarrassing things. Most of them would be horrified if they knew I had seen them like that. So here's a word of advice for *everyone*: never post anything you don't want public. Pretty much any information can be accessed, even on a "private" site.

A university student recently killed a student passenger while she was driving drunk. While she was awaiting trial she posted a picture of herself *drinking* with friends. Somehow the judge got hold of those pictures and was of course furious that the student was flaunting her drinking after such a tragic accident. He threw the book at her, and she'll now be spending years in a prison cell, in large part due to the documented fact that she continued to drink even after the horrendous accident.

Clearly, it's hard for any young person to absorb completely how public and permanent something posted online can be; for someone on the spectrum, the dangers of the Internet are even more confusing. They may clearly understand rules that are black-and-white, but when it comes to shades of gray, they may be easily manipulated, fooled, and led into poor judgment.

You need to monitor your child's Internet use closely to make sure she understands that *anything* she posts may be seen by others or forwarded. Have frequent conversations about the dangers of the Internet, using examples and exploring potential consequences of online actions, and always teach positive and appropriate Internet manners.

CLAIRE

Ah, the joys of trying to filter or monitor your child's Internet access. What fun we've had with that.

We've tried. Lord knows we've tried. We're always worried that our kids will accidentally stumble onto a site that will forever sear some sick image onto their tender little brains. (I'll never forget the time I wanted to take the kids to a farm and innocently typed "cherry picking" into a search engine. I was stunned when the results appeared—apparently those words have a meaning I wasn't aware of.) So we've tried several age-appropriate filters to keep their Internet viewing safe. And you know what happens? The filters filter out everything, even the Web sites we approve of and including the ones they need for homework (like, for example, their school Web site). So then our kids come to us, rightfully complaining that they're being blocked from everything they need to do online. Pretty soon we're teaching them the password that allows them to access things that are blocked—and then we're wondering what the point of blocking it is if they know how to go around the blocks.

Not that it matters—my kids aren't idiots and they know there are plenty of other ways to access the Internet, including simply using my computer when I'm not around. They'll always be more technosavvy than I am, so I'm fighting a losing battle if I think I'm going to protect them with computer-generated filters and blocks and the like. Anyway, they all have friends whose parents don't control their access, so they can get access to anything they want at other people's houses.

So we're not going to win this battle through technology. No, the only way we're going to protect our kids is by talking to them at great length and with annoying frequency about the dangers of the Internet. And that's just what we do.

Just recently I joined a social networking Web site, and while the kids were watching over my shoulder, I checked out some young relatives' Web pages. My children's jaws fell open, as did mine, when we saw some of the stupid stuff these perfectly intelligent kids had posted, like photos of themselves drinking, fondling members of the opposite sex, and generally making fools of themselves. But it was good—it gave me the chance to talk to my kids about how if an old relative like me could stumble across these photos, so could the kids' parents, future employers, potential girlfriends/boyfriends, and so on. I think my kids got it (the visual aids helped). And, of course, Rob and I have stated and restated that lesson many times. Many, many times. At least a google times.

We have other set speeches too. If we walk by when the kids are exchanging instant messages with a friend, we frequently stop to remind them that there could be another person reading over their friend's shoulder and so they should never say anything they wouldn't want someone else to read. (And to be especially careful if someone says something like "What do you think of Diana?" because I've heard too many stories about "Diana" being right there watching the answer, or at least having the answer forwarded to her.) We also have a whole lecture *about never communicating in any way with anyone you haven't met personally. Andrew once responded to e-mail from some-one who claimed to be a friend of someone he knew only dis-tantly. We refused to let him continue to interact with this stranger. As we always tell the kids, anyone can claim an ac-quaintanceship online and pretend to be someone he's not, so don't respond unless it's an established friend with an e-mail address you recognize. And of course there's the granddaddy of all Internet-related advice:* never agree to meet with someone you met online. *Never, never, never.*

Our kids have heard our advice so often that sometimes when we launch into it, they'll start saying it for us, to get us to stop already. Fine with me: it means they've been listening. Are we being overly cautious? Probably. Are we going to relax a lit-tle? Never.

DR. KOEGEL

Use It for Good, Not Evil

It's up to you to ensure that your child will utilize what's best about the Internet without getting trapped by its dangers. Don't assume he'll automatically know the difference between what is appropriate online behavior and what is not. Before any problems arise, talk to him about staying positive or neutral in e-mails and instant messages rather than gossiping in ways that may be hurtful (and passed around). Let your child know that many teens and young adults are contacted by complete strangers, some of whom are predators. Make sure he understands that spending too much time online may ultimately harm his real social life. And finally, make sure your child stays fairly busy with activities out in the real world. If you find that computer time is gradually taking over his life, pull the plug (so to speak). In short, it's up to you to make sure that your child's computer is a useful and not a harmful tool.

ANDREW

I am the kind of guy who is on my computer a lot. I am on my computer a lot mainly because I think that computers are amazing nowadays and there is a lot you can do on them. Whenever I am on my computer, I like to play flash games, look at news about my interests, IM, e-mail, watch videos on YouTube, and chat with friends through Facebook.

A lot of the time, I try to follow my parents' rules about the computer and I do, although every once in a while, I may end up chatting with someone whom I do not know who pretends that he or she is a friend of mine when that person is actually a hacker. I do not like to talk to people who pretend to be others on the computer, but sometimes I am out of my mind and really think that those people are who they say they are (mainly the names of friends whom I know).

It is also hard for me when friends of mine like to look at inappropriate stuff online and it is hard for me to say no when I feel that it really is not right to do. I almost never disobey my parents' rules nowadays, but I used to when I was twelve. When I was twelve, I used to look up pictures of naked people on Google, since I thought that was funny. But after my parents found out that I was being immature on the Internet, they did not trust me anymore and that resulted in about three or four years without Internet in my room. I thought that it was really unfair but I definitely learned a lesson from that.

I do have suggestions about Internet use for other teenagers: first of all, listen to what your parents say and be smart about what you do online; second, do not chat with anyone you do not know and also do not chat with anyone who you assume is pretending to be someone else; last, if you are worried about somebody who seems unsafe online, in my opinion, the best idea is to honestly tell your parents about it—if they don't trust you, though, then talk to a therapist about it privately.

If I had to choose between hanging out with a friend or doing stuff on my computer, it would really depend on what I am up to. If I am really awake and feel like doing something active, then I would prefer hanging out with a good friend. If I am really tired and feel like a couch potato, then I might prefer doing nothing but sitting at my computer and playing games and checking news.

Every once in a while, I like to play video games. I like to play mostly shooting and adventure games. My least favorite video games that I like to play are sports games. I also like my cell phone and iPod, but probably my iPod more. I have the iPod touch which has Internet on it and many more applications that make it feel more like a mini high-quality laptop, although it is also touch screen.

I really like electronics that have high performance and can do many things. I also like my cell phone, because I can call, text message, take photos, and record videos on it. My phone flips in two directions and has a small keyboard on it, which is great for text messaging.

Out of my computer, video games, cell phone, and iPod, it would probably be easiest for me to give up my cell phone, because there aren't great graphics on it and it also does not have great Internet access. The Internet on my phone is slow and expensive, but my computer has fast Internet, high performance, and a really good flash player. It also stores about 200 GB, which is a great capacity for a desktop computer.

Frequently Asked Questions

My teenage son is looking at online porn—I can tell from checking the Web history. My husband laughs and says that at that age he did the same kind of thing and we should just let him keep doing it. But it makes me uncomfortable. Should we let him go ahead or insist he stop?

The problem with OK'ing this activity is that you may inadvertently be rewarding a pattern of behavior that leads to destructive behavior down the road. We have had underage kids develop such a fascination with pornographic material that they ended up ditching school to seek it out. One high school boy got arrested for truancy when he left school to go to a local bookstore that had adult materials (yes, the bookstore called the police). Again, finding alternative activities may be helpful for your son.

When my daughter gets home from school, she goes right to the computer and starts playing games. I try to get her to stop and either go outside or do her homework first, but she insists she needs the decompression. Is there anything wrong with letting her play on the computer for an hour or so before doing anything else? It genuinely seems to relax her.

Some potential problems with her dashing to her computer every day after school are (1) she may be doing this instead of spending time with other kids her age; and (2) she may never get around to her homework. We all know that the computer can suck you in and provide endless hours of entertainment. If she's doing this at the expense of socializing with kids her age and learning from her peers, I would pull the plug. Or if she's never getting around to her homework because, heck, it's just a lot more fun, then I would only let her use the computer when she finishes her homework.

A kid who claims to be a friend of a friend starting instant messaging my daughter. She said the new girl was really nice but I was a little worried when I looked at the IMs because I felt that the girl was trying to lead her into saying negative things about other kids and expose some embarrassing truths about herself. It might just be friendly, but I'm uneasy about it. How should I handle this?

Kids can be mean to one another, and adolescents can adjust their own stories slightly to make themselves more appealing to their peers. If you have discussed the rules and the potential negative consequences, hopefully your daughter will steer clear of potential problems by simply not saying anything negative. If it is a hoax, the other kid will eventually give up if your daughter doesn't make the mistake of saying anything potentially harmful or embarrassing. But remember, kids have to be constantly reminded of the rules. Not in a nagging and irritating way, but in a mature, adult way. Growing up is also a time of learning and experience, and they all will fail here and there as they learn for themselves about complex social interactions.

5. Improving Coexisting (aka Comorbid) Conditions

Whenever my daughter sits down to work at her desk, she has to make everything line up perfectly—laptop, papers, lamp, and so on. She reminds me of that detective with OCD on TV. Do you think she could have OCD? That would be pretty unfair when she already has autism!

CLAIRE

Andrew worries a lot about germs (see what he had to say about personal hygiene earlier in this section if you don't believe me). He didn't get that from me—I have to be the most relaxed mother in the world about that stuff. The other kids and I are always sharing glasses and food (and, inevitably, viruses), and I don't make them wash their hands nearly as often as they should. So the germophobia is unique to Andrew, who adamantly refuses to drink or eat out of anything someone else has used.

He's very concerned about washing his hands every time he sneezes. Unfortunately, the poor guy has mild allergies and sneezes fairly frequently. He had one disastrous outing to the Third Street Promenade, where public bathrooms are in short supply and where he wound up dragging his friend up and down the street for half an hour looking for one because he had *sneezed once. I've since encouraged him to carry a small bottle of Purell when he goes out, so he can sanitize his hands without needing to find a bathroom. This has helped—a little bit. He still prefers to wash his hands if he sneezes (which is admirable) but he doesn't feel it as a burning need the way he used to. Or maybe he's just learned to postpone the washing until there's a convenient way to do it (when we're out, he still tends to rush off to any available public restroom to wash his hands). But this habit, and several others, make me wonder if he could fall on the OCD spectrum in addition to that other spectrum we've been talking about.*

DR. KOEGEL

Unfortunately, many older kids and adults with autism develop other conditions that are in some way related to the autism. These may develop because some of the characteristics of autism can lead to different but related challenges. For instance, repetitive and restricted interests might lead a teenager to hoard everything related to that particular interest (say, train schedules, if he likes to read them). Lack of socialization might lead a young adult on the spectrum to develop habits or behaviors that would have been socialized away by a group of peers. An adolescent on the spectrum might develop some feelings of depression as she improves and realizes that she doesn't have many friends.

If you've noticed that your child has any of the symptoms described on the following pages, you'll want to be active in intervening, just as you have been throughout her life. Seek out a specialist in the area of autism who understands how to use applied behavior analysis and can teach pivotal responses to help with these extra challenges that sometimes appear in adolescents and adults on the spectrum.

Here are some conditions that frequently arise in conjunction with autism and suggestions on how to work with and hopefully improve them:

Hoarding

I'm not sure whether hoarding stems from the strong desire for the preservation of sameness that many people on the spectrum feel (see page 360 for more on that) or from a desire to own everything related to a favorite restricted area of interest (as we mentioned earlier) or from something else entirely, but a subgroup of adolescents and adults on the spectrum hoard things. Some hoarded objects are common, like magazines or newspapers that they think they might want to read in the future, but sometimes they're more unusual. I heard of one boy on the spectrum who even kept nails in a drawer—not nails construction workers use, but his own fingernails!

If your child is showing a tendency to hoard, you'll need to step in and make it a goal to start sorting through and discarding things. The best way to go about this approach is to help your child make a list of the hoarded items, organizing them into a hierarchy of things that are the most difficult to part with and those that are the easiest to part with. For example, he may insist that he's not ready to get rid of his train magazines or toy model trains, but he's sort of OK with discarding the weekly train club newsletters. So you'd start by getting rid of those first. As your child is successful, gradually work up the list. I've also done the two-for-one technique, where each time a new item is purchased, my client has to get rid of two less desired but hoarded items. If your child is reluctant to get rid of *anything*, you may need some kind of positive reinforcement ("We'll go on that special outing if you throw out those papers") or self-management system ("Give yourself a star every time you toss a magazine, and when you have ten stars, we'll go out to dinner") to get him to actually dump the stuff. (See Section I, Chapter 2 for more information on self-management.)

"Obsessive Compulsiveness"

We all use the terms *obsessive* or *OCD* in loose, sometimes joking ways to refer to our own or our family's rituals, habits, or interests. I often joke about my husband's being "obsessed" with sports cars. But OCD *is* a very real psychiatric anxiety disorder that can be debilitating to people. It generally involves distressing and intrusive thoughts and related compulsions that serve as an attempt to neutralize these thoughts, for example, "The house will burn down if I don't check the stove repeatedly to make sure it's off."

We all know people who worry about germs, but it's a serious problem when it gets to the point where these fears significantly interfere with a person's normal routine. We had a college student (not on the spectrum) who was so worried about germs that she scrubbed her apartment so often her hands were constantly bloody.

When it comes to kids on the spectrum, some people believe that although their behaviors *look* like OCD, they actually aren't, because they don't have the obsessive thoughts, just the compulsive behaviors. I have talked with many people on the spectrum who will say that they repeatedly count their money, work out formulas, or line up things in perfect order just because they like it that way and it gives them pleasure. While some appear to be bothered if these activities are interrupted, many report that there is no anxiety involved—that is, they don't experience any anxiety or distress related to these behaviors. So there is a theory that these behaviors are remnants or symptoms of restricted interests or ritualistic behaviors (like self-stimulatory behaviors) that we see so often in children on the spectrum and not actual obsessive-compulsive behaviors that we would see in other patients with psychiatric disorders.

We once did a study that utilized the intense interests of kids with autism to create group games and activities, to help improve social interactions. When we submitted the article, it was titled "Using the Obsessions of Children with Autism to Improve Peer Socialization." Well, I have to tell you that the reviewers raked us over the coals for using the word *obsessions*! We had to change "Obsessions" to "Repetitive Ritualistic Interests." It was an educational experience, and I realized how easy it is to casually reference anxiety disorders that are extremely complex and serious. And that's why we put it in quotes at the top of this section.

Regardless of the underlying reason for these types of behaviors, they generally interfere with a person's life and therefore require

intervention, and a number of different strategies have worked to reduce them. The first is simply providing rewards when your child
doesn't engage in the behavior. (If he's an adult, he could self-reward.)
For example, I worked with one young man on the spectrum who repeatedly drove in circles around the block after leaving his home. He
reported no anxiety associated with this activity and simply stated
that he enjoyed it. However, he was often late to events, meetings,
and appointments as a result of driving around the block too many
times. We developed a reward system and created a little chart for
him to fill out: he gave himself a check every time he left his home
without driving around the block, and when he completed the chart,
he treated himself to one of the rewards. This was successful in
breaking a habit that had continued for many months.

Self-management is a great strategy for reducing repetitive behaviors. We often set up situations in which the opportunity for the repetitive behavior is present, then have the person evaluate how well
she avoided engaging in it (remember to keep it positive).

We have also had success with incompatible behaviors. For example, we're currently working with a boy who's very bright and constantly solves math problems. He'll solve a series of progressively more
difficult equations in his head, along the lines of $2 \times 2 = 4$, $4 \times 4 = 8$,
$8 \times 8 = 64$, $64 \times 64 = 4{,}096$ (I had to do that last one on my calculator), but he can—and will—go into the multimillions. The problem
was that he used to get upset if someone tried to stop him from finishing his calculations once he'd begun. Our intervention was to
bring him to new places and redirect him to talk about activities and
items in the new environment while ignoring the repetitive math problems. We pretty much bombarded him with comments, questions, and
games ("Watch me, I'm going to walk backward—tell me if I'm going
to bump into anything," "Oh, look, there's a flock of birds flying over-
head," and so on), while totally ignoring anything having to do with
math calculations. He has greatly decreased his math solving and is
beginning to engage in improved social interactions. And we've done
some parent education, so his parents are able to incorporate the procedures at home and have seen changes there too.

Finally, in a case like Andrew's, where he so strongly feels the need to wash his hands after sneezing, we can use a desensitization program if it starts to affect his daily life and get him used to waiting a longer time—until it's convenient—to wash his hands. We would also need to teach him a replacement behavior because the delay alone probably wouldn't eliminate his anxiety altogether.

Preservation of Sameness

Many kids on the spectrum are inflexible about certain things and have to have everything a certain way. For example, they might get upset if you take a different route to school, rearrange the furniture, or change the way their belongings are arranged. If your child is already having a problem with needing to have something in a certain order or a certain way, it may get out of hand as he gets older. This is okay if it doesn't interfere with normal functioning, but occasionally it does.

For example, I worked with one young adult who lived in her own apartment and didn't want a single thing changed in it. Unfortunately, after a few years of neglect it *really* needed fixing but she was unwilling to make any changes. Just taking the first step into her front door, you could tell that not a thing had been changed in years. She also never got rid of anything—shoes, old bottles, magazines. . . . Her apartment was excessively cluttered. That wasn't a problem per se, but the fact that she became irritated with anyone who suggested she clean or organize *was* a problem.

I wanted to encourage her to fix up her apartment, but at first I couldn't hit on a strong enough reinforcer that would be more important to her than just keeping things as they were. Then I realized that she was interested in dating. By promising to introduce her to eligible guys once her home was fixed up, we were able to persuade her to replace broken and outdated pieces of furniture. I will admit that this has been very difficult for her but little by little she has started to work on the apartment. At the same time, we gradually started getting her together with other young adults who have similar interests, and she has invited a few people to her place. She doesn't have a boyfriend yet, but I'm confident that eventually she'll meet the right person, and although she might not be viewed as the greatest housekeeper, her apartment is no longer a disaster.

Depression

As interventions have improved, we're starting to see a large group of adolescents and young adults who succeed academically, get jobs, and even establish a career—but who just don't have many friends. They tend to be a little quirky, mostly because they haven't had enough social interaction throughout their lives and really never developed a group of friends or even one best friend. Feeling socially isolated, some become depressed. Unfortunately, depression is a vicious cycle: when they become depressed, they don't make an effort to get out and do things, and so they fall deeper and deeper into the rut of social isolation.

We have found it very helpful to provide supported community opportunities for depressed people on the spectrum. In other words, we find out what activities they like and gradually introduce them to these activities in a supported way so that they'll experience success. For example, we enrolled one young adult who likes dancing in a ballroom dance class along with a therapist. No one else knows that the partner is a therapist, but her support allows him to meet other single people without having to do it all on his own. Another one of our clients goes to museum art shows every month with a cousin.

Again, you need to get people on the spectrum who are experiencing depression into social settings where they're likely to experience success. First, though, you need to do a functional analysis to try to figure out why that person is depressed. We've had people tell us about that spiraling downward cycle—where they aren't making friends, so they spend more time alone, which makes them more depressed. If this vicious cycle can be addressed, life can get better, not worse. Finding the right therapists who will actually help your child get the skills he needs to be successful socially can make a difference.

While depression may be related to variables other than social isolation, it has appeared to be socially related in just about all of the adolescents and adults on the spectrum whom I have met who are experiencing it. Some of our adults come in already taking antidepressants or other mood stabilizers, but we generally try to fade them quickly, because our goal is to teach the person those missing behaviors that are causing them to become socially isolated. In fact, we have had some adults come to us on so many medications that we don't feel as if we know the real person.

Medications may help some, but most of our clients express a desire to be chemical free and are eager to learn to remedy the social behaviors that are causing their isolation. If someone is missing key behaviors, the medications won't miraculously teach them how to show self-control when dealing with a stressful situation or how to keep a nice back-and-forth conversation going. And until those behaviors are learned, the social isolation that's causing the depression and/or anxiety is unlikely to improve.

Anxiety

Some individuals who experience repeated failures socially can begin to feel anxiety about socializing and may start to avoid any activities that might potentially involve socializing (which, of course, are most activities outside the home). As with depression, this creates a vicious cycle. The worst thing a person who is already having social anxiety can do is to shut himself out of all society.

One successful approach we've used is to have our clients rate on a scale how comfortable they would feel in different social situations, using a large list of community activities as a reference. We generally like to focus on a positive comfort level rather than asking them how anxious they would feel, because we really want them to think about which situations are comfortable for them and not about the ones they want to avoid. We usually try to estimate the number of people who are likely to be in those settings (one person, a small group of people, a large group of people), the particular company they would like to have (going with a therapist or alone), and the specific setting (their home, a movie theater, a restaurant, and so on). If we start with the situations where they feel most comfortable, such as going to a movie with one person, or going to a sports event with a few people, then gradually and systematically work up to the situations where they feel less comfortable, they usually can experience success without anxiety and are more likely to want to continue these outings.

Frequently Asked Questions

My son refuses to go out with us when we're visiting friends or relatives and rarely goes out by himself. My husband says to leave him alone, that he's old enough now to decide for himself and he seems perfectly happy at home by himself. And it's true he doesn't exactly seem depressed—he's not crying or talking about being unhappy. He's perfectly cheerful, but his lack of interest in doing anything other than going to school and coming right back home worries me. Do you think I should take some kind of action or should I leave him alone because, as my husband says, he seems happy enough?

> If your child isn't doing anything outside of the home except going to school, he's differing drastically from his peers. My concern is that he isn't learning how to socialize and isn't developing friendships. Because he enjoys being at home, you may want to start by having some of his school buddies come over to your home to engage in some activities that your son likes. If it turns out that he gets along perfectly well with his peers but just likes being at home, your problems are solved. But if he isn't able to get along with his peers, I would worry that hanging around home all the time is just putting him further behind socially. In that case, you'll want to develop a comprehensive program with the school and carry over social activities outside of school. Remember, learning to get along with peers will help him with work, friendships, and potential relationships.

You said we should do something about compulsive behaviors if they interfere with normal life, but what if they don't? My son does have some lining-up sorts of behaviors, and has to brush his teeth and wash his face in the same order and in the same way every morning and night, but he only does these things when he's alone. Do I have to do anything about them?

> If they aren't a problem for him or anyone else who interacts with him (or who might in the future), then you can probably leave these behaviors alone. But having said that, I believe you should keep an eye on them. Little problems can turn into bigger ones, and if they appear to be getting worse over time, you should definitely be concerned and start intervention.

My daughter's very anxious about how other people regard her when she's out in public. Just the other day, she thought a waitress "didn't like her" because of the way she ordered her dinner. (She does speak in an unusual way, but I don't think the waitress was bothered by it—she was just brusque because she was in a rush.) These fears can ruin an outing. She'll suddenly get very nervous and quiet and whisper to me that someone at the next table is staring at her peculiarly or something like that. She's been teased a lot at school so maybe that has something to do with it. Do you have any suggestions for handling this? I'm worried it's really affecting her willingness to go out socially.

> If your daughter is reacting to nonexistent criticism, you'll need to teach her a different way of thinking about others' feelings. For example, when she orders, you may want to prompt her to consider that the waitress may have thought how nice it was that she ordered so quickly. Or if she thinks someone is whispering about her, you may want to teach her that they're probably talking about how cute she is. Changing these thoughts may help her to learn that other people's motives aren't always malevolent. However, if people *are* making fun of her, you may first need to work on the areas that are drawing attention to her. For example, if she speaks in an unusual way, you may want to work on prosody (see Section II, Chapter 2 for how to do that). Second, encourage her to talk to people who can help. If it's happening at school, she can talk with a counselor or special education staff member who might be able to help.

Third, teach her to deal with it differently. For example, if the waitress is short with her, have her ask if everything is OK. If someone is laughing, have her ask "What's so funny?" and teach her at times just to ignore it and self-instruct with a "Who cares?" attitude. Having lots of strategies in her repertoire should make these situations easier.

An Afterword for Educators
by Robert L. Koegel, PhD

You'll catch just about any father of an adolescent saying, "It seems like just yesterday that I was walking around the delivery room . . ." and time may blur even faster for parents of kids on the spectrum who have every minute filled to the brim with therapies, playdates, parent-teacher conferences, IEPs, priming, and the like. In fact, it's hard to believe that Andrew, who seemingly yesterday was nonverbal and struggling with communication, is now contributing eloquent essays with thought-provoking honesty to this book.

Kids do grow up so quickly. We can see that the epidemic of kids diagnosed with autism spectrum disorders is now approaching adolescence. And as a society, we're not prepared. As the peak of the tsunami begins to hit, parents are realizing that while things are most certainly better for young children on the spectrum and intensive early intervention has improved immensely, the conditions for adolescents and young adults still leave a lot to be desired. Because of the gap between when a research study comes out and when we see it implemented in the real world, books that translate research to practice are essential. Lynn and Claire have written just such a book, as they describe the pivotal response approach to intervention in a practical and user-friendly way. These scientifically sound techniques, where individuals' motivations are considered at the heart of every activity, result in extraordinarily widespread and generalized changes that happen very rapidly.

Fortunately, this approach does not rely on punishment, but instead relies on specific intrinsic motivations and desires in order to produce huge improvements. Contrast this new Pivotal Response approach described by Lynn and Claire with approaches used in the recent past (and unfortunately even in some places during the present time), where individuals are tied to their beds in four-point restraint and given high-voltage electric shocks and other forms of painful or humiliating punishments. Many of us have seen reports of these horrendous procedures described in documentaries and news reports on television. But it is one thing to read or hear about incidents like these, and it is another thing to live them. Therapists and parents alike were destined for grief and anguish knowing that while the procedures worked, albeit short term, they offered no dignity or self-respect for the person on the spectrum.

So again, while older approaches to eliminating behaviors such as aggression, constant arguing, or stereotypic self-stimulatory behavior may have been met with the dreadful fate of a painful punishment, this newer approach examines the intrinsic motivation for the behavior. Armed with that knowledge, intervention can be designed that replaces the maladaptive behavior (such as arguing) with an appropriate behavior that will accomplish the same function—a long-lasting fix that is by far less painful and infinitely more respectful of the individual undergoing the intervention. In short, the scientifically based improvements described by Lynn and Claire in this book make a remarkable difference in the quality of life and happiness of not only people with autism, but also everyone around them.

However, the authors do not stop there. Once they have tackled motivation, so that the individuals on the spectrum want to work hard to improve and make the effort to interact socially, Claire and Lynn go on to show that it is possible for the adolescent or young adult with autism or Asperger's to take a large self-regulatory role in his or her own road to improvement. This makes a huge difference in the person's self-dignity, independence, and autonomy. When the goal of the individual on the spectrum is dating, a relationship, and marriage, he can be even more motivated to take a major role in his own intervention. We have seen many young adults who have recognized that they need to take an active role in learning the thousands of social nuances that go along with social conversation. They begin to actively work with their intervention providers and family members in order to change entrenched clusters of behaviors, eliminating the need to address each individual behavior alone by relying on an external intervention provider. At that point, when the person on the spectrum begins to take charge of his life, we can sort of take a backseat and watch the miracle of this person's life unfold before our eyes. Such changes are ones that are likely to last and be truly meaningful.

Thus, the heart of this book relies on building the critical pivotal areas of self-motivation and self-confidence to improve the lives of individuals on the spectrum. And Lynn and Claire show how such an approach gives dignity and respect to the individuals, treating them as people first and not as people with disabilities.

When one reads the descriptions in this book, it is obvious that most individuals with autism and Asperger's syndrome initially (without intervention) appear very unmotivated to change their behavior due to a seeming learned helplessness. That is, they seem to think they cannot do things that they in fact are actually capable of doing. Further, while they seem to desperately want friends, they appear to lack confidence in their ability to make friends, and therefore put their effort into avoiding the very social interactions they so desperately require. But once self-motivation is addressed as a pivotal core area for intervention, quick and long-lasting improvements take place with a natural and generalized result.

This book also recognizes that people on the spectrum sometimes have extreme attentional problems. They may attend to too few cues, and to incorrect cues, missing critical social information necessary for positive interactions that are critical for social competence. Lynn and Claire describe how motivation to attend to social cues can rapidly result in dramatic intervention gains. Joint attention to stimuli, with shared emotions regarding those stimuli, produces such a rapid and widespread improvement that one suspects that critical neurological changes may be occurring in the remediation process. This is a major breakthrough. Although Lynn and Claire do not say it themselves, their work suggests that, at least in some cases, it may not be wrong to be thinking in terms such as "to cure" or at least "to overcome" the symptoms. Lynn and Claire describe the approach that seems to work at the very basic heart of the disability.

It also is very important to note that in many cases Lynn and Claire report that the individuals receiving treatment improved very rapidly, almost instantaneously. This suggests that the desired behaviors may have been in their repertoire all along, and what was needed was not to teach them from scratch, but rather to find a way to motivate the performance of behaviors. For example, instead of teaching a person how to play a game, the authors suggest that it is important to show the person how to have fun with the game, and then the individual will rapidly motivate herself to acquire the necessary skills to play the game.

Thus, it appears that the individuals with Asperger's and autism disorders may have a learned helplessness, and may actively avoid the responses that are necessary for their long-term happiness. The authors show in this book that learned helplessness is a pivotal area, and that once remediated, extremely rapid and natural improvements occur, resulting in a greatly improved quality of life for all of the individuals involved. Lynn and Claire show not only how to make improvements in these people's lives, but also how it is possible for them to achieve happy and fulfilling lives as adults. This is critically important for all concerned: the individuals with the disability, their friends and families, and for all of the society members with whom they interact. Happiness is not a small goal, and Lynn and Claire have taken on the challenge to show that there is reason for all of us to have hope!

Resources

If this book left you with questions, concerns, a desire for more information, and/or a motivation to plunge into making positive changes for individuals on the spectrum, then we want to help you continue on your journey. Here are some suggestions for where you can go from here.

Our Clinic and Research Facilities

The Koegel Autism Center at the University of California, Santa Barbara (UCSB), keeps expanding exponentially. We continue to research Pivotal Response Teaching methods, which have been shown to result in widespread positive improvements on a variety of symptoms of autism, and to improve the intervention available to children and adults on the spectrum. We also have an annual PRT conference at UCSB that focuses on the latest and greatest research findings. In addition to the Autism Center, we now have a Center for Excellence in Asperger's Studies. This was started with funding from Eli and Edythe L. Broad. The Eli and Edythe L. Broad Center for Asperger Research is conducting research and intervention with the purpose of developing a model that can be disseminated nationally, and is moving toward the long-term goal of becoming the largest and most comprehensive clearinghouse in the world on intervention for Asperger's syndrome. Information on this new center, as well as the UCSB Autism Center, can be found at www.education.ucsb.edu/autism.

Manuals and Books

The following manuals can be ordered from our Web site (www.edu cation.ucsb.edu/autism):

How to Teach Pivotal Behaviors to Children with Autism

This manual addresses the subject of pivotal behaviors, such as motivation, that produce widespread positive effects on many other behaviors, including overall emotional responses and learning, and decreasing disruptive behavior. It's also available in Spanish.

Facilitating Play Dates for Children with Autism and Typically Developing Peers in Natural Settings

This manual is designed to help teach those who work with children with autism how to facilitate play dates with typically developing peers. It outlines simple steps for setting up play dates with peers and promoting positive interactions during play dates. It's easy for families and professionals to use in home and community settings.

Teaching First Words to Children with Autism and Communication Delays Using Pivotal Response Training

Even though this book focuses on teens and young adults, it's never too late to give first words a try if your older or adult child is nonverbal. This manual describes Pivotal Response Teaching procedures as they apply to children with autism or related severe communication delays learning their first words. The manual focuses specifically on the pivotal area of motivation in children as they learn their first words and how to use them spontaneously and independently.

Understanding Why Problem Behaviors Occur: A Guide for Assisting Parents in Assessing Causes of Behavior and Designing Treatment Plans

This manual gives details on how to perform a functional analysis. It will help you recognize the function of the behavior that an individual is displaying, and use that information to replace the behavior with one that is appropriate.

Increasing Success in School through Priming

This book was originally written for younger children, but the same procedures work with older children on the spectrum who are included in regular education classrooms. It gives more details on the priming procedures described in this book.

How to Teach Self-Management to People with Severe Disabilities

Even though the book includes the words *severe disabilities* in the title, the self-management works with mild and moderate disabilities, too. This manual is also available in Spanish.

Procedures for Working with Paraprofessionals to Improve Socialization for Children with Autism

This manual may be interesting to those who want to expand on the existing in-home services for families by creating a program to increase the social opportunities for children with autism or related disabilities in inclusive settings, including after-school and summer camp programs. It outlines the recruitment and training of paraprofessionals to assist with social interventions, so that children with autism or related disabilities can gain access and successfully integrate into community settings and programs.

Overcoming Autism. L. Koegel and C. LaZebnik (Viking, 2004)

If this book was helpful, you may want to read our first book, *Overcoming Autism*. We focus more on younger kids in that book, but a lot of the tips are useful with older children who still have some remnant behaviors that need to be addressed. Browse through it at the bookstore and see if anything is helpful.

**Pivotal Response Treatments. R. L. Koegel and L. K. Koegel
(Paul H. Brookes Publishing Co., 2006)**
If you like more scientific reading with lots of references, you might
want to pick up a copy of *Pivotal Response Treatments*. This is often
used as a college textbook and includes much of the scientific background and studies that went into developing the procedures described in this book.

Journals

While journals may have jargon and just too many details, they are
still a great way to get the latest information and groundbreaking
studies. There are so many wonderful journals out there, but here are
a few that are especially helpful for individuals on the spectrum.

Focus on Autism and Other Developmental Disabilities
PRO-ED
8700 Shoal Creek Blvd.
Austin, TX 78757-6897
Web site: www.proedinc.com

Journal of Autism and Developmental Disorders
Subscriptions/articles through Kluwer Academic Publishers:
Journals Department
101 Philip Dr.
Assinippi Park
Norwell, MA 02061
Email: kluwer@wkap.com

Journal of Positive Behavior Interventions
Subscriptions/articles through PRO-ED
8700 Shoal Creek Blvd.
Austin, TX 78757-6897
Web site: www.proedinc.com

Research and Practice for Persons with Severe Disabilities
Subscription/articles through the Association for Persons with
    Severe Handicaps (TASH)
29 W. Susquehanna Ave., Suite 210
Baltimore, MD 21204

Organizations

The following organizations may help you. Many have annual conferences. If you join them, you can get their regular newsletters. Some of
them have journals, too.

- Association for Behavior Analysis (ABA)—www.abainter
  national.org

- Autism Society of America (ASA)—www.autism-society.org
  ASA also has local chapters in many cities

- The Association for Persons with Severe Handicaps
  (TASH)—www.tash.org

- Association for Positive Behavioral Support (APBS)—www.
  APBS.org

- Autism Speaks—www.autismspeaks.org

Index